# REAGAN
## REMEMBERED

## BY GILBERT A. ROBINSON

BEAUFORT
BOOKS

# REAGAN REMEMBERED

Library of Congress Cataloging-in-Publication Data On File

For inquiries about volume orders, please contact:

Beaufort Books

27 West 20th Street, Suite 1102

New York, NY 10011

sales@beaufortbooks.com


Published in the United States by Beaufort Books

www.beaufortbooks.com


Distributed by Midpoint Trade Books

www.midpointtrade.com


Printed in the United States of America


Interior design by Mark Karis

Cover Design by Brayton Harris

Cover Photo by Michael Evens; National Archives 198600

# ACKNOWLEDGMENTS

It is rare in Presidential history to find a single volume that includes personal accounts written by such a varied group of individuals, all of whom have worked, some more closely than others, with a President during his administration. I am indebted to all my former colleagues in the Reagan administration for their generous participation.

I am especially grateful for the advice and counsel of Edwin Meese III, Chief of Staff during Reagan's California governorship, later Counselor to the President (cabinet rank) and U. S. Attorney General. Jim Baker, Chief of Staff in the President's first administration and then Secretary of the Treasury, also provided support and was most helpful in getting the book off the ground. As you will see, Ed Meese also contributed the Introduction, and Jim Baker supplied the Epilogue.

At the suggestion of Dr. John M. Templeton, Jr., I have included many of President Reagan's major speeches, especially those mentioned in the text. In addition, a generous donation from the Templeton family will underwrite distribution of copies of *Reagan Remembered* to selected schools throughout the nation.

Finally, I want to offer thanks to executive editor Brayton Harris, and to Diane Patrick and my assistant Estelle Candia, who helped me in so many ways during the collection and publication of these anecdotes.

— GILBERT A. ROBINSON

# CONTENTS

Positions noted are those held during service with Ronald Reagan

151
**ROGER W. ROBINSON, JR.**
*Senior Director of International*
*Economic Affairs, National Security*
*Council 1982-1985*

160
**WILLIAM BENNETT**
*Secretary of Education 1985-1988*

162
**HELENE VON DAMM**
*Secretary to President Reagan*
*1981-1982 / Director of Personnel*
*1981-1982 / Ambassador to Austria*
*1984-1989*

165
**LOUIS J. CORDIA**
*Special Assistant for Federal Activities,*
*Office of the EPA Administrator*
*1981-1983*

168
**JOHN BLOCK**
*Secretary of Agriculture 1981-1986*

172
**FAITH WHITTLESEY**
*Ambassador to Switzerland 1981-*
*1983, 1985-88; Assistant for Public*
*Liaison 1983-1985*

176
**ELAINE L. CHAO**
*Chairman, Federal Maritime*
*Commission 1988-1989*

178
**MAX L. FRIEDERSDORF**
*Assistant to the President for Legislative*
*Affairs 1981-1982, 1984-1986*

180
**E. PENDLETON JAMES**
*Director, Presidential Personnel*
*1981-1982*

182
**MURRAY WEIDENBAUM**
*Chairman, President Reagan's Council*
*of Economic Advisors 1981-1982*

184
**JOSEPH WRIGHT**
*Deputy Director, Office of Management*
*and the Budget (OMB) 1982-1989*

185
**FRANK FAHRENKOPF**
*Chairman, Republican National*
*Committee 1983-1989*

187
**PETER H. DAILEY**
*Ambassador to Ireland 1982-1984*

# FOREWORD

## EDWARD MEESE III
### Counselor to the President 1981-1985 / Attorney General 1985-1988

"Leadership is the capacity and will to rally men and women to a common purpose and the character which inspires confidence." That definition of leadership, proclaimed by British Field Marshal Bernard Montgomery, is an accurate description of Ronald Reagan, the 40th President of the United States, whose vision and commitment brought together the people who have provided the remembrances contained in this book.

This unique collection of stories, experiences, and commentary illustrates how a team of dedicated people, motivated and directed by an exceptional leader, came together "to change a nation, and instead . . . changed a world," as President Reagan commented in his farewell address.

It was my privilege to serve in the White House as Counselor to the President during the first term, and as the Attorney General, in the Department of Justice, during the second term. It is now a pleasure to join my former colleagues in this recording of history from behind the scenes of our Nation's Capital.

The contributions to this book represent the work of over seventy people—Cabinet officials, White House staff members, assistant department secretaries, and various others who served during the Reagan years. Written from a variety of vantage points, there are anecdotes and narratives about how the President and his team worked together to successfully deal with so many complex and diverse challenges. Look at just a representative few of the topics covered in the book:

- Government employees who violated the law and their oaths of office.

- The threat of nuclear war.

- The quest for revised intellectual property laws to contend with accelerating changes in science and technology.

- The changing conditions for the relationships with the Soviet Union and its rapidly changing leaders.

- The need to work with sometimes hostile members of Congress to benefit all the citizens of the Country, regardless of politics and philosophy.

The recollections in this volume are from those who were actually on the scene and participated with the President in the making of history. To appreciate the depth of their feelings and their commitment to their leader, it is important to understand the background and history of the Reagan era. It starts with an examination of how the President's policies and decisions affected the United States, and indeed the world. Most historians have cited three primary achievements as most significant:

- Revitalizing the economy.

- Rebuilding the Nation's defense capability and enabling the Free World to win the Cold War.

- Reviving the spirit of the American people.

When President Reagan took office in January of 1981, the country was in serious trouble in terms of both domestic conditions and national security concerns. An economic crisis gripped the nation, characterized by massive inflation, high unemployment, severe energy shortages, and stagnant business growth gripped the nation. Inflation rates of 12.5 percent and interest rates of over 20 percent were not uncommon, and the number of people out of work was surging toward 10 percent of the normal work force.

At the same time, major foreign and defense challenges threatened America and its allies in the West, as the Soviet Union continued a pattern of aggression, subversion, and intimidation throughout the world. The international tensions and threats to peace—even the specter of nuclear war—were a constant worry.

To make matters worse, our military capabilities had deteriorated during the 1970's, in the wake of the unsuccessful end to the Vietnam War. In the minds of many in our nation, as well as those in other countries, we were becoming neither a reliable ally to our friends nor a credible deterrent to our enemies.

In the face of such daunting problems, the spirit and confidence of the American people had reached an uncharacteristically low ebb. Many feared that our basic institutions were in jeopardy. The out-going President had declared that the people were in a "malaise," while some pundits were predicting that our system of capitalism and free enterprise had reached its peak, as they saw socialism advancing around the globe. Even the superiority of our basic political values, such as liberty and democracy, were viewed with uncertainty, as some influential "experts" contended that a "moral equivalency" existed between totalitarianism and freedom, both being just two different types of government that would have to live side by side in the future.

Ronald Reagan came to office with a very different vision for the future of America and the world. As a successful governor of California he had faced serious challenges before, and as president he immediately initiated a series of bold strategies to deal with the country's plight.

In the economic realm he established a four-point program: first, to reduce income tax rates, across the board, to stimulate economic activity; second, to eliminate unnecessary and burdensome government regulations that were stifling business and industry; third, to maintain stable monetary policies, which had been contributing to the financial uncertainty; and fourth, to slow the growth of federal spending, which was burgeoning out of control.

The results of this dramatic change in economic policy achieved the desired results: rapidly reducing inflation and unemployment, strengthening the economy, and beginning the longest and strongest period of peacetime economic growth in the history of the nation. The most important part of this achievement was the financial relief brought to the American people and the improvement of the well-being of millions of families.

In the field of national security, President Reagan likewise introduced a series of critical steps. Working with Congress, he rebuilt our national defense capability, modernizing our military weapons and material, improving the pay and living conditions of the men and women in the Armed Forces, and upgrading our intelligence systems. These changes were accompanied by his personal demonstration of leadership as commander-in-chief, as he visited military installations, conferred regularly with the Joint Chiefs of Staff, met with key commanders and units, and showed Congress and the public his personal support for the Armed Services.

On the foreign policy front, the President developed a new strategy in coping with the Soviet Union. He engaged the Iron Curtain forces on a moral plane, identifying Marxism-Leninism as an evil force in the world. He strongly criticized the plight of the captive nations and the oppressed peoples who were suffering under Communism. He also quietly made it known to the Soviet leaders that any further aggression would be resisted by the free nations of the world. And, most importantly, he began to provide support, both rhetorically and materially, to freedom-fighters in Poland, Nicaragua, Afghanistan, Angola, and other similar situations to roll back the existing Soviet aggression. In carrying out these various aspects of his national security strategy President Reagan's purpose was to counter Soviet hegemony and to promote "peace through strength."

These military and foreign policy initiatives, and the strong leadership of Ronald Reagan among his international colleagues, accomplished a result that, during most of his presidency, the foreign affairs "experts" said couldn't be done: the ultimate victory in the Cold War and the implosion of the Soviet Union. Thus our President had fulfilled his prediction, given when he outlined his strategy for contending with the Soviets, that the free nations would "consign Marxism-Leninism to the ash heap of history."

Throughout the implementation of his economic and national security strategies, Ronald Reagan regularly talked to the American people, explaining the actions being taken, encouraging their support for the legislation he was seeking from Congress, and reporting the progress being made. It was this regular communication in a forthright way, delivered with the President's continuous cheerfulness and optimism, which had a major impact on how the people of our country regarded our improving situation. The combination of this encouraging communication and the successes both in the domestic economic scene and in world affairs served to revive the spirit of the American people. Ronald Reagan called it "the recovery of our morale" and said it was one of the "great triumphs" that he was "proudest of."

By the end of the first Reagan term, he successfully campaigned on the theme that it was "morning in America," and that our country was "respected again in the world and looked to for leadership."

One of Ronald Reagan's greatest concerns, long before he became President, was the issue of nuclear weapons. He had often declared his belief that "a nuclear war could not be won and should never be fought." But he vehemently did not agree with those anti-nuclear activists who believed that the United States should unilaterally abandon its nuclear arsenal, as a so-called "moral example" to other nations, and then depend upon diplomacy and treaties to prevent a nuclear attack.

He was equally adamant against the then-existing policy of "Mutually Assured Destruction." This concept was that both sides in the Cold War held nuclear weapons pointed at each other's cities, so that if one side launched an attacking missile, the other could immediately retaliate, thus resulting in massive destruction to both sides. Ronald Reagan believed this was not only flawed as a reliable protection, but was morally wrong. He likened it to "two cowboys standing face-to-face in a western saloon with cocked pistols aimed at each other's heads." He didn't think that policy inspired confidence as a defense against weapons of mass destruction.

Instead Ronald Reagan believed that a defensive shield must be developed to make nuclear weapons obsolete. He made the analogy to other types of offensive weapons over history. In response to spears and arrows, warriors used individual shields to protect themselves. Likewise, defensive measures such as armored vehicles and anti-aircraft weapons were invented to counter other offensive threats. After consulting with scientists and military experts, the President directed the Joint Chiefs of Staff to conduct research into the potential of nuclear defense and to include the subject in their strategic planning recommendations. A similar project was assigned to a task force of the National Security Council Staff.

After an extensive study, the Joint Chiefs reported to the President that development of a nuclear missile defense capability was not only feasible, but was what they called a "a moral imperative." Armed with that recommendation, Ronald Reagan launched a missile defense program, which he denominated the "Strategic Defense Initiative."

To show our Soviet adversaries that we would not use this system as part of an offensive effort against them, Reagan stated that when SDI became a reliable shield against a nuclear attack, we would share the technology with other nations.

The Ballistic Missile Defense development program continues today, but without the name "SDI" and with limited resources. Unfortunately, since the Reagan days the program has often been underfunded by Congress and some recent administrations. I believe that if the SDI program had been continuously supported since

1983 with the same emphasis and resources given it by Ronald Reagan, we would have an operational and reliable missile defense system in existence today.

President Reagan took another major step against nuclear war during his second term. From his first days in the White House he had been opposed to a Cold War situation in which the Soviet Union and the Western Allies were to have intermediate range nuclear missiles positioned against each other in Europe. By 1981, the Soviets had already deployed their weapons and the U.S. was scheduled to emplace its missiles as part of the NATO defense plan. Early in his first term, Ronald Reagan suggested that the U.S. not position its weapons if the Soviets would remove theirs, thus creating a zero-zero balance. He reasoned that this would lessen tensions and protect against an accidental launch or some other untoward event. When the Soviets refused, the U.S. had no course but to carry out the NATO plan and install the missiles. But Ronald Reagan never gave up. In conversations with General Secretary Gorbachev, and through other diplomatic efforts, he reiterated his proposal to mutually remove the nuclear weapons.

Finally the Soviets were persuaded to agree and in 1987, when Gorbachev came on a visit to America, he and President Reagan signed a treaty which caused the intermediate range weapons to be removed on both sides. This was the first time an entire class of nuclear weapons was eliminated from employment.

There were many other successful initiatives during the two terms of the Reagan presidency, including among them:

- Restoring the Constitutional role of the States and protecting them against usurpation of their authority by the Federal government.

- Preventing Federal regulations that interfered with strengthened family.

- Combating illegal drugs and significantly reducing drug abuse in the United States.

- Appointing judges, at all levels of the Federal Judiciary, who were committed to fidelity to the Constitution.

These actions were part of the extensive efforts over the two Reagan terms to restore the Constitutional government, enhance our domestic and economic situation, and protect our national security. They provide the background for the many accounts of the President's stewardship as the Nation's Chief Executive.

As the vignettes in *Remembering Reagan* recount the activities of what has been called the "Reagan Revolution," the question has been asked, "How was one man able to accomplish so much?" An important part of the answer lies in his clarity of vision and goals, his single-minded focus on his objectives, and his leadership in engaging and inspiring the people who served in his administration.

No modern president other than Dwight D. Eisenhower used the Cabinet, and through it, the departments and agencies of the Executive Branch, as effectively as Ronald Reagan. Following a pattern he had initiated as Governor of California, he used the Cabinet System as the principal forum for decision-making. Meeting on a regular basis with the entire Cabinet, he also created smaller cabinet councils to deal with specific issue areas. The statutory National Security Council was integrated within this system. In this way, the President was able to continually make known to his top officials his policies, plans, and expectations, and also to receive regular feed-back and views from all of them, encouraging their ideas on all issues, whether or not a particular subject fell within a specific Cabinet member's portfolio. He often said, "The more information I get the better the decisions I can make."

A symbolic aspect of the give-and-take of Cabinet deliberations was the jelly bean jar which always sat in the middle of the cabinet table. When the discussions sometimes became argumentative amid intensive controversy, the President would reach over, select a jelly bean and pass the jar around the table. This immediately mitigated the tension and restored calmer reflection.

The extensive use of the Cabinet was augmented by other steps to communicate with the Reagan Team. An annual meeting of all Presidential appointees, gatherings of sub-Cabinet officials, and several other events were established to enhance internal presidential contact and promote teamwork and unity of endeavor.

These and other similar motivational and unifying measures enabled the President to maintain operational focus, encourage cooperation, and inspire exceptional effort among the members of this Administration.

In this book, the great initiative and hard work of Gil Robinson has produced an important contribution to history. Like the accomplishments of the 1980s, *Reagan Remembered* is the result of a team effort. It has brought together those who were privileged to be part of a special Administration, to provide their memories of an exceptional era, and to commemorate the outstanding leader they served.

# 1

## GEORGE H. W. BUSH
### Vice President 1981-1989

t is inordinately hard to distill eight wonderful and challenging years spent working with a man I admire down to an anecdote or two. For starters, Ronald Reagan was one of the most decent men I have had the privilege to know. He would no sooner fly to the moon than walk past a waiter or a doorman without saying "Hello!"

One afternoon I recall visiting with a group of disabled California teenagers, which was part of the regulatory work we were doing on disability issues at the time. We were having such a good visit that I checked President Reagan's schedule, and finding nothing on it, took the kids down to the Oval Office to see the President. He spent about an hour with these kids, who were there without any appointment. To me, it showed how informal and comfortable Ronald Reagan was with people from every walk of life. He was compassionate to the core.

On another occasion, our regulatory reform group was working to accelerate the elimination of lead from gasoline, and there was a full Cabinet meeting to consider the decision. There were no real objections going around the table, when President Reagan observed that lead—which was eventually recognized as one of the greatest industrial poisons—was originally considered a technological marvel of the first order when it was introduced in the 1920s. Looking around at the blank faces staring back at him, the President remarked tongue-in-cheek that he was, of course, the only one in the room old enough to remember the introduction of lead.

A final recollection comes from when I visited President Reagan in the hospital after the assassination attempt in 1981. I was ushered into the President's room, but he wasn't in bed. I looked around wondering where he could be.

Then I heard his familiar voice, "Hello, George." It was coming from the bathroom. The door was open so I delicately peeked in, and found President Reagan on his hands and knees on the floor. Alarmed, I quickly asked, "Mr. President, are you all right?" He smiled and said, "You see, I was in here and I spilled some water on the floor. I don't want the nurses to have to mop it up. I'm enough of a nuisance to them as it is. So I'm just wiping it up. Be with you in a second." That's the sort of man Ronald Reagan was.

*George H. W. Bush also served as the 41st President of the United States, 1989-1993*

# 2

## GEORGE SHULTZ
### Secretary of State 1982-1989

There was an unexpected breakthrough with the Soviet Union. After one of my trips to Japan, China, and South Korea, I arrived back in Washington in the middle of a snowstorm and was lucky to be able to land at Andrews Air Force Base. The Reagans were snowed in at the White House so Nancy invited my wife and me to come over for supper. During the course of the evening, President Reagan asked me for my views about the Chinese leaders. He also knew that I had dealt with Soviet leaders on numerous occasions.

I realized that he had never had a real meeting with a major Communist leader and that he wanted to have one. I told him that Ambassador Dobrynin would be coming to my office the following week and asked if he would like me to bring Dobrynin over for a meeting.

The president was enthusiastic and said the meeting would only take ten minutes because he simply wanted to say that if the Soviet Union's new leader, Yuri Andropov, was interested in doing business, he was ready. The meeting lasted ninety minutes and covered a variety of topics. President Reagan spoke eloquently on the subject of human rights, Soviet Jewry, and the Pentecostals who had rushed into the U.S. Embassy during the Carter administration and were still there.

"If you can do something about the Pentecostals or another human rights issue," Reagan told Dobrynin, "we will simply be delighted and will not embarrass you by crowing." Dobrynin and I took up the Pentecostal issue and, after some exchanges, we were confident that if the Pentecostals left the U.S. Embassy, they would be allowed to go home and eventually emigrate. Within two or three months, the Pentecostals and their families—some sixty people in all—were allowed to leave the Soviet Union. The president kept his word and did not crow. He learned that he could make a deal with the Soviets and they would carry it out, and the Soviets learned that, even with the great temptation every politician faces to take credit for accomplishments, President Reagan could be trusted to keep his word.

Another example of President Reagan's skill as a negotiator and his reputation of delivering on his promises involved one of his trips to Germany. At a meeting in the White House, Chancellor Helmut Kohl of Germany said that he and President Mitterrand of France had met at a cemetery where French and German soldiers were buried. The photograph of their handshake improved the relationship between the two countries. President Reagan agreed to do the same when he came to Germany on a scheduled trip.

The Germans chose to arrange the meeting at the cemetery at Bitburg, and the initial White House scouting report indicated this would be acceptable. When members of the press swept snow off the gravestones, however, they discovered that members of the SS were buried at Bitburg. A huge controversy ensued. Elie Wiesel, a Holocaust survivor, said of Bitburg, "That place, Mr. President, is not your place. Your place is with the victims of the SS." We tried to change the venue of the meeting to another place in Germany, but Kohl and the Germans resisted, insisting on Bitburg. So, having made a commitment, President Reagan went to Bitburg.

Later, I stopped in London and met with Margaret Thatcher. She said that no other leader in the free world would have taken such a political beating at home in order to keep his word. One thing was clear: If Ronald Reagan made a promise, he would deliver on that promise.

Ronald Reagan liked to have fun. I recall a trip to South America that we took together when he was president. The secretary of state works hard on such a trip; there are endless meetings, dinners, and press conferences at the end of each day. After our last stop, I boarded Air Force One, had a drink and a light dinner, and then tilted my head back and went sound to sleep. President Reagan came back and saw me, called for a photographer, and posed imploringly in front of me. The next week, I received a White House photo showing me, out cold, and the president pleading with me. The caption was, "George, wake up! The Russians are coming."

# A. B. CULVAHOUSE
## Counsel to the President 1987-1989

I n March 1987, President Reagan appointed me Counsel to the President of the UnitedStates (better known as White House Counsel) upon the recommendation of Senator Howard Baker, the President's new Chief of Staff. The immediate challenge was to assist the President in responding to and cooperating with the investigations into the so-called Iran-Contra Affair conducted by Independent Counsel Lawrence Walsh and by a U.S. Senate Select Committee and a House of Representatives Select Committee sitting jointly.

The Iran-Contra investigations focused on the "diversion" of approximately $4million in proceeds from the covert sale to the Iranian Government of U.S. military arms, which was used to fund the Nicaraguan Resistance forces ("Contras") seeking to overthrow the Sandinista regime. The diversion of the Iranian arms sales proceeds to support the Contras occurred at a time when U.S. law provided that "no funds available" to the CIA, Defense Department and other agencies and entities "involved in intelligence activities" could be expended to support military or paramilitary operations in Nicaragua.

From November 25, 1986, when Attorney General Ed Meese publicly announced the discovery of the Iran-Contra affair by a team of Justice Department investigators, the central issue became whether President Reagan knew about and approved the diversion of funds. In press conferences, interviews and in an appearance before a special review board, President Reagan adamantly stated that he was unaware of the diversion.

We assembled in Counsel's Office a large team of lawyers, analysts and archivists to examine the thousands of documents and electronic notes relevant to Iran-Contra. We reviewed the President's schedule, telephone logs, and his personal diary; we interviewed numerous White House and N.S.C. staff; and my Deputy and I interviewed President Reagan on 13 separate occasions (the President began each session with a lawyers' joke). The President was firm and confident that he was unaware of the diversion of funds; and we found no evidence to the contrary. Thus we were reasonably comfortable that the President's recollection and statements were accurate, but it is a lawyer's job to fear that your client's recollection will be challenged, credibly or not, by others.

Our principal reservation related to Admiral John Poindexter, who had been the President's National Security Advisor. Poindexter was aware of the diversion of funds, and on seven occasions had short meetings with the President without others in attendance. We explained to the President that Admiral Poindexter was under great pressure by the investigations and might be tempted to suggest that during one of those meetings the President orally authorized his actions. President Reagan's response was that "John Poindexter is an honorable man, a Navy officer, and he won't lie."

In early May 1987, Senator Warren Rudman, the Vice Chairman of the Senate Select Committee investigating the Iran-Contra Affair, informed me that Admiral Poindexter, in a deposition by the Committee while under oath, had testified that President Reagan was not aware of, and did not approve, the diversion of Iranian arms sales proceeds to the Contras. I received Senator Rudman's consent to give a confidential briefing to President Reagan, Vice President Bush and Chief of Staff Baker, which I proceeded to do in the Oval Office. Upon being advised of AdmiralPoindexter's testimony, the Vice President and Howard Baker both expressed gratification and relief, as did I. President Reagan visibly reacted to our expressions of relief, as he responded, "Why are you so surprised? I told you all along I did not know about the money going to the rebel forces."

From that point on, I had no doubts whatsoever that President Reagan was unaware of the diversion of funds. More profoundly, I realized that the President's confidence that Admiral Poindexter, as a "man of honor," would be truthful, was shaped by the fact that Ronald Reagan was the most honorable of men.

**4**

# FRANK C. CARLUCCI
National Security Advisor 1986-1987 / Secretary of Defense 1987-1989

As we all know, Ronald Reagan hated nuclear weapons. Periodically, he would tell us to get rid of them, and periodically, I and my predecessors, as well as George Shultz, would explain to him that, given Soviet conventional superiority, nuclear weapons had kept the peace for over thirty years. The President persisted and it is a good thing that he did. One morning he came down for the National Security briefing and started again. I guess I was in a somewhat mischievous mood because instead of giving him the standard lecture, I told him that "If you move to do that Margaret (Thatcher) will be on the phone in five minutes." "Oh," he said, "I don't want that." And the discussion ended!

The SS-20 was a short range missile that the Soviets had deployed as an existential threat to Western Europe. As a result, the West, basically the U.S. and Germany, deployed the Ground Launch Cruise Missile (GLCM) and the Pershings. When the Soviets indicated they would negotiate arms control issues, Ronald Reagan made a startling proposal—the so-called "Zero Option." The Zero Option meant that we would remove the GLCMs and the Pershings and they would dismantle the SS 20s. This led to the INF negotiations led by George Shultz, in which I participated. It led to the first reduction in nuclear weapons in the history of the world. End result? The remaining stock of these missiles: one is in a museum in Moscow and one is in a museum in Washington.

Ronald Reagan's relaxed style is legendary but I found out early on in my tenure as National Security Advisor that he could be quite sharp. I guess forceful is a better term. We were on a visit to Canada and President Reagan was particularly fond of Prime Minister Mulroney. I had been negotiating separately with Derek Burney, Mulroney's Chief of Staff. Following memos from the U.S. bureaucracy, I was standing firm on key issues such as northwest passage and NAFTA. As the Presidential limousine pulled up to Mulroney's house for lunch, Reagan called me over and said "Be nice to the Canadians." We were having a pre-lunch conversation during which I followed my bureaucratic talking points. Mulroney, sensing disagreement among us, suggested we caucus in a separate room. There, George Shultz and I, sitting on different sides of the President, started to argue. The President listened for a brief time, then turned and poked his finger at my chest. "I told you to be nice to the Canadians," he said. "Do it." With that, I went out and found Derek Burney. I asked him to clarify the Canadian position "because it's now ours." Thus, the relations moved on and the visit was a great success.

# 5

## JAMES C. MILLER III
### Director, Office Management and Budget 1985-1988

very month or so the President would invite the Congressional Leadership down to the White House for a discussion of issues. The meetings were held in the Cabinet Room, with strict seating protocol. Outward from the President would be the Speaker, Majority Leader, and Minority Leader on one side, and the Senate Majority Leader, Minority Leader, and Majority Whip on the other. Members of the President's staff, including any cabinet members present, would sit against the wall. This day, in early 1986, the President called on Chief of Staff Howard Baker to discuss some legislative matters, on Secretary of Treasury Jim Baker to discuss the soon-to-be-met statutory limit on federal debt, and me to discuss the budget. After we had all finished our presentations and had answered questions, the President said, "That's right. We have to do something about all this wasteful spending. It's getting away from us. Too much pork."

"Right, Mr. President," said someone, and most began pushing their chairs away from the table.

But the President wasn't finished: "We just have to do what the people elected us to do—get rid of all that non-essential spending, get rid of programs that don't work, and cut taxes."

At this point, Speaker Tip O'Neill's face was as getting red as a beet, and he blurted out, "There you go, Mr. President, cutting programs for the poor, the downtrodden, the disenfranchised."

"There you go, Tip," said the President, "spend, spend, spend."

"There you go, Mr. President," said the Speaker, "you bail out all your rich buddies with tax cuts while leaving the poor to wither on the vine."

"No, your answer to everything is government—more spending and more regulation," said the President. At this point, there were scared looks all around the room. Two Titans were going at each other, and the mice were about to get stepped on.

Out of the blue, Senator Alan Simpson shouted, "All right, all right. Enough, you two." And magically, there was silence. Both Titans looked like a kid who had just been caught with his hand in the cookie Jar.

"Well, Tip, I guess we had better get back to work," said the President.

"You're right, Mr. President," said the Speaker. And the meeting ended as though nothing had happened.

Initial cabinet meetings were pretty formal affairs, with each member of the cabinet being asked for their advice on the issue at hand. At one such meeting, the issue was whether the President would issue an Executive Order allowing some deterioration in the quality of air in Wilderness Areas, in order to permit limited commercial development. President Reagan asked each for their advice, in turn. Almost everyone urged him to sign the draft before him, but some things he said about open spaces and pristine air indicated he was disinclined. In a final attempt to change the President's mind, Secretary of Energy Jim Edwards exclaimed, "Mr. President, I still don't understand why bears need cleaner air to breathe than us humans."

As the laughter broke out, President Reagan responded, "Jim, have you ever smelled a bear?"

On several occasions there was a threat of a government shut-down, as Congress demanded tax increases as part of continuing appropriations, and the President refused. One day, as appropriations ran out and we came to the "magic hour" when we had to notify all non-essential federal employees to go home, I was in the Oval Office, pacing up and down, and grousing about what had become a frequent, fruitless, and senseless routine. Suddenly the President turned to me, put his hand on my shoulder, and said, "Jim, Jim, just settle down. Let's close 'er down and see if anybody notices!" (The next day Congress relented, the President signed appropriations without tax increases, and government went on as usual.)

On September 29, 1988, the President signed a revised version of the Gramm-Rudman-Hollings law in a small ceremony involving Congressional leaders in the Rose Garden. Early in the day I had received a draft copy of his remarks and had read it carefully. As I had predicted, it was a statement that indicated he was signing the bill only with great reluctance and that he scolded Congress for giving him such bad choices [i.e., agree to tax increases or cut defense]. In one place, the President wrote that some in Congress thought they had put him in a box between taxes and defense. He went on to recall the incident in World War II during the Battle of the Bulge when an American general and his troops were surrounded; the Germans demanded surrender and the general replied with one word: "Nuts!"

The next few lines in the draft read something to the effect that those who thought the President would go along with cutting defense or raising taxes were wrong. As a play on "Nuts" I wrote in a suggested change to the text, so that the passage read, "To those who say we should weaken America's defenses: They're nuts. To those who say we must raise the tax burden on the American people: they, too, are nuts."

I had no doubt that if the president read that line it would become the "sound bite" that appeared on the evening's network news shows. But in truth, I didn't think it would get past the speechwriters, much less past the President. During the afternoon ceremony, my position was on the front row at the right end. You can imagine my surprise and delight when, standing there looking over the president's shoulder, I saw that, in the next lines after the story about the general, that he had kept the speech as I had amended it. And, as I had anticipated, that was the sound bite that led the network news shows that evening.

Later, Howard Baker, the President's Chief of Staff, asked me what I thought of the President's remarks, and I told him I thought it was good and appropriate that the president indicate his sentiments about the matter. Baker told me that he had been "positively scared" that one or more of those congressional leaders were going to bolt the session because of being dressed down so severely.

By law, once each year the President must convene a cabinet-level meeting to review the safety of our stockpile of atomic weapons. The presentation is made by the Secretary of Energy, since the Department of Energy (DOE) is in charge of all warheads.

One year, as part of his presentation, Energy Secretary John Herrington wanted to show President Reagan a "dummy" warhead—to demonstrate just how small one can be and therefore the need for everyone to be particularly vigilant in protecting our stocks from theft.

Secretary Herrington had his staff take over to the White House an example on a gurney, covered with a black drape. As the DOE staff rolled the gurney in the basement door of the West Wing, the metal set off alarms. When the Executive Protection Service (EPS) officer on duty asked what was on the gurney, the DOE staff replied, "an atomic warhead." Understandably, this set off a different sort of alarm. After the DOE staff hastily explained what was up, the EPS officer said, "OK, let me see it."

To which the DOE staff replied, "You can't. You aren't cleared to see this." The impasse was broken only when Secretary Herrington personally intervened and had the gurney cleared through.

President Reagan's sense of humor is the stuff of legend, and he loved a good joke even when the joke was on him.

On almost every Monday when he was in town, the President lunched with his Senior Staff, where he would address longer-term issues, how his message was getting out, and the administration's relations with Congress. Since the President seldom complained about anything, we were surprised one day when he arrived grumbling about something.

Quickly, it became apparent the President was upset that some in the media were making too much of his age. "They say I can't see," he said. "Why I have a contact in one eye for distance viewing and no contact in the other eye, so I can read." He then put his hand over one eye and said, " I can see distance with this eye," and then switching hands said, "And I can read with this eye.

"And," he added, "they say I can't hear . . . Here, wait a minute," he said, and promptly took out small hearing aids from each ear and placed them on the table. "Now, somebody say something," intoned the President.

It so happened that I was sitting directly opposite the President. Without hesitation, I caught his eye, and with great energy pointed at my watch, pointed at the door, and pointed at others in the room, all the time pretending to speak but not uttering a sound. After an awkward pause, the President caught on and delivered a belly-laugh. Others were not so sure, at least at first. "Uh-oh, Miller's gone," said one. But I was so sure about President Reagan's sense of humor that I never thought twice about making a career decision.

## 6

## COLIN L. POWELL

General, U.S. Army (Retired) / National Security Advisor 1987-1989

One morning early in 1988, shortly after I became President Reagan's National Security Advisor, I went into the Oval Office to discuss a problem with the President. We were alone. He was sitting in his usual chair in front of the fireplace with a view of the Rose Garden through the beautiful glass-paned French doors. I was sitting on the end of the couch to his left.

I don't even remember what the problem was. But it involved a not-uncommon fight between the State and Defense Departments, made more complicated by significant Commerce, Treasury Department, and Congressional interests. I described the problem at some length and complexity to the President, underscoring that it had to be solved that day.

To my discomfort he kept looking past me through the French doors without paying much attention to my tale of woe. So I talked a little louder and added more detail. Just as I was running out of gas, the president raised up and interrupted me: "Colin, Colin, the squirrels just came and picked up the nuts I put out there for them this morning." He then settled back into his chair and turned back to me. I decided the meeting was over, excused myself, and went back to my office down the hall in the northwest corner of the West Wing.

I had the feeling that something important had just happened. I sat down, gazed out my windows across the North lawn and into Lafayette Park across Pennsylvania Avenue, and reflected on it. And it became clear.

The President was teaching me: "Colin, I love you and I will sit here as long as you want me to, listening to your problem. Let me know when you bring me a problem I have to solve." I smiled at this new insight. In my remaining months with him, I told him about all the problems we were working on but never asked him to solve problems that he had hired me and the rest of the team to solve. Reagan believed in delegating responsibility and authority, and he trusted those who worked for him to do the right thing. He put enormous trust in his staff. The President's approach worked for him most of the time. But it could also get him in trouble as the Iran-Contra debacle demonstrated.

On another morning in 1988, I went into the Oval Office with another problem. U.S. naval forces in the Persian Gulf were chasing Iranian gunboats that had threatened them. Our ships were approaching the Iranian 12-mile limit and Secretary of Defense Frank Carlucci wanted authority to break that limit in hot pursuit of the boats. President Reagan was sitting behind his desk, calmly signing photos knowing that we were in action. He trusted our ability to manage the situation and keep him informed. He looked up as I approached and locked his eyes on me. He knew he was about to be handed a Commander-in-Chief problem to solve. I laid out the request, with all the upsides and downsides, potential consequences, press needs, and Congressional briefing strategy. He took it all in and simply said, "Approved, do it." I conveyed the answer to Frank. We chased the boats back to their bases and the action was over.

President Reagan's approach offered an example of how the leader at the top has to step outside the pyramid of the organization to see the wider view, as from atop the highest hill of the shining city. He was always at what I call a higher level of aggregation than the rest of us. One morning in 1988, the President's entire economic team marched into the Oval Office to discuss a problem. The Japanese, who were then doing well economically, were buying up lots of U.S. properties—even icons of American real estate like Rockefeller Center and Pebble Beach resort. Congress was starting to stir, the public was buzzing, and the purchases were causing economic and security concerns. "Something has to be done and done now," said the team. They quietly waited for the President to respond. He did.

"Well," he said, "they are investing in America, and I'm glad they know a good investment when they see one." The meeting was over. Reagan once again demonstrated his confidence in America. He was above our ground-level view.

On many occasions during our time together, I brought Reagan presidential decisions that he would think through, question, analyze, and make. He was always available for Oval Office decisions. But he was happier if problems could be solved at a lower level.

One of my most treasured mementos, and the only signed picture I have from Reagan, shows us sitting side-by-side in front of the Oval Office fireplace. We are leaning toward each other examining charts I am using to explain some issue. He later inscribed that photo, "Dear Colin, if you say so, I know it must be right." Gulp.

*General Powell went on to assignments as Chairman of the Joint Chiefs of Staff 1989-1993, and as Secretary of State in the George W. Bush Administration 2001-2005 Some portions of this anecdote appeared in Powell's memoir,* It Worked for Me, *published by Harper, 2012.*

# 7

# CHRISTOPHER COX
### Senior Associate Counsel to the President, 1986-88

resident Reagan is known as the "Great Communicator" for good reason. His clearly reasoned arguments and ability to cut to the heart of the matter won him not only the presidency in two electoral landslides, but also many important policy arguments during his two terms. Providing U.S. assistance to the anti-Communist opposition in Nicaragua was one of those key victories.

In the summer of 1986, with Soviet arms and personnel flooding into Nicaragua, and Cuban, East German, and Bulgarian advisors at their side, the Sandinistas were building the largest standing army in Central American history. The country had rapidly become a police state, with thousands of political prisoners in facilities run by Cubans, Russians, Bulgarians, East Germans, and North Koreans. The government crushed press freedom, suspended all civil rights, and murdered political dissenters.

Confronting the reality of a Soviet military beachhead inside our defense perimeters, about 500 miles from Mexico, President Reagan asked Congress for $100 million in aid for the freedom fighters resisting Sandinista rule. Months earlier, the Senate approved the legislation, and this week it was to be the House's turn to consider the proposal. The vote was expected to be close.

On Monday afternoon, with the vote scheduled for Wednesday, Chief of Staff Don Regan phoned the Speaker of the House on behalf of the president. He asked for the opportunity for President

Reagan to address the House to make a personal appeal for the aid legislation. The call didn't go well. Democratic Speaker Tip O'Neill bluntly told him no—and Regan was hopping mad.

A few minutes later, I got a breathless call from Don Regan asking: "Can he do that?" The question, at bottom, was one of Constitutional prerogative. Understandably, the search for an answer had quickly led to the Office of White House Counsel. One of the truly enjoyable aspects of serving as Senior Associate Counsel to the President was that my law practice routinely included questions about the respective roles of the Article I, II, and III branches, as well as a multitude of fascinating constitutional arcana. While I was reasonably certain I knew the answer to this one, I promised to do some quick research and get back promptly.

What I learned that I did not previously know is exactly how often presidents had addressed one chamber of Congress. But while President Reagan's request was backed by precedent, it was not, as a matter of law, the president's right to address the House of Representatives. The Speaker was well within his rights to deny the president's request, impolite and graceless as that might be.

My quick-and-dirty legal opinion was not cheerfully received. The White House press secretary, Larry Speakes, put out a statement saying that President Reagan was "deeply disappointed" by Tip O'Neill's refusal of his request.

President Reagan and Speaker O'Neill had a warm personal relationship—the two Irishmen often shared lunch—but when it came to politics both were also fiercely competitive. Undoubtedly the Speaker believed he had gotten the better of President Reagan in this way. As so often happened, this underestimated Ronald Reagan. When he learned of Tip O'Neill's snub, the president wasted no time with recrimination. Instead, he immediately asked, rhetorically: "They have televisions up there, don't they?"

With that, the plan was hatched to go over the Speaker's head to the American people. Twenty-four hours later, President Reagan delivered a compelling address to the nation—directing it very explicitly to the House of Representatives—that was carried by every network. His closing argument urged the members of Congress to believe, with him, that "even the humblest campesino has the right to be free."

The quintessentially Reagan peroration was inspiring:

> My fellow citizens, Members of the House, let us not take the path of least resistance in Central America again. Let us keep faith with these brave people struggling for their freedom. Give them, give me, your support; and together, let us send this message to the world: that America is still a beacon of hope, still a light unto the nations.

When the vote was called in the House the following day, Speaker O'Neill was in the chair. But he was not in control of the outcome. The Democratic-controlled House passed President Reagan's requested legislation, 221-209. Voting with almost all House Republicans were no fewer than 51 Reagan Democrats.

They did indeed have televisions up there.

*Full text of President Reagan's remarks will be found at page 341.*

During my final year working in the White House, in 1988, I went back to California to run for Congress. That was a much more difficult undertaking than I had imagined. While having worked for President Reagan was certainly an advantage, the fact I had been back East in that den of iniquity, Washington, D.C., was occasion for my 12 Republican primary opponents to label me a carpetbagger.

There were many pressing local issues in our congressional district, and the other candidates, including the mayor of the largest city in the district, were ostentatiously focused on how Congress could help the folks back home. Not to be outdone, I drafted legislation during the primary to ensure that the highway taxes Californians paid to Washington were actually spent on highways (the supposedly dedicated highway "trust fund" was routinely raided by Congress for general revenue purposes). I promised to introduce my bill once elected.

To attract attention to my legislative plan, I asked President Reagan's head of the Federal Highway Administration, Ray Barnhart, if he would travel to California and hold a news conference with me. To my everlasting delight, he agreed. We arranged that he would fly into John Wayne Airport in Newport Beach, and our news conference would be held the following morning.

Ray Barnhart's arrival the night before our scheduled media event gave us the opportunity to have dinner and talk about the campaign. It also gave me a chance to get to know him better personally. I took the opportunity to ask him how he came to be involved with President Reagan.

"During the 1976 campaign," he said, "I was the co-chair of the Reagan campaign in Texas. That's what first brought me to Governor Reagan's attention."

"You were head of the Texas campaign!" I blurted out. I was enormously impressed, since the Reagan triumph in Texas that year was legendary. On the eve of the primary election, the *New York Times* had predicted that President Ford and Governor Reagan would roughly split the delegates, which were awarded separately by congressional district. In the event, Reagan carried every district and won 100 percent of the delegates statewide—an unimaginable triumph.

"How did you do it?" I prodded him. "Your strategy must have been brilliant, and Governor Reagan must have been enormously grateful he followed your advice."

"Not exactly," Ray told me. "Governor Reagan was always his own best political strategist. In honesty I have to report that in several cases, he completely rejected my advice and followed his own lights."

I asked him for an example, and he told me how, weeks before the May election, he called Governor Reagan with great news.

"We've just gotten you into the largest church in Houston! This is the most coveted prize for anyone running statewide in Texas," he told the Governor. He was certain that his stock would rise immensely for having pulled off this coup.

But Governor Reagan demurred. Ray was shocked. "You don't understand," he pleaded. "This is an exceptional opportunity. Thousands of conservative voters will see you and millions more will read about it. The venue couldn't be more prestigious."

Barnhart said the Governor's response was polite but firm. "I'm a very religious person," Governor Reagan told him. "But I don't wear it on my sleeve. And I never want to use religion for political purposes."

That was that. The candidate had the final word, and the event never took place.

Ray Barnhart died in 2013, justly credited as the prime architect of the pivotal victory that sent 100 Reagan delegates to the 1976 Republican National Convention. He had served as a state representative and went on to become Republican State Chairman before being appointed Federal Highway Administrator by President Reagan.

When he passed away, I couldn't help but think of this story, and how few other politicians would have made Governor Reagan's choice. One recalls President Clinton obtrusively carrying his Bible to church during the impeachment hearings, or President Obama taking to the pulpit in the Vermont Avenue Baptist Church in Washington. Somehow, Ronald Reagan sensed the balance that most Americans prefer to see struck: national leaders who respect religion enough to resist the temptation to appropriate it for secular purposes. It is a valuable lesson for all of us.

Having worked for President Reagan in the White House nearly to the end of his second term, one of my great joys was to be able also to serve in Congress during his Administration. Under the terms of the 20th Amendment to the Constitution, following a presidential election the new Congress convenes on the first Monday in January, whereas the new president does not take office until January 20.

Before he handed over power to George H.W. Bush, President Reagan took advantage of this overlap with the new Congress by making a personal visit to the House.

Perhaps remembering the slight he received at Tip O'Neill's hands in 1986, the president accepted Minority Leader Bob Michel's invitation to address the House Republican Conference from the House floor. It would be the president's opportunity to deliver a valediction to the many men and women with whom he had worked so closely, and who proudly called themselves Reagan Republicans.

President Reagan's trip to the House that January afternoon was a thrilling occasion for me personally. It was a passing of the baton: he talked somewhat wistfully about how we in Congress could carry on the work he had begun.

This private audience with President Reagan in the House chamber, where some of the most dramatic legislative events in American history have taken place, had a special intimacy about it. This was not the larger-than-life President delivering the State of the Union address to packed galleries under the glare of klieg lights, but a very human individual standing where we Members typically do when addressing the House, from one of two microphones in "the well," the area on the floor of the chamber immediately in front of the three-tiered Speaker's rostrum.

The assembled Representatives were visibly moved by his inspirational and very personal speech. But most of the Members, including me, were privately distracted by one slightly embarrassing faux pas that he committed. Evidently not having been briefed on protocol in the House, he was speaking from the microphone on the left side of the rostrum. By tradition, members of the Democratic Party speak from the left side of the aisle and members of the Republican Party speak from the right.

By this time, I should have known better than to underestimate President Reagan.

His use of the microphone on the Democratic side was entirely purposeful. Midway through his remarks, as he reflected upon the political odyssey that saw him progress from Democratic supporter of FDR and Truman to the Republican standard bearer of the late 20th century, he announced: "I did not leave the Democratic Party. The Democratic Party left me." He had said this many times before, but never in such dramatic fashion. As he spoke these words, he strode across the aisle. He continued with the balance of his remarks from the Republican side.

The Members erupted in applause and gave him a standing ovation.

*U.S. Representative, 1989-2005*
*Chairman, U.S. Securities and Exchange Commission, 2005-2009*

# 8

## WILLIAM H. WEBSTER
### Director, FBI 1978-1987/ Director, CIA 1987-1991

In acknowledgement of President Reagan's confidence in and support of the FBI, we decided to make him an Honorary Special Agent of the FBI. It was of course purely ceremonial, but gave him a reason to come to our headquarters and meet with a few thousand FBI employees.

The investiture took place on a platform in the courtyard of FBI headquarters. I made some relatively brief remarks and handed the President his official badge, which had been mounted in a fairly heavy display case.

The Secret Service had warned me that because of the March 1981 assassination attempt (from which recovery had been slow) they did not want him to carry anything heavy. Accordingly, once he had had the opportunity to admire the presentation, I approached with my hands out, and said, "The Secret Service wants me to take this now."

Well, he held the case in both hands and raised if over his head, way out of my reach. The audience suddenly realized what was happening and broke out in a cheer. Whereupon the President, triumphant, carried the case with him as he left the platform and proceeded to a reception we had set up inside the building.

In a symbolic sort of way, this was typical of his approach to "problems"—with good humor but the force to do what he thought was right.

1987—following the death of CIA Director Bill Casey—I got a call from President Reagan asking me to move over and become Director of Central Intelligence. Just at that moment I was on short notice to testify before Congress on the FBI's budget, and needed a bit of time for cogitation. I promised an answer, later in the day. Well, after some consultation with my family, I called Chief of Staff Howard Baker, and said, "I would be honored."

The next morning I was in the Oval Office to accept the offer; the President explained this was basically an opportunity for the media to get some photos of the occasion. However, because it was the birthday of long-time White House correspondent Helen Thomas, she would be allowed to ask one question. Naturally, we all expected it to have something to do with me or the CIA—logically, both—but the question she asked was a stunner: "Mr. President what you think about members of your staff referring to the first lady as 'a dragon lady'?"

There was a moment of somewhat shocked silence; the President grew red-faced (call it, a bit of the Irish showing through) but his response was simple and quiet: "Well, they ought to be ashamed of themselves."

Helen tried to go on, "It was your chief of staff . . ."

The President cut her off. "No, Helen, no." And the session was over.

Again, typical Reagan, expressing his loyalty to his wife, his chief of staff, and all other members of his staff. Not negotiable.

Toward the end of his second term, Ambassador Claire Booth Luce hosted a small party for the President in her Watergate apartment, and I was privileged to be among the guests. A quick but strong storm interrupted for a moment, knocking out the lights, but Claire assembled some candles and the party continued in this more relaxed and intimate atmosphere.

The subject of Reagan's probable successor came up—Vice President George Herbert Walker Bush. The President, clearly relaxed, was totally candid. He reminded us all that, years before, George Bush had been his most vigorous opponent for the presidential nomination. At that time, some of his campaign staffers had urged him to take Bush as his vice presidential candidate and others had been strongly opposed, the contest had been too bitter, how could these two ever work together?

Reagan said, nonetheless, that putting Bush on the ticket was the right thing to do. What struck me was how he now spoke of his former rival. How loyal he had been throughout his term in office—Bush never challenged him in a meeting or in public. By agreement, they reserved Thursday noon to have a private lunch together where the vice president could express himself on any subject in any manner . . . but it always was "private."

President Reagan said he could not have asked for more in a vice president and was deeply grateful to Bush for all he had done. Another example of Ronald Reagan's own loyalty.

**9**

## WAYNE VALIS
Special Assistant to the President 1981-1983

Ronald Reagan on Time Management. In January 1981, at the beginning of the Reagan Administration, a group of mid-level and senior White House aides met after the phones stopped ringing and the meetings of the day were over, at about 6 or 6:30 p.m. in the Roosevelt Room, across the hall from the Oval Office. They intended to strategize on coalition and lobbying efforts for the President's Economic Recovery Program. Many of these Reaganauts had served in the Nixon and Ford White Houses, and were used to working until 9 or 10 p.m. every weekday night.

At about 7 p.m. or so, the door nearest the Oval Office opened, and, to our astonishment, the President popped in. Usually, he left the Oval Office by about 6 p.m. to meet Nancy, relax, and have dinner. For some reason, that evening he had returned to the Oval Office and was told that some of his staff were meeting across the hall.

Reagan stepped in. Dapper, immaculate, and looking splendid as always, the President said, "Well, why are all of you working so late?"

To the all-male group, he added, "Don't you have wives or girl-friends? It's getting late. I know they say 'Hard work never killed anybody,' but I say, Why take the chance?"

He then told us he was going back to see Nancy, and left. We were in shock. For a minute, nobody spoke. While we pondered this appearance, the door swung open again. And again, it was the President.

"Oh, and fellas…One more thing. When I was Governor, I learned that people who always worked late at night…were usually just bad managers."

The President said goodbye and left. Message received. I think it was presidential aide Red Cavaney who broke the silence. "Why don't we break up, go home, get refreshed, then come back tomorrow?" No one demurred.

The Future under President Reagan—1981-1983. During 1980, the conservative publishers Arlington House, led by conservative academic Dick Bishirjian, contracted with me to edit and co-write a book featuring essays by conservative leaders known for having close ties to then-Governor Reagan. It was to be titled "The Future Under President Reagan." It was written "on spec;" if Reagan lost, the chapter contributors and I would get nothing; if Reagan won, Arlington House would speedily publish the book, hopefully in time for the inauguration.

Throughout the year, we worked on the essays. Aram Bakshian, who was to become the President's first chief speechwriter and head of the speechwriting office, prepared a chapter on "The Once and Future Reagan." Jack Kemp wrote a chapter on "Economics, Inflation and Productivity;" James C. Miller, who was to serve as Reagan's OMB Director, prepared "Regulatory Reform Under Ronald Reagan." Bob Carlson, Reagan's California Welfare Director, who became a senior Reagan domestic policy advisor, wrote "Taming the Welfare Monster;" General Dan O. Graham, the inventor of High Frontier and the "Star Wars" defense plan, wrote "National Defense Policies of a Reagan Administration;" Gerald Hyman, John Lenczowski, David Wheat, Jeff Eisenach, Larry Korb, Dale Tahtinen, Pedro SanJuan, and Joachim Maitre all contributed sections. I wrote several chapters, including: "Ronald Reagan: The Man, The President;" and "A Reagan Presidency: The Congress and the Courts."

Immediately after Reagan won the election, Arlington House furiously went to work finishing the book, and, before Christmas,

"The Future Under President Reagan" was published.

To my great surprise, in early 1981, "The Future Under President Reagan" outsold the *New York Times'* election book on President Reagan. At the corner of Pennsylvania and 17th Street, the then-bookstore stocked massive pyramids of the book in their show window. The sight of these gorgeous blue books, with a wonderful picture of Ronald Reagan on them, with my signature underneath, sent my 36-year-old head spinning. Full of myself, as young men are, I began escorting dozens and dozens of unsuspecting friends and visitors to the White House past the bookstore; each time, I would be "shocked, shocked" to see "my book" in glorious heaps in the window. All of them would buy copies, often in bulk, for their friends, which I would modestly autograph.

Basking in my newfound glory as an author, and as a newly-minted Special Assistant to the President—with White House mess and car and driver privileges—one day to my surprise I was called by Helene von Damm, Reagan's closest personal aide, his Executive Assistant (later his Director of Presidential Personnel, and Ambassador to her homeland, Austria). I had never been called by Helene or the President. Helene instructed me that the President wanted several copies of the book.

I flew from my office in the Old Executive Office Building (now the Eisenhower) to the rarified atmosphere of the West Wing. After waiting a short while, I was ushered in to give two copies of the book to the President. He thanked me for the book, looked over the chapters, leafed through the book, and said, "Oh, no pictures. You know, I like pictures." I apologized for the lack of pictures and told him I loved pictures, but that Arlington House was saving a little money and scrambling to get the book out on time. He put the books on his desk, thanked me, and my brief meeting was over.

Two years later, I was to have a second brief conversation with the President about this book. On January 27, 1983, Elizabeth Dole's staff had official portraits taken with the President in the Oval

Office. Just as the White House photographer was snapping the first group photo, a terrible, loud, gutteral noise shocked all of us. We all flinched. The picture was ruined. Well, almost ruined.

The President laughed. "That was me. I learned that trick in Hollywood, from my old friend, the actor Fredric March. If you make a loud noise, and keep smiling, you'll be the only one in the picture to look good. Everyone else will look startled." Then we all laughed, and took a great group photo. He also told us some other Hollywood lessons. The President said that when he announced that he was running for Governor, that Jack Warner, the head of Warner Brothers, said, "No, no—that's all wrong. Jimmy Stewart for Governor; Reagan for best friend." The President also said that Jack Warner gave him some advice about running for office: "Remember Ronnie, the secret to politics is the same as the secret to great acting: Sincerity. And once you learn to fake that, the rest is easy."

When it became my turn to have my picture taken, I showed the President a copy of *The Future Under President Reagan*, and told him that I had never gotten him to sign a copy of my book. The handsomest 71-year-old man in the world said that he remembered getting a copy several years ago, and said that it was a good thing he'd hired a "fortune teller" as part of the White House staff. He asked "Oh, by the way, how did I do?"

I told him that the authors predicted that he would restore the American spirit; confront the Soviet Union; rebuild America's defense forces; cut taxes; eliminate or reduce unnecessary regulation; and effectively work with, or defeat, the Democrats in the Congress. The President smiled broadly during my one-minute presentation. He said "Well, Wayne, if I do all that, I'll have been a pretty good President."

He did. And he was.


Ronald Reagan: Unending, Wonderful Surprises. Ronald Reagan had great affection for President Sandro Pertini of Italy. On Thursday, March 25, 1982, President Pertini made his first visit to America, as part of a State visit to the White House. Pertini and the Italian authorities had intervened in several anti-terrorist, anti-American incidents. So the President insisted on bringing Pertini for a State dinner. The Italian, one of the few world leaders older than the President, became close to Reagan's heart, so the arrival ceremony was even more warm and enjoyable than normal. In his diary, Reagan described their first meeting: "He's 84 & a terrific old gentleman. He loves America—very touching moment on the way to the W.H. He paused by the Marine holding our flag and kissed it." Forever after, the President was a great Pertini fan.

Almost everyone on the White House staff attended and enjoyed the arrival ceremony. After it all ended, mid-level and senior staffers settled in for a normal, hectic day; for at the time, the President was negotiating unusually difficult budget and tax battles with the Congress and business leaders—all with very differing and strong opinions on taxes. A little after 2:00, we all received notices that commissioned officers (Special Assistants and above) were immediately to report to the East Room, where the President had something important to tell us.

I regarded this as a little ominous. In the fifteen months of the Reagan Presidency, nothing like this had happened, except when the President had been shot. We all scurried as rapidly as possible to the East Wing, which had been set up for the entertainment portion of the Pertini state dinner, which was to take place later that night. Everything seemed slightly disjointed, and some of us political staff members prepared for the worst. We were seated on the golden, beautiful, but fragile wooden chairs used by guests for East Room ceremonial occasions. The President soon arrived, beaming, and exuding his almost-hypnotic charm. He strode to the small riser and podium that were set up near the famous, full-length Gilbert Stuart painting of Washington. The President, looking amazingly handsome for a man of any age, much less one of 71, took the stage; but what was really unusual was that he was accompanied by his elegant and lovely bride, Nancy. We had never been jointly addressed by the Reagans.

As he began talking, the President's grin got wider and wider. Obviously the Reagans were thoroughly enjoying a joke that they were putting over on us. The President in mock seriousness announced that today was important because there was going to be a state dinner for the Italian President that night. This made no sense, and we continued to be mystified. Reagan turned to Nancy and said, "Honey, why don't you tell them?"

Nancy Reagan took over the microphone. "I thought it would be nice to let you in on a little secret." Two of her close friends were going to be providing the entertainment for the state dinner, and she thought it would be better for them if they rehearsed before a live audience. She said, "Ron and I hope you'll be willing to sit through their rehearsals and help them out a little bit."

Without further ado, she introduced Frank Sinatra and Perry Como, who came out from the Green Room. The President and Mrs. Reagan went over to the piano, where four hand microphones had been prepared, and we were treated to the loveliest of banter between the four. Frank, famously the Chairman of the Board, teasingly took over. He said he would do anything for his girlfriend Nancy. The Reagans loved it. So did everyone. For over an hour, we heard singing, jokes, teasing, and the most charming entertainment from the greatest entertainers of the 20th century, in a really intimate setting. The President and Nancy, and Frank and Perry, made us feel like we were in a private supper club.

For days after, at odd hours of the day and night, a thought would come to my mind: "I really love this man." Thirty-two years later, I often have the same thought.

Helping U.S. Citizens: Prompt Payment Reform—1982. As the government greatly expanded after WWII, it began contracting and subcontracting for services with small, minority, disadvantaged, and large businesses. To the horror of these private sector vendors, the government began delaying payment of its bills, sometimes for months and months. Although the IRS and Federal Government demanded immediate payment from citizens, tacking on 20 percent penalties that compounded monthly, the government began the practice of acknowledging its debts to private vendors but simply not paying them. These vendors could not sue the U.S. government; there were no penalties for the delays; and the government soon began using delay as an "accepted, normal money management practice." Contractors and subcontractors began clamoring for change, and in 1971 created the PPC, or Prompt Pay Coalition, which butted its head against the government, to no avail.

In 1981, the Coalition, headed by Kenton Pattie, brought its complaint and proposed remedy to the Reagan White House. Unfortunately, the career bureaucrats in both the Office of Management and Budget and the U.S. Treasury were deaf to the appeals; they decided to make no change in the "accepted money management" system. Private vendors and small businesses would receive no redress. The bureaucracy was adamant. I believed that the government position was unjust, and I also thought, more importantly, that should Ronald Reagan learn of it, he would make a major change.

I decided to try an end run. Despite the risks of offending the Treasury Department and the OMB, I decided to include a representative of the Prompt Pay Coalition in a White House meeting with the President that was discussing the 1982 TEFRA tax legislation. At the tail end of a strategy session in the Cabinet Room, a small businessman told the President of the problem of government tardiness in paying its bills. At that time, the U.S. Government was late on paying private vendors over $50-100 billion, a huge sum, especially during the recession of 1980-81, which featured 20 percent interest rates and 10 percent unemployment. Businesses were stretched to the breaking point.

The President listened, and couldn't believe that the situation was true. He turned to Treasury Secretary Don Regan and asked, "Don, does the U.S. Treasury not pay due bills to private citizens—on time?" Regan, who had been briefed by his bureaucracy, reluctantly acknowledged, "Well, Mr. President, you see, we have accepted and customary payment procedures, to safeguard the public treasury."

The President was incredulous. "Is it our policy not to pay the government's bills on time? Is this true?"

The Treasury Secretary and the OMB Director reluctantly began to respond. The President cut them off. "The policy of this government is to pay its bills on time, especially to private citizens. They have to pay their tax bills on time, so it's only fair. The policy of my Administration has just changed. Now work this out, and report back to me."

On Thursday, May 13, 1982, in the Rose Garden, the Prompt Payment Act was signed into law by Ronald Reagan, in a small business ceremony. Henceforth, the U.S. Government was going to pay its bills on time, to private citizens, or be subject to fines and penalties. What was sauce for the goose was going to be sauce for the gander. Ronald Reagan's innate sense of justice, equity, and fairness had reversed decades of unfairness by the U.S. Government.

Budgets, Spending Cuts, and Tax Increases. 1982 was a very difficult year for President Reagan. The recession continued; budget deficits were projected to reach $128 billion, the largest peacetime deficit ever; the stock market dropped by 10 percent during 1981, and Wall Street was very nervous for 1982. Deficit hawks within the Republican party were calling to repeal part of the 1981 tax cut. Democrats urged an increase in business taxes. Many were urging spending cuts—GOP leaders wanted cuts to domestic programs and entitlements, the Democrats to defense. Conservative business leaders, including the U.S. Chamber of Commerce and leading small business associations, were opposed to any tax increase.

Paul Volcker was conducting a tough monetary policy to squeeze out inflation, which had risen to 13.5 percent, the highest in U.S. peacetime history. And the President was supporting Volcker, despite damage to his popularity and approval ratings. Thus there was castor oil and unpleasantness for Democrats, Republicans, and Conservatives alike—and especially for the President.

In an effort to find a way out of this dilemma, the President decided to arrange an extensive series of listening sessions with Wall Street, Main Street, and small and large business leaders. He had to find a bipartisan solution. Tip O'Neill and Democrat leaders contacted the President, pledging to support such a bipartisan program.

Jim Baker and Elizabeth Dole assigned me to arrange these meetings with the widest array of business leaders. Throughout early spring and summer 1982, many such meetings occurred, culminating on May 11, 12, and 13, with six Presidential sessions.

Participating in all six, I had an up close and personal view of the President in action. Finally, the President decided to rescind part of the 1981 business tax cuts. He believed this was the only way to convince the Federal Reserve, Wall Street, the financial markets, and a bipartisan majority in the Congress, that he was finally going to put the economy on the right track. So the President, despite his own anti-tax philosophy, and deepest instincts, agreed to the 1982 TEFRA economic legislation.

The President now had to announce his decision to a Cabinet Room full of top U.S. business leaders. The meeting was opened by Jim Baker, Don Regan, and Dave Stockman, who summarized the economic situation for the leaders and prepared the group for the President and his decision.

In the Reagan White House, everything was like clockwork. Nothing and no-one was ever late. And now the time came for the President to enter, and there was no Ronald Reagan. I was seated behind Jim Baker, in a chair next to the window, looking out over the Rose Garden. Baker finally turned around to me and said, "Wayne. Go get the President. Now."

I left the Cabinet Room and went into the Oval Office to summon the President. I said, "Mr. President, it's a little past time."

President Reagan, almost wearily, said, "I know. It's time." He got up and started walking over to the Cabinet Room. "But you know, I really don't want to do this."

I froze. Panic set in. I debated saying something to the President, but I realized he was talking to himself. I waited.

"I don't really want to do this damn thing." The President never, never swore. Even in his diaries, the President would write "d—n" or "h- - l." He was always a gentleman and never in the slightest used profanity.

Happily for me, the President took a few more steps toward the Oval Office. "I hope they know, I want the most spending cuts and the fewest tax increases. That's the only way they convinced me to do all this." We were now at the door to the Oval Office.

"Well, I guess they're ready for me."

I said, "Yes, Mr. President, these are your strongest supporters. They will back you no matter what you do."

He responded, "Well, okay. Here we go. Let's do it, then."

The President walked through the door. The transformation was unbelievable. A tired, somewhat discouraged 71-year-old-man suddenly turned into an impossibly handsome, vigorous, enthusiastic, energetic political leader. He gave a tremendous pep talk. He was most enthusiastically FOR this program. It was the only way ahead for America. It would transform the U.S. economy. It would bring back prosperity. He talked for about ten minutes and closed with a gentle but firm admonition to them to begin lobbying the undecided Congressmen and Senators. There was dialogue around the room, and pledges of support. And the President in the most genial and inspiring way, told them, "Remember, they don't have to see the light; they only have to feel the heat. Let's go, on to victory."

Years later, Reagan's diaries were published. Here's what he said about May 11, 1982:

> Demos. have come up with House proposal for budget. It would add $150 bil in taxes & make most if not all it's savings in defense. Met with 3 groups—Indie Bus. Men, leaders of Trade & Bus. Associations, and some top C.E.O.'s. All seem gung-ho to support our plan. I leaned on them to start pressing on their Reps and Senators."

It was vintage Ronald Reagan. After months of debate and political warfare on Capitol Hill and within the business community, the new Reagan budget and tax proposals passed the House and Senate and were signed into law by the President. The stock market surged, from about Dow Jones 900 to 2200, and it didn't stop there. The Reagan prosperity continued for almost two decades, eventually setting the stage for a Dow Jones Industrial Average at 16,000. Interest rates dropped precipitously. The economy soared. One of the largest economic booms in U.S. history began. It was captained and orchestrated by the Gipper, one of the most masterful political leaders of the 20th century, in whose shadow we still live.

Ronald Reagan, Father of American Energy Independence —1983. Ronald Reagan inherited a disastrous economy. Un-employment was over 10 percent; inflation reached 13.5 percent; and interest rates briefly touched 20 percent—virtually killing economic activity in America. There had been lines at the gas pump. U.S. dependence on foreign oil increased; and bizarre labyrinthine regulation of natural gas severely distorted production and price of that valuable energy source.

By 1983, the economy was in much better condition. Reagan had the stock market humming, jobs were being created, and the President was ready to tackle the problem and opportunity of natural gas production and regulation.

In his diary for Tuesday, Feb. 8, 1983, the President described a meeting in the Cabinet Room "on deregulating gas." Vice President George H. W. Bush, an experienced Texas oil man very familiar with and committed to solving the natural gas problem, and new Energy Secretary Donald Hodel, briefed the President. Again, in his diary, the President wrote, "Hodel is going to work with our leaders in Cong. to come up with a package to deregulate & at same time protect consumers. Under the present (Dem.) control plan there are 28 dif. classifications of gas price & it has still gone up about 50 percent."

The President told Vice President Bush and Secretary Hodel

to move full speed ahead. He committed his administration to the task of energy deregulation. A Reagan SWAT team was created to produce legislation and get it passed. Consisting of the Vice President; White House staffers Fred Khedouri and C. Boyden Gray; and Energy Department leaders Hodel, Danny Boggs, Ted Garrish, and Jim White, the team devised a plan to transition the regulated system to a functioning, free market system. The battle was joined. Opponents raised the specter of rising prices following decontrol, but the Energy Information Agency predicted deregulation would do the opposite. The President's proposed legislation carried the day intellectually—even being described by *The New York Times* as "an elegant solution." Unfortunately, intellectual merits don't always translate into Congressional votes.

Although the legislation did not pass the Congress during Ronald Reagan's tenure, the foundation for its future passage in the next administration was laid. During these years, I worked with the private sector deregulation coalition and the leadership of the Natural Gas Supply Association to pass the legislation. In 1989, soon after Ronald Reagan had departed for California, President George H.W. Bush had the pleasure of signing into law the deregulation envisioned by President Reagan.

This successful policy change has led to a 25-year boom of natural gas in America. The glimmers of the future discussed in that 1983 Cabinet meeting have resulted in one of the most spectacular energy explosions and the transformation of the natural gas market. As the Reagan Administration predicted, supplies soared and prices dropped. In 2014, America is on the threshold of energy independence. The U.S. has become the Saudi Arabia of natural gas. By removing the shackles of regulation on the natural gas market, the energy legacy of Ronald Reagan lives on.

Privatization—1985-87. President Reagan was a big believer in the power of the private sector. His philosophy was that private business was more efficient than government in performing economic functions. One example of government failure that galled the President was Conrail, a government-owned and operated freight railroad that consistently lost money and had to be subsidized. The President was determined to sell it. Transportation Secretary Elizabeth Dole was put in charge of getting it done. The big obstacle was senior Democrat Congressman John Dingell of Michigan, whose father had come to Congress during the 1930's, died, and was succeeded by his son, John. Dingell was a New Dealer, Chairman of the Commerce Committee, who inspired fear in his adversaries. He used all the powers of government to intimidate his opponents.

Regarding Conrail, and similar government-owned entities, liberal Democrats believed if an entity or a business was profitable, you should tax it; if it moved, you should regulate it; if it didn't make money, and it couldn't move, you should subsidize it. Thus, they fought bitterly to keep Conrail on the federal payroll.

The battle between the Democrat anti-privatizers, on the one hand, and, on the other, the Coalition of Americans for Privatization (CAP—made up of Ronald Reagan, Elizabeth Dole, Republicans, Boll Weevil Democrats, and private sector leaders), in favor of privatization, went on for over a year. It was bitter. On January 23, 1986, the President personally went to work on winning this battle. As the pro-privatization coalition leader, I organized a meeting in the Old Executive Office Building for the President and Secretary Dole. We rallied over 100 CEOs to get active on Capitol Hill to privatize Conrail. The President and Elizabeth Dole did fabulous jobs in rallying these troops. CAP, led by Citizens for a Sound Economy President Rich Fink, American Business Conference CEO Jack Albertine, and small business leader Dirk Van Dongen, organized a massive lobbying campaign on the Congress. Ultimately, it was decisive.

Finally, in a series of Congressional votes, Dingell, Dan Rostenkowski and Tip O'Neill agreed on a compromise. Ronald Reagan had triumphed. To help the Democrats save face, the privatization legislation was limited to Conrail only; other federal assets, such as the Tennessee Valley Authority, would remain federalized. Secretary

Dole, a North Carolinian lady of intellect, charm, graciousness, and beauty, repeatedly conferred with the lordly, forceful, and commanding Dingell. She again reassured him on the TVA and other government-owned entities.

In October 1986, the only successful major privatization legislation in the history of the U.S. was signed into law. In March 1987, Conrail was sold for $1.65 billion—real money, back in 1987. On Friday, April 3, 1987, at 11:35 a.m., there was a little party in the Roosevelt Room including Fink, Van Dongen, Albertine, Jim Burnley, Wayne Vance, and Valis. DOT Secretary Elizabeth Dole brought a gigantic, three or four foot-long check, in the amount of $1,575,000,000, made out to the U.S. Treasury, the purchase price for selling Conrail.

We had a wonderful intimate party with the President, who was overjoyed at the first victory for his privatization principle. The President looked over the check and remarked on how big it was, especially to someone who had gone through the Depression. He turned to Elizabeth, "Well, Elizabeth, you have done a great job. This was a terrific victory. Now how much do you think we could get for selling the Tennessee Valley Authority?"

Postscript: Fifty-eight percent of Conrail's assets were purchased by the Norfolk Southern Corporation, and the remaining 42 percent by CSX in 1998. Both freight railroads are solidly profitable and are regarded as providing excellent service to a wide variety of shippers. The President's philosophy on privatization was proven and has turned out to be wildly successful. The Tennessee Valley Authority, alas, is still federally owned, and continues to lose hundreds of millions of dollars annually.

Goodbyes—1983-1994. In early 1983, the President appointed Elizabeth Dole as Secretary of Transportation. Her successful White House outreach staff was now broken up: scattering to different agencies or joining the private sector. I opted for the private sector. The Washington Post wrote a dishonest article about how disgruntled Special Assistant to the President Wayne Valis was leaving in disgust. I wrote a sharp rebuttal, setting Post reporter Juan Williams straight. The day after the Post published my rebuttal, I received the following letter:

Dear Wayne,

I've been given a copy of your letter to the editor of the Wash. Post, March 21st. I just want you to know how much I appreciate your generous words and your statement of loyalty to and approval of what we are trying to do. You warmed my heart with your put-down of Mr. Williams and made me very proud.

Thank you & God Bless you.

Sincerely, RR.

The President's generosity to me continued. Several days later, I received an invitation to the State Dinner for Sultan Qaboos of Oman. A day or two later, Jim Baker informed me that I would have a farewell audience for ten minutes with the President at 10:50 a.m. on April 15, 1983. In the Oval Office, the President told me how much my coalition formation work meant to the victories of Reaganomics. He then went to his desk and presented me with a lovely, heavy, bronze Ronald Reagan service medallion, which he gave to some aides and strong political supporters. Jim Baker told the President that I was still going to be on his team in the private sector and would be helping him put together coalitions on economic and regulatory issues, as needed. We briefly recalled our victories, posed for photos, shook hands, and said our goodbyes. My White House days with Ronald Reagan were over.

Later, I wept at the thought of leaving the side of this great man.

In November 1993, I received an invitation to go to the Reagan Library as part of three or four dozen relatively senior Reagan aides, to have a Christmas party and photo op with the President. The rumor was that the almost 83-year-old President's health was failing. On December 11, 1993, at the Reagan Presidential Library in Simi Valley, California, we were seated in a small auditorium at about 10:00 a.m. Reaganauts Jim Miller, Jim Watt, Don Hodel, and others made remarks and led us in some dialogue about our service in the Reagan White House. At 11:40, the President appeared, still looking very good, but appearing slower and grayer than when I had last seen him two years earlier. The President delivered remarks. There was then dialogue with him, followed at 12:15 by a reception and then photos and a leave-taking. I knew then that I would probably never see this inspirational figure again. I told him that the greatest honor in my professional life had been serving as a corporal in his army. Looking at the nametag, the President said, "Well, Wayne, the honor was mine." I was never to speak with him again.

In November 1994, eleven months later, the President issued his letter to the American people about his impending Alzheimer's. In it, he famously said, "I now begin the journey that will lead me into the sunset of my life. I know that for America there will always be a bright dawn ahead."

# 10

## KENNETH M. DUBERSTEIN
### White House Chief of Staff 1988-89

The old speaker of the House, Tip O'Neill, used to say he didn't like compromising with Ronald Reagan because every time he did, the president would get 80 percent of what he wanted. President Reagan would tell us "I'll take 80 percent every time and come back next year for the remaining 20 percent. That's what governing is all about."

In the immediate tragic aftermath of the 270 marines losing their lives in the barracks in Lebanon, President Reagan convened a secret briefing of the bi-partisan congressional leadership upstairs in the residence of the White House. The topic was not what they expected—it was about the rescue mission in Grenada. There were lots of good questions raised by Senators Byrd and Baker, by Speaker O'Neill, Majority Leader Wright and Republican leader Bob Michel. At the end of the briefing by the Chairman of the Joint Chiefs and the Secretary of Defense, President Reagan said that it was his decision to launch the invasion at 5 AM the next morning. In spite of the varying views expressed, the leaders all came together. As they rose from their seats and shook hands, I will always remember Tip O'Neill patting President Reagan on his elbow and saying "God Bless You, Mr. President."

As we looked at the Berlin Wall shortly before the President's electrifying speech at the Brandenburg Gate, President Reagan was overtaken with emotion as he confronted the crosses painted on the wall where people had died trying to escape to freedom. The President turned to West German Chancellor Helmut Kohl and me and simply said, "This is the only wall built to keep people in, not keep people out." Fifteen minutes later, he delivered the signature line of his presidency—"Mr. Gorbachev, tear down this wall."

# 11

## DAVID R. GERGEN
### White House Director of Communications 1981-1985

Any White House staff that wants to understand how a President can govern effectively at home and lead with strength overseas would do well to study the Reagan years. Certainly Ronald Reagan taught me more about presidential leadership than anyone I have known—and often by surprise. Everyone who had the privilege of working with him in those days has a treasure trove of stories. Let me offer just one.

It took place in the third year of his presidency when it was his turn to play host to leaders of the G-7 nations in their annual spring summit. Mike Deaver—the best choreographer of modern White Houses—persuaded Reagan to locate the summit in Colonial Williamsburg. It was a congenial setting that allowed Reagan to recall the early ideals of the Republic and to give the other leaders a taste of early America. All, that is, except the French—Mike, as I recall, thought the French had been haughty to us when they hosted a year earlier and in compensation, housed them somewhere in East Jesus.

The more serious challenge, as we on staff saw it, was how to prepare the President for the substance of the talks. World leaders were still taking his measure and the dragons in the international press corps were just waiting for him to make a gaffe so they could pounce. Surely, he would have to be as well versed on substantive detail as our crack advance team was on logistical detail.

So, we on staff beavered away preparing lengthy briefing papers for every meeting. And that raised a second challenge. Ronald Reagan had a habit of reading at a very deliberate pace. Once he had finished reading, he had excellent recall of details but still, it took a while. Some thought that dated back to his movie days when he read slowly to memorize a script.

Our challenge was that if we gave him too much to read, he would often stay up late and wake up tired the next morning. He didn't seem to mind but boy, Nancy sure did. She was a glorious enforcer for him. I had learned that during the campaign when I had been responsible for preparing briefing books for him in advance of the debates. The day after I handed him a thick one, Nancy gave me hard stares. Staff quickly learned, you didn't want to get cross-threaded with Nancy.

About half-way through that summit, Reagan had a very tough day ahead—one-on-one bilaterals with a series of world leaders—Thatcher, Kohl, Mitterand, Mulroney and the like—and for each of them, he would need a briefing paper of 15 pages or so. Moreover, he had to host at least one plenary session—more pages and pages. His briefing book was turning into "War and Peace."

So, it was with some trepidation, as I recall, that chief of staff Jim Baker (the best!) gave Reagan the briefing book late the after-noon before and urged, "Mr. President, try to go over this material quickly, Please, please don't stay up late reading it." "All right, Jim," he said reassuringly and off he went.

The next morning, Reagan joined our staff team for breakfast around 7:30 a.m. and he looked like he had been hit by a truck. His eyes were puffy and he was walking slowly. "My God," I thought to myself, "he was up half the night with that damn briefing book." "

About 20 minutes into the eggs, he got that "Aw, shucks" look on his face—one so memorable even today—and said, "Fellas, I've got a confession to make. Last night, I sat down with your briefing book, which was good. I appreciate you doing it.

"But did you know," he went on, "that "The Sound of Music" was on TV last night? That's one of my favorite movies, so I watched it. It went on pretty late. I'm sorry I never got through the briefing papers!"

Instantly, fears of Nancy disappeared—how could she hold *us* responsible? —but other fears shot up: How was he possibly going to get through all these meetings without benefit of our elaborate briefings? Were we heading toward a gaffe heard round the world? What would those dragons do to us?

That's when Reagan—once again—taught me something about him, and about leadership. As it turned out, he was better that day than we had almost ever seen him. Fortified by a relaxing movie, breakfast and a few laughs, he was absolutely on his game. Instead of getting down in the weeds in conversation, he stayed above the tree line, sharing long-term aspirations and plans with other leaders. His visitors clearly appreciated the easy flow of conversation and talking through long-term visions. Even the journalists outside reported favorably.

What I found about Reagan was that he was not only comfortable in his own skin, he was serene. He had enough experience and success in life to be well anchored as a person. And as someone who had served for eight years as chief executive of the biggest, most complex state in the country—a state that if it were a country would have the 7th largest GDP—he also knew how to get things done as President. Those are invaluable assets in the White House.

His leadership lessons for me that day were also clear: we on the staff should get over the arrogance that often comes from working in the West Wing, thinking that only if a president listens to you personally can he get things right. Sometimes on staff, you must be willing to recommend a different course than what a President wants—to speak truth to power, and yes, to speak conscience to power—but always remember who is in charge. He or—one day, soon, I hope—she got there by winning the votes of millions upon millions of Americans; you didn't.

The other lesson Reagan underscored for me in Williamsburg is that the place of the leader is not down in the engine room of the ship, trying to turn each of the many dials, focusing on all the details. The place of the captain is up on the top deck—looking out over the horizon, setting the course, steering the ship. Reagan was always most comfortable at the foc'sle.

Some years ago, the Chinese leader Zhou En-lai was asked whether Napoleon had been a great general, and he famously replied, "I can't answer that question. It's too early to tell." Historians tell us in the same way that it is too early to make lasting judgments about Ronald Reagan. But those of us who had the privilege of working for him do know this: he wasn't perfect, just as we certainly weren't. But he came to the White House when most Americans despaired about governance of the country; a string of presidents had seemingly failed and there was serious talk about rewriting the Constitution. Within weeks of taking office, Americans said—as they had about FDR—we have a leader in the White House again. He restored hope, rebuilt pride—and made us smile once more.

*David Gergen is Director, Public Leadership Center, Harvard University Kennedy School of Government*

## 12

## FRED F. FIELDING
### Counsel to the President 1981-1986

In July 1985, the Chief of Staff called me to go with him to the Oval Office; a routine medical check-up had disclosed that President Reagan needed surgery to remove a cancerous intestinal polyp. I briefed the President on the option of exercising the 25th Amendment, since the operation would require that he be completely sedated for a period of time. It became apparent that he was intrigued by the fact that if he chose to exercise the Amendment and temporarily transfer his powers to his Vice President, it would be the first time in history that a President had done so. His expressed concern was that since he was to be incapacitated for such a relative brief period of time, this might set a precedent that would restrict the options of a future President. No final decision was made except that we would meet in his room at Bethesda Naval Hospital the next morning, but it was clear to me which way he was leaning.

The exercise of the Amendment requires a Presidential letter, so that evening I prepared not one, but two letters. One draft formally advised the Speaker of the House and the President Pro Tem of the Senate that he was exercising his prerogative under Amendment XXV to temporarily transfer his powers to the Vice President. The other draft acknowledged the 25th Amendment, but explicitly recited his belief that the drafters of the Amendment did not intend it to apply to brief and temporary periods of incapacity such as this. However, the letter then went on to direct that upon his sedation the Vice President was to assume the President's duties and power "consistent with my long-standing arrangements with Vice President George Bush, and not intending to set a precedent binding anyone privileged to hold this Office in the future..."

In his hospital bed, with Nancy by his side, he reviewed both drafts and, not surprisingly, picked the latter one. That draft satisfied him but it also satisfied the formal Constitutional requirements for a Transfer. As in so many other instances in my dealings with him, in situations involving Executive power, President Reagan's two threshold questions were (1) was it the right thing to do, and (2) would it be setting a precedent unduly impinging on a successor's ability to exercise his or her own judgment. Here he had satisfied himself and accomplished what needed to be done, in his own way.

The postscript to this hospital-bed meeting came as I was leaving. He asked me to call Vice President Bush to tell him what he had decided to do, and then added with that wonderful sparkle in his eye "but tell George that Nancy doesn't come with the transfer."

*Fred Fielding also served as White House Counsel to President George W. Bush, 2007-2009.*

# 13

## MALCOLM S. "STEVE" FORBES
### Chairman of the Board for International Broadcasting 1983-1989

When I was head of the oversight agency for Radio Liberty and Radio Free Europe, I hosted a dinner at Forbes headquarters with President Reagan as guest of honor and after-dinner speaker. The desserts were already set on the tables, and just as everyone began to eat the first course, Reagan ate his dessert. I guess he realized that this might look a bit strange, so he explained. "When you are the after-dinner speaker, they always call on you to come up to the podium and start speaking, just when the audience begins dessert. If the desserts are on the table and you haven't already had yours, it won't be waiting for you when you've finished speaking . . . it will have been cleared away. So if you like dessert, you should eat it first."

The October 1986 Reykjavik summit meeting, between Reagan and Soviet President Mikhail Gorbachev, was generally viewed as a failure, because Reagan did not get the concessions he sought to allow development of an anti-missile defense system (colloquially known as "Star Wars").

Reagan told me, "why." Something he had learned in his Hollywood days, negotiating as head of the Screen Actors Guild: when you are involved in hot and heavy negotiations, spread out over several days, and you have come to some level of agreement . . . at the last moment, when everyone is exhausted and just patting each other on the back about what a grand success they had enjoyed, one side or the other will slip in something—one last bit of business—expecting it to move on through, in the camaraderie of the moment.

In this case, Gorbachev wanted to insert a few simple words in the overall agreement—words that would stymie Star Wars development. Reagan expected the move, and refused. As he told me, "Always keep your eye on the ball, never lose sight of your real objective. Don't let 'mood,' he said, "trump 'substance.'"

In 1992, we celebrated the 75th anniversary of the founding of Forbes magazine, which by coincidence had been in the same year, 1917, as the Russian revolution. The founder of Forbes—our Scottish immigrant grandfather who came to this country with little money and a lot of ambition—would certainly have been delighted, had he been around in 1992, to know that his creation outlasted that of Vladimir Lenin—i.e. the Soviet Union.

We held our party at Radio City Music Hall—packed with 2,000 civic leaders, friends, supporters, and employees. We thought it would be fitting to have President Reagan (the man who brought down the Soviet Union) and Mikhail Gorbachev (the last General Secretary of the Soviet Communist Party) to highlight the program. Well, for some reason, Gorbachev and his wife Raisa got into high dudgeon. They thought he should be the headliner, not a supporting act, and he refused to participate. They appealed to me, and to Reagan . . . and I let President Reagan handle the matter. He heard them out, agreed that Gorbachev had been a great leader, but, well, this was a party, the celebration of a company's anniversary, not a geo-political event, etc. etc. In the end, Reagan's deft touch worked. The man was a master of diplomacy. And, in the event, Gorbachev enjoyed a rousing ovation, the crowd chanting "Gor-by, Gor-by."

Reagan was interviewed by Rowland Evans and Robert Novak about the time that some of his cabinet officials and White House staff were known to be in acrimonious disagreement over one issue or another. He was asked, "How do you deal with all this seeming disarray?"

He told a story, about two psychiatrists who commuted together to work, every day. One was an old hand, the other was young and newly-arrived in the profession. At the end of the day, every day, the young man was exhausted, emotionally drained because of all of the issues he had to handle, assess, deal with. The old man was always calm and serene.

Finally, one day, the young man couldn't stand it anymore. He said to the old hand, "Every day, I am washed out, distressed, and you just sail along. How do you do it?"

The old hand said, simply, "I don't listen."

**14**

# ELIZABETH DOLE
## Secretary of Transportation 1983-1987

To have worked for President Ronald Reagan and to have been a part of an administration that truly changed the course of history for the better was an experience that I will forever treasure. I have countless special memories of my seven years in the administration, but there are two "Reagan remembrances" that stand out.

The first occurred during my service as Assistant to the President for Public Liaison. President Reagan and I were alone in a "holding room," as he awaited the call to go on stage to deliver a speech. As the two of us talked, I couldn't resist the opportunity to pose a question I had long wanted to ask.

"Mr. President," I said. "You have the weight of the world on your shoulders, and yet you're always so gracious, so kind, so thoughtful of others. You are never flustered or frustrated. How in the world do you do it?"

President Reagan leaned back in his chair, and said, "Well, Elizabeth, when I was Governor of California, it seemed that every day there was someone standing before my desk describing yet another disaster or crisis. The feeling of stress became almost unbearable, and I had the urge to look over my shoulder for someone I could pass the problem to. One day I realized I was looking in the wrong direction. I looked up instead of back, and I'm still looking up. I couldn't face one more day in this office if I didn't know I could ask for God's help and it would be given."

Though I believe that the private conversations I had with President Reagan should remain private, I have taken the liberty to share that story on many occasions. I do so because it eloquently explains that what we do on our own matters little. What counts is what God chooses to do through us. President Reagan knew life is more than a few years spent on self-indulgence and career advancement. It's a privilege, a responsibility, and a stewardship to be met according to His calling.

My second memory involved not something that President Reagan said; rather, it involves something he didn't say. One of the tough battles of my time as the President's Secretary of Transportation was the effort to remove National Airport and Dulles Airport, gateways to the nation's capital, from Congressional control. Many Senators and Members of Congress—including my husband—told me that it was an effort destined to fail. Administrations of both parties had proposed the idea eight times since 1948, and each time it went absolutely nowhere.

The ninth time, however, was to be different. It took three years of hard work to gain Congressional approval, and there were instances when powerful Capitol Hill leaders urged President Reagan to tell me to give up or back off. It might have been politically beneficial for him to do so, but he never said a word to me, because he knew that our proposal was the right thing to do. Today, of course, Reagan National Airport and Dulles International Airport are hailed as models of success. History, as it has so often, has proven that President Reagan was correct.

# 15

# PETER M. ROBINSON
### Special Assistant / Speechwriter 1983-1989

One day a few years ago, I visited Bill Clark at his ranch near Paso Robles. As Judge Clark and I talked, I found myself wanting to ask not about Reagan's policies but about his interior life. What had Clark, the man who was probably closer to the President than anyone outside the Reagan family, seen in the chief executive that would have been hidden from an ordinary member of the staff such as me? The private, inner Reagan—what had he been like?

"He was a man of prayer," Clark said.

Reagan, Clark explained, prayed in all moods and in all circumstances. Even during government meetings, Reagan might offer a brief, silent prayer. "I could usually tell when he was in communication with our Lord," Clark said, chuckling. "When he was leaning back his head and looking at the ceiling, that's often when he was praying."

Flying with Reagan from Sacramento to Washington for a governors' meeting in 1968, Clark was startled to see the captain emerge from the cockpit, then walk down the aisle to find him. "He said, 'Mr. Clark, you might want to tell this to the governor. We've just received word that Martin Luther King Jr. has been shot and killed.' " Clark stepped back to inform Reagan, who was seated in a row behind him. "I expected him to say something, but he was silent," Clark said. "He just looked down at his feet." Clark returned to his seat. When he glanced back a moment later, Reagan's head was bowed, his lips moving. "He was in prayer."

When in 1982 Leonid Brezhnev died, Clark joined the President and Mrs. Reagan in walking the couple of blocks up Sixteenth Street from the White House to the grim old mansion that served as the Soviet embassy. Once each of them had signed the book of condolences, the President made a suggestion. "He looked over at me with that wonderful catbird grin of his," Clark said, "and he asked, 'Do you think they'd mind if we just said a little prayer for the man?'" The President, Mrs. Reagan, and Clark bowed their heads. Then Reagan asked the blessings of God on the deceased leader of a nation devoted to atheism.

Reagan's favorite setting for prayer? The outdoors. "He didn't need a church to pray in," Clark explained. "He referred to his ranch as an open cathedral with oak trees for walls." On trail rides, Clark and Reagan would often recite the famous prayer of St. Francis of Assisi that opens, "Lord, make me an instrument of Thy peace." Sometimes," Clark said, "the President would look around and say, 'What a wonderful place for prayer.' And sometimes he'd just look up at the sky and say, 'Glory to God.'"

If only the President had time, he could write all his speeches himself—that, I learned when I joined the speechwriting staff, was the correct reply to any reporter who asked about my job. It sounded good, and I certainly said it often enough. But I couldn't help wondering if it were true.

Then in late 1983, James Watt, the secretary of the Interior, made a remark belittling affirmative action, and, in the furor that followed, Watt found himself forced to resign. The President felt for the former secretary—Watt may have said something stupid, but he'd been a loyal member of the administration all the same—so Reagan decided to devote one of his weekly radio talks to a review of Watt's accomplishments. Never learning of this decision, the speechwriting office sent the President a radio talk that dealt with the economy, not Watt. The President solved this problem by writing a radio talk of his own.

When the President's draft reached the speechwriting office for fact-checking, we passed it around. Single-spaced on a yellow legal pad, the draft ran to two pages in the President's own handwriting. It was relaxed and conversational, a perfect little piece of oratory. But what struck me was the way it looked. It was clean. The draft contained only two or three rewrites, each an instance in which the President had crossed out only a single word or phrase. Whereas we speechwriters always rewrote extensively, crossing out so many paragraphs, adding and dropping so many words and phrases, and scribbling so many new passages in the margins that our secretaries often had trouble making out our changes, Ronald Reagan had simply sat down and written what he wanted to say.

It was true. If only the President had time, he *could* write all his speeches himself.

*The above are excerpts from Peter Robinson's book,* How Ronald Reagan Changed My Life *(HarperCollins Publishers Inc., New York, 2003) The first begins on page 186 and the other on page 121.*

*The President's Radio Address of November 26, 1983, will be found at page 329.*

## 16

## JAMES S. ROSEBUSH
Deputy Assistant to the President and Chief of Staff to the First Lady

The White House Correspondence Office was staffed with many volunteers and they had the almost impossible job of answering, mail in the most knowledgeable way. Sometimes they would ask us specific questions to be able to more accurately answer the questions that came in from across the world.

One day someone from the Correspondence Office asked me if I knew what the President's favorite hymns were. Rather than speculate, I decided to ask him directly. "Well, Jim, yes I have several but I would have to say my two favorites are: "In The Garden" and "Sweet Hour of Prayer." Then he sang them to me in that quiet low voice—and he knew every word in a way that said to me that he used these hymns like prayers. They were not strangers to him.

It happened that these hymns were also favorites of my dad and I had heard them many times as well—they are really old, what we used to call Tennessee Ernie Ford hymns—referring to a 1950s country recording artist. When I thought about the words of one of them it seemed to me that they really summed up Ronald Reagan's unique relationship with God. The chorus of *In The Garden* contains these words: "And He walks with me, and He talks with me, And He tells me I am his own; And the joy we share as we tarry there, None other has even known." This confirmed for me the view that Ronald Reagan had a very special relationship with God which was really

a daily walk and talk and something that he kept most private—
a part of the unknown Ronald Reagan.


*Author of the forthcoming book (2014 Hachette Publishers)* Decoding
Reagan: His Rules for Communication, Leadership, Faith, and
America

# 17

## ARAM BAKSHIAN, JR.
### Director, Presidential Speechwriting 1981-1983

His Faith. President Reagan was the least preachy but most spiritual of the many political leaders I have worked with over the years. As I learned in collaborating with him on scores of speeches, he had a deep and abiding faith in his Maker, and referred to it often in simple, direct words. But, like his approach to politics, his approach to religion was "big tent" rather than divisive, humble rather than self-righteous.

Early on I noticed that whenever he referred to Jesus, it was always as a figure representing the Son of God to some, a great moral teacher to others. Whenever he invoked God's blessing on America—which he often did—it was the God of all mankind, not the God of any one group. And it was a God he believed he owed his life to after narrowly escaping death from an assassin's bullet, a God he felt had saved him for some higher purpose ... a purpose which, ultimately, led to the fall of the Iron Curtain and the end of the Cold War.

A few scoffers made much of the fact that President Reagan did not regularly attend formal worship services. What they didn't know was his reason: He knew how disruptive a presidential appearance, complete with security entourage and media mob, could be to ordinary worshippers. His respect for them was much more important than "photo ops" and media events using houses of prayer as a backdrop for presidential publicity, and his schedulers acted accordingly. "Natural" is the first word that comes to mind when I think of Ronald Reagan. He was calm, unaffected, kindly, confidant, and observant … and he always had a ready laugh. All of which made you love the guy. My initial encounter with him was long before I was tapped to take over the White House speechwriting office in 1981. It was the autumn of 1976 and I was responsible for writing supportive speeches for Jerry Ford's presidential campaign. One of the GOP notables we tried to recruit was then California Governor Ronald Reagan. Lyn Nofziger, who was also part of the campaign organization—and had been an early aide to Ronald Reagan in California—said there was no way RR would do a recorded national endorsement for Ford after the bitter, bruising convention fight. I decided to give it a try anyway, drafted a short radio spot and got him on the phone. Governor Reagan liked my draft and, ever the GOP team player, recorded it flawlessly without any edits. A smart, quick, ungrudging gentleman was my first impression of him then, and close exposure afterwards never changed it.

Our paths didn't cross again until I was tapped to handle the arts and humanities liaison for his incoming administration and, in the fall of 1981, was asked to take over the Office of Presidential Speechwriting. I had already been a White House speechwriter for Presidents Nixon and Ford so the job wasn't new to me, but working for President Reagan was. We talked about things. We met regularly. We had a direct line via memos that could not be intercepted, and automatic phone access. I always felt that I understood him and he understood me, no questions asked. All of which probably helps to explain one of our collaborations that has since become a presidential trademark for most of his successors: the "hero in the gallery" ploy.

On the wintery evening of January 16, 1981, I was sitting in my office suite in the Old Executive Office Building trying to think of a good way to end the President's State of the Union address. There had been earlier drafts by other writers, but nothing really did the job. Then history intervened. I had the evening news on and an Air Florida flight had just crashed into the ice-laden Tidal Basin. People were drowning, including a lady who couldn't keep her grip on a lifeline from a helicopter. As she began to sink, a young bystander dived into the icy water and rescued her. His name was Lenny Skutnik, a very junior employee at the Library of Congress.

I'd been looking for some kind of unifying theme, something real and touching, to tie together the State of the Union which was about an American future worthy of our heroic past. Bingo, there it was: For those who say America's best days are behind us, there are everyday heroes all around us, like Lenny Skutnik. Here was an ordinary guy, an average American, who responded in a truly extraordinary, heroic way to someone in need.

President Reagan loved it and cut the trite earlier ending to the speech, noting "we've got to go with this." Needless to say, he carried it off like the champ he was; it became the triumphant end of the State of the Union address with Lenny Skutnik sitting next to the First Lady in the gallery, to a massive ovation . . . it also became the forerunner of a seemingly endless procession of sometimes hackneyed later "heroes in the gallery" speeches by future presidents that almost make me regret the original.

That was just one example, but President Reagan was always open to new ideas, new approaches. Mainly, I think, because, unlike so many politicians I've known, he wasn't insecure. He knew who he was and what he believed in long before he entered the White House. One of the first things he told me as his Director of Speechwriting was, "Aram, always tell me if you think I'm wrong." I only had to do so on a few occasions, and then about minor, misremembered details, but the fact that the most powerful man in the world had the humility—and inner self-confidence—to ask that of a subordinate goes a long way to explaining what made Ronald Reagan a leader who was both great and good.

*Aram Bakshian, Jr., was Director of Presidential Speechwriting for Ronald Reagan (1981-1983) after having served as an aide to Presidents Nixon and Ford. He was also in charge of the selection process for the Medal of Freedom, America's highest civilian award, in the Reagan White House. His own writing on politics, history, gastronomy and the arts has been widely published in the U.S. and overseas.*

# 18

# RICHARD V. ALLEN
National Security Advisor 1980-1982

R eflection on Reagan Abroad, 1978. In the long run-up to the election of 1980 and in the requisite preparation, Ronald Reagan intensified his reading, writing and speaking activities. The prime example of this activity is reflected in his daily five-minute radio broadcasts, carried by many radio stations and heard by millions. These were compact, substantive, policy-oriented broadcasts, always with a specific prescription.

To extend his contacts and gain fresh insight into then-current major international problems and opportunities, he decided to take several international trips.

He visited Tokyo and Taipei in April 1978, where the former governor held substantive meetings with government and business leaders. The Reagans then traveled back to the United States via Iran, and he began work on his report of the visits and integrated his findings into a dozen forthcoming radio broadcasts.

The second trip was to Britain, France and Germany in November 1978. A formal request for the Governor to meet with the Labor Party's Prime Minister, James Callaghan, was surprisingly declined, but he met with the Foreign Secretary, David Owen. On the other hand, Conservative opposition leader Margaret Thatcher was eager to meet, along with Winston Churchill, grandson of the famous wartime British prime minister. Reagan was very enthused about the spirited long meeting with Thatcher, and it established the basis for the later warm working relationship when both were in office. Lady Thatcher was, by design, his first state visitor. He also had meetings with leading UK journalists and spoke at a fundraising event for Republicans Abroad, a part of the Republican National Committee.

In Paris meetings with President Valery Giscard d'Estaing and Prime Minister Raymond Barre had been requested. These two leading personalities had no time for Governor Reagan, and he was referred instead to a third level official in the Foreign Ministry. Reagan took all this with his characteristic good grace. Mayor Jacques Chirac did not hesitate to accept a meeting, but unfortunately had an auto accident the day before Reagan arrived in Paris, and was in the hospital with a broken leg. Reagan did meet a group of leading intellectuals, journalists and influentials, and considered the visit a success.

On to Bonn, then the capital of divided Germany, where Reagan met with Chancellor Helmut Schmidt, a Social Democrat and man of intellect and talent. The meeting was detailed and interesting, quite formal and points of obvious disagreement were muffled. There were also other meetings with government officials as well, and a productive session at the Konrad Adenauer Foundation, a part of the German CDU, Christian Democrat Union. A meeting with the CDU Opposition leader, Helmut Kohl was a much warmer and in-depth meeting than with Schmidt.

The encounter paved the way for a second meeting, this one at the White House in 1981 with Reagan as President and Kohl still Opposition leader. He became Chancellor in 1982, and remained in the post for 16 years. To this day and in retirement, Kohl, the Chancellor who succeeded in reuniting Germany and had been a reliable partner for Reagan and the U.S., remains Reagan's strongest supporter.

From Bonn the party flew to Berlin, for Reagan a centerpiece of the trip.

It is unusual that Reagan had never visited Germany (although Nancy had), and he was especially eager to see the city. He crossed into East Berlin, and at the famous Alexanderplatz Reagan witnessed twoEast German "Volkspolizisten," People's Police, stop an ordinary citizen carrying shopping bags. They forced the man to drop the shopping bags and raise his hands, while one poked his machine gun into the hapless man's stomach and the other used the barrel of his gun to probe the contents of the shopping bags. The scene enraged Reagan.

The visit to the Berlin Wall was clearly the most memorable stop in Berlin. Reagan viewed it at the spot where a young student trying to escape through the thick barbed wire that was rolled out before the actual concrete block wall was built. That student, Peter Fechter,was shot multiple times by the Grenzpolizei, border police, and was left hanging on the barbed wire, bleeding and calling for his mother until he died. It was an infamous incident about which Reagan knew, and he was moved by the story.

The small Reagan party approached the Wall. His reaction was not unexpected: for what seemed the longest minute he stared intently at the Wall as though he were mentally reviewing the tragedies that it had caused, his body stiffened, hands tightly clenched and his jaw set. And then he turned slightly, not taking his eyes off the Wall, and said in a low, almost growling tone: "We've got to find a way to knock this thing down!"

Nine years later. On June 12, 1987 as President he would stand at that Wall before the Brandenburg Gate, accompanied by the man he had met as opposition leader in 1978, Helmut Kohl, now Chancellor of Germany, and declare to the world and directly to Mikhail Gorbachev, "General Secretary Gorbachev, if you seek peace, if you seek prosperity for the Soviet Union and eastern Europe, if you seek liberalization, come here to this gate. Mr. Gorbachev, open this gate. Mr. Gorbachev, tear down this wall!"

That speech is among the most remarkable and memorable of the Twentieth century. Reagan had retained his initial 1978 impressions of the Wall, and when it came time to prepare his 1987 speech, he wanted this central thought retained in his formal remarks. His speechwriter for this trip, Peter Robinson, a gifted professional (now at Stanford University's Hoover Institution), actually flew to Germany to sample local opinion.

As Reagan worked with Peter Robinson on versions of the speech, several White House staffers, joined by the State Department, objected to including the appeal to Gorbachev to "tear down this wall." It was deemed "provocative." Reagan stuck to his own ideas on the matter.

The simple fact is: Reagan wanted the powerful line kept in, and continued working with aide Peter Robinson. After all, he would be making a basic restatement of what he uttered spontaneously in November 1978, nine years earlier, but now aimed specifically at Gorbachev; it was what he believed, and he hadn't changed his mind! And it wasn't Gorbachev who knocked down the Wall, nor was it Reagan; it was the people of East Germany in 1989, after Reagan had left the presidency, who had been encouraged by the words of the Leader of the Free World. The Reagan Berlin speech may be called "The Great Accelerator" of the end of the Cold War as we had known it. If he were with us today, he'd disagree sharply with those who proclaim "Reagan won the Cold War without firing a shot." He'd allocate the credit where it was due, and be proud to accept his share.

Among President Reagan's greatest assets were his candor, his conviction, his dedication to principle and especially his consistency and his gift of conveying profound thoughts in simple, understandable language anyone could comprehend.

*Full text of The Speech: page 352.*

*Richard Allen is a Senior Fellow at the Stanford University, Hoover Institution*

# 19

# ARTHUR B. LAFFER

Member, President Reagan's Economic Policy Advisory Board

1981-1989

My Godfather was a man named Justin Dart, who in the 1970s and beyond was conceivably one of Ronald Reagan's best friends and closest confidants. Jus, (as he was called) was at one time CEO of Walgreens, Rexall, and Dart/Kraft. He was also a well-known king-maker in California and U.S. politics. What may not be so well known was that Jus's second wife and mother of three of his 5 children, née Jane O'Brien, or as he called her "Punky," was also at one time a Hollywood starlet.

When Jane was dating Jus she told him that one of her best friends, another starlet named Nancy Davis, was also dating an older divorced man, an actor, and that the two girls would like to go on a double date together. Jus asked Punky the name of the actor Nancy was dating and when Punky replied that it was Ronald Reagan, Jus recoiled in shock and said that he would never go on a double date with that "left wing bastard." (I paraphrase; I believe his characterization was a bit more colorful.)

Obviously, Punky prevailed and Justin Dart and Ronald Reagan became fast friends and both married their respective starlets.

After Ronald Reagan's famous 1964 speech in support of Presidential candidate Barry Goldwater (*see page 223*), there was a lot of buzz about what the future had in store for Ronald Reagan's political career. By this time, Ronald Reagan was a full-fledged and adored member of, for want of a better word, the Los Angeles Country Club and Rancheros social set. A subgroup of the social set got together and agreed that Ronald Reagan should run for Governor of California in 1966, against the incumbent Governor Edmund G. (Pat) Brown. If re-elected, it would have been Pat Brown's third term as Governor.

Justin Dart carried the request to R.R., who said that he didn't really want to run for Governor because all he would do was to run around asking people for money to finance his campaign, and raising money for a political campaign didn't appeal to him. Justin Dart and R.R. agreed that to run a successful gubernatorial campaign in California at that time would cost about $700,000.

A few days later Justin Dart once again met with R.R. only this time Justin presented R.R. with seven checks for $100,000, each from different members of Reagan's future Kitchen Cabinet and asked if now R.R. would agree to run for Governor.

The rest is history. Reagan beat Pat Brown by more than 1,000,000 votes and served two terms in Sacramento.

1977, Puerto Rico. I did an economic study under the auspices of Governor of Puerto Rico Carlos Romero Barceló. While Puerto Rico may be small relative to the entire United States, the economic principles under which it operates are the same as those in the U.S.—and the results were crystal clear.

Governor Romero Barceló wanted to institute supply-side economic tax reform for Puerto Rico. His dream was to create prosperity in the impoverished island economy. Earlier in his career, Governor Romero Barceló had won election for mayor of San Juan—with a platform of cutting property taxes—and became a hero. Next, he ran for Governor, again promoting tax cuts, against an incumbent left-wing governor who believed in increasing, not reducing, taxes; his name was Rafael Hernandez Colon, but he was widely known as "La Vampirita," the "little vampire" and "La

Adiciónal," the "addition."

Now, he wanted to take real action; thus, the study. Why me? He said he had checked with economists up and down the East Coast, to see if they knew of any economist who believed cutting tax rates and balancing the budget would work. They all said "Oh no! No one's dumb enough to believe that you can cut tax rates and balance the budget except for Dr. Laffer in California." Then he added, "That, Professor Laffer, is why I'm calling you! "

I did the study, and the governor began making changes. Before—legend has it—there were only two people in all of Puerto Rico who reported incomes over $50,000 a year. Tax evasion was rampant. You need to understand that Puerto Rico, while using the dollar as currency, was not governed by English Law, but operated under Spanish Law, where deliberately not paying your taxes is a civil offense, rather than a criminal offense. So, if you're caught cheating on your taxes, you just have to pay the money you owed (plus fines, or course); not like our system, where you could actually go to prison.

The governor cut the highest marginal income tax rate, 87.1 percent, to 50 percent, which became the centerpiece of his plan. Many other taxes were also cut in the process, and a boom ensued—such as Puerto Rico had never seen before. Growth replaced stagnation.

I used "Puerto Rico" in many discussions with presidential candidate Ronald Reagan. The policies Puerto Rico adopted and the economic results were compelling, to say the least. Here is one of the Puerto Rican examples that Reagan really liked:

> Pretend you're running the Hilton Hotels Company, which includes the Caribe Hilton (in San Juan, Puerto Rico) and the Miami Hilton. These two hotels are maybe 80-90 miles apart. Also imagine both hotel managers have done a great job, and the company wants to give both hotel managers a bonus of $50,000 after tax. The relevant question to the company is, what would the pre-tax cost to the Hilton Company have to be to give the Caribe Hilton manager, who pays taxes at the 87.1 percent tax

rate, an after-tax bonus of $50,000? For the Caribe Hilton, you'd have to give the manager approximately $400,000 pre-tax in order to get an after-tax bonus of $50,000, whereas, to give the same after-tax bonus to the Miami Hilton manager, the Hilton Company would only have to pay $100,000. The difference in costs between $100,000 and $400,000 for the same bonus is *not* small. Tax rates really matter.

You can understand by this example why the Hilton Company would be more reluctant to invest in high income tax rate locations, rather than low income tax rate locations. Governor Carlos Romero Barcelo understood this concept as well, and that is why he pushed for tax reforms in Puerto Rico. By the time we had fully implemented the Puerto Rico tax reforms, the highest marginal income tax rate was 50 percent.

Ronald Reagan easily grasped the concepts and the results. With actual real test cases like this—bolstered by California's Proposition 13, Proposition 2½ in Massachusetts, Pete Du Pont's tax reforms in Delaware, and the major tax cuts in Guam, I was able to witness a full metamorphosis of Ronald Reagan into a pro-growth supply-sider. I knew he had majored in economics in college; now I saw that he actually enjoyed the subject!

The plight of "inner cities." In the early 1970s, I wrote about "Enterprise Zones" for the poor minority and depressed areas of some of our nation's largest cities. The solutions I proposed were strictly supply-side in nature. I lifted the idea from international economics literature, where free trade zones existed in ports and harbors, to attract businesses, create jobs, and increase incomes. These businesses wouldn't have to pay domestic taxes when they re-exported imported products.

Throughout the years, I had discussed these ideas extensively with both Congressman Jack Kemp (a dedicated economic conservative and, in 1996, the unsuccessful Republican candidate for vice president) and Ronald Reagan, when I was advocating, analyzing, and drafting my thoughts on Enterprise Zones. I had also discussed them perhaps even more intensely with a number of Democrats, including California Governor Jerry Brown. What amazed me was just how invested Jack Kemp and Ronald Reagan were in the idea of redressing the plight of the inner-cities. They really wanted to make a difference. To others, the idea of helping the inner-cities was little more than a paragraph in a speech.

As a professor at the University of Chicago, located on the south-side of Chicago, I noticed every morning, black women catching trains going out to the suburbs, while white men would take the same trains running in the opposite direction and get off in down-town Chicago to work. Something was gravely amiss.

In intuitive terms, the principles of Enterprise Zones are straight-forward. Imagine two locations, A and B, where taxes are being raised in B and lowered in A. People, jobs, and incomes will flow from B to A. What I wanted to accomplish was to have jobs and incomes being created in and flowing into the Enterprise Zones following the tax cuts and other pro-growth policies.

The key here was to address the paucity of jobs and persistent poverty in the inner city ethnic communities by stimulating location-specific economic growth. If poor people couldn't travel to the businesses, then we had to entice businesses and jobs to travel to where poor people live.

The first part of my proposal, which I published in the *Los Angeles Times*, was that there should be no payroll taxes, either for employees who both lived and worked in the Enterprise Zones, or for the employers who set up businesses in the Enterprise Zones. As a point of fact, even with no payroll taxes, there wouldn't really be much by way of lost tax revenues, because not many people were working or paying payroll taxes in the Enterprise Zones anyway.

The second part of my proposal was reduced corporate and personal income tax rates for entities who both reside and work in the Enterprise Zone. The third part of my proposal would require a thorough review of all building codes, regulations, restrictions and requirements to make sure they weren't anti-growth. At the time, most of those requirements and regulations were adopted solely as SOPs (standard operating procedures), and amounted to little more than featherbedding for city and union workers. In order to remain on the books, each and every building code, regulation, restriction, and government requirement would have to demonstrate *real* purpose. Codes in the city of Chicago were just humongously complicated as well as perverse.

The fourth and final part of my proposal was to eliminate the teenage minimum wage for the residents of the Enterprise Zone. These kids don't get their requisite skills to earn above the minimum wage by going to prep school like I did, or by going to Yale or getting their MBA or PhD at Stanford like I was able to. These kids really had to learn requisite skills with on-the-job training. And, if at a young age they don't get that first job, after awhile they become unemployable, and after becoming unemployable they become hostile, and after becoming hostile, you have to spend a fortune to protect yourselves from them. So I proposed there'd be no teenage minimum wage in the inner cities.

The neat thing about all of this discussion was that both Jack Kemp, who spent a lot of his life playing football with minorities and people from lower-income communities, and Ronald Reagan— who had a very different background—just loved the idea. Both Ronald Reagan's and Jack Kemp's support for Enterprise Zones really showed their compassion for and their understanding of not only incentives, but also how those incentives could be used to make a material difference in the lives of people who had not had all the advantages in life. Ronald Reagan and Jack Kemp really did care.

Ronald Reagan's view of what makes the world work went through a dramatic transformation between his campaign in 1976 and his campaign in 1980. In 1976, Ronald Reagan lost the Republican nomination to Gerald Ford. At the convention, Ronald Reagan was somewhat desperate, as was demonstrated by his choice of Richard

Schweiker of Pennsylvania as his running mate, even though Reagan had not secured the nomination. *(For a somewhat different view, see page 227)* Reagan ultimately lost the nomination to Ford by only a few delegates. Ford went on to be defeated by Jimmy Carter. That's all history.

The difference between Reagan in 1976 and Reagan in 1980 is beautifully illustrated by his answers to reporters' questions in New Hampshire, in both 1976 and 1980. One of the questions went something like this: "Governor Reagan, you've proposed this $90 billion tax cut. How are you going to pay for the lost revenues?"

Reagan's response in 1976 was that the $90 billion of revenue lost from the tax cuts would be offset by eliminating waste, abuse, and fraud in government spending.

There are two important features of his answer in 1976 that should be noted: first, the tax cut was a dollar amount, not tax rates, and second, the funding of the revenue losses from the tax cuts was to be carried out by cutting government spending. That was his mindset in 1976.

By 1980, he was asked pretty much the same question again, "What about this $90 billion tax cut you're proposing? How are you going to pay for the revenue losses?"

Reagan responded, "No, no, no. I'm not proposing a 90 billion dollar tax cut. This is a 30 percent across-the-board cut in tax rates."

The reporter, in essence, said, "Well, a 30 percent cut in tax rates or a 90 billion dollar tax cut, there's really no difference."

Reagan again asserted, "This is a tax *rate* reduction," to which the reporters again asked, "Well, how are you going to fund the deficit created by the tax rate cut?"

Ronald Reagan then retorted, "What do you mean the deficit created by cutting tax rates? We'll have so much more growth, output, employment and production that tax revenues are not going to fall by nearly as much as people think they will, and, in the long run, tax revenues may very well increase with a tax rate cut. And number two, we're going to have a significant reduction in spending because there will be less need for food stamps, fewer poor people, fewer people unemployed, etc. It's going to have two effects: fewer revenue losses and less need for spending. This tax rate cut will, in due course, pay for itself."

By 1980, Ronald Reagan frequently used himself as an example. Back in the day when he was actively making movies, the highest marginal income tax rate was an unbelievable 91 percent. In any given year, after he reached the 91 percent tax bracket, he stopped making movies for the rest of the year. As a consequence, other people would be out of work as well. The tax rate / tax revenue curve that bears my name ("Laffer") should really be called the "Reagan Curve."

That was the difference between Ronald Reagan in 1976 and Ronald Reagan in 1980—a huge transformation, where he had clearly come to embrace the supply-side perspective.

Late 1979 or early 1980. There were about 12 of us meeting with presidential candidate Reagan at the Beverly Hills Hotel. The Governor asked Dick Allen (future National Security Advisor) to summarize U.S. foreign policy over the post WWII era.

In his inimitable humorous style, Dick summarized the post WWII era as one where the U.S. harassed its allies and cajoled its enemies. The Governor was taken a little aback by Dick's brief summary and asked Dick to repeat what he had just said. Dick repeated that the U.S. had cajoled its enemies and had harassed its allies over the post-war era.

The Governor then queried what the consequences of those policies were. To which Dick replied we have almost no allies left, sir, but we have lots and lots of enemies.

Without a moment's hesitation, Reagan retorted: we would have to reverse those policies, now wouldn't we? We will have to make our allies rich and prosperous with "supply-side" economics and scare the bejabbers out of our enemies with "star-wars."

I knew exactly at that moment that we had won World War Three.

I don't know if the phrases "supply-side" or "star-wars" were the exact words he used, but that's what he meant.

Reagan discovers the power of . . . reducing taxes. A couple of weeks after President Reagan took office, he convened an Oval Office meeting to discuss the proposed legislative agenda for the Reagan Administration's first term tax proposals. There were perhaps a dozen of us, soon joined by President Reagan accompanied by Dick Wirthlin, who was a long-time ally and pollster, and the legendary Mike Deaver. The President said he would like to make sure his tax legislation *exactly* fit the promises he had made in the campaign—nothing more, nothing less.

Then, to my surprise, the President asked, "What *exactly* did we promise on tax cuts during the campaign?" He went on to say that he knew he had promised a 30 percent cut in taxes, but did he say "tax rates," or just "taxes?"

With that, both Wirthlin and Deaver popped up and said, "Sir, you never mentioned tax rates. All you did was mention taxes."

There were two ways to consider a 30 percent tax cut. One was to cut tax rates by 30 percent, leaving the highest earned income tax rate at 35 percent. The other way was to increase income thresholds for each tax bracket, leading to a 30 percent cut in taxes, but leaving tax rates unchanged—i.e., the highest rate would still be 50 percent. This was what the President chose to do: to move the brackets out, rather than cut tax rates by 30 percent. The highest marginal income tax rate at that time on earned income was 50 percent—which would (and ultimately did) stay at 50 percent.

So much for "earned" income . . . but there was another category. During the early stages of the Nixon presidency, a tax distinction had been made between earned and unearned income, which carried on up to President Reagan. Unearned income was basically interest and dividends, while earned income was wages and salaries. The highest tax rate on unearned income was 70 percent, which the President had not discussed during the campaign.

The President had no real intention of (and, in fact, did not campaign on) cutting the unearned income tax rate, either. What had happened to the unearned income tax rate during and after the campaign came from a Democratic congressman from Michigan named William Brodhead, who sat on the Ways and Means Committee and the Budget Committee. Congressman Brodhead proposed an amendment to the President's tax bill that would eliminate the distinction between earned and unearned income, thus cutting the highest tax rate on unearned income from 70 percent to 50 percent. All income would be taxed the same, irrespective of source.

Although President Reagan had an aversion to allowing amendments to his tax bill, he told us he liked the Brodhead amendment, and, if all the rest of us agreed to it, he was willing to make an exception. Of course, we all thought that was a great idea, and the distinction between earned and unearned income was dropped. The unearned income tax rate went from 70 percent down to 50 percent as soon as the tax bill was signed into law. This change was amazingly good for the economy.

There also was an unintended drop in the capital gains tax rate, solely as a consequence of accepting the Brodhead amendment. The official formula for calculating the tax on capital gains was to exclude 60 percent of all capital gains from any taxation, and then tax the remaining 40 percent at the unearned income tax rate. So, if you had $100 in capital gains, $40 would be taxed at the 70 percent rate, which comes out to a maximum 28 percent tax rate on capital gains. By dropping the highest unearned income tax rate from 70 percent to 50 percent—with the formula of the same 60 percent of all capital gains exclusion—now the $40 of capital gains would be taxed at a maximum tax rate of 50 percent. Therefore, the capital gains tax rate effectively dropped from 28 percent to 20 percent. Again, none of this was part of Ronald Reagan's campaign proposal.

One other discussion topic at our Oval Office meeting was the indexing of income tax brackets for inflation. This had been a part of the President's campaign. Instead of calling for an immediate indexing of all tax brackets—remember that, in 1981, inflation was in the double digits—indexing was deferred until 1985.

While I was genuinely disappointed we didn't get a lot more, the President's 1981 tax bill was still a great deal better than what existed at the time.

As time passed and the results of the 1981 Tax Act became more and more clear, Reagan bought into the power of tax rate cuts more and more. It was really the 1986 Tax Act where he fully implemented the Reagan / supply-side agenda. The highest income tax rate on any form on income was lowered to 28 percent, from 50 percent. The highest corporate tax rate was lowered to 34 percent from 46 percent, and a whole bunch of deductions, exemptions, and exclusions were eliminated to make the bill statically revenue neutral. This was the single best tax bill since the nation started taxing income in 1913.

Ronald Reagan's true genius of persuasion was nowhere more apparent than the 1986 Tax Act. In the Senate, the bill passed 97 to 3. Can you imagine the likes of Democratic Senators Alan Cranston, Howard Metzenbaum, Al Gore, Bill Bradley, Joe Biden, Chris Dodd and Teddy Kennedy voting for tax cuts like those, let alone Democratic House members Barbara Boxer, Harry Reid, Dick Durbin, Chuck Schumer, and Charlie Rangel voting for it?


President Reagan's First Encounter With Margaret Thatcher. After his terms in office, President Reagan was at my house in Rancho Santa Fe, California, on several occasions. At this one occasion, I had a small gathering of people to meet with him, and he was describing how he first met Lady Thatcher, shortly after he took office.

The conversation went something like this: President Reagan said "I want to tell to you about the first time I met Margaret Thatcher—now, this wasn't really the first time I met her. As you know, Arthur, Justin Dart had an apartment in London. On one occasion, I was at a party in Jus' apartment, and I guess then-member of parliament Margaret Thatcher was there as well. I don't remember meeting her—I knew she'd been there, but we had no interchange. The first *real* meeting with her was at my first G7 meeting."

The G7 meeting was being held in Ottawa, Canada, and, typical of Ronald Reagan, when he mentioned that it was the G7, he stopped and said, "G7, so that's the U.S., U.K., France, Germany, Italy, uh… let's see… Canada and—oh yes, that's it—Japan." He was very proud he'd gotten all seven—he loved doing stuff like that. It was very endearing.

He said, "We went up to Ottawa, Canada, and I was the 'new kid on the block.' I got in there, and I had been told by staffers that, at these meetings, everyone went by their first name. I walked in to the meeting where everyone was already seated, and I raised my hand and said 'Hi everybody, I'm Ronnie!'"

I could just see Ronald Reagan doing this because that's the type of wonderful, unpretentious man that he was. So, continuing, Ronald Reagan sat down and joined the meeting. Right off the bat, Canadian Prime Minister Pierre Trudeau, the host of the meeting, started being rude to Margaret Thatcher—in Reagan's words, "he was just plain rude."

And Reagan said, "I was there, and Trudeau was clearly being rude to Margaret Thatcher, and I thought Trudeau's behavior was inappropriate. Remember, though, I was the 'new kid on the block,' so I didn't say anything, but the smoke was starting to fume up from under my collar." (Remember those cartoons from the 40s and 50s, where the smoke shoots out of a cartoon character's collar when he gets angry? Well, smoke was coming up from under Ronald Reagan's collar.) He didn't say anything in the meeting, however.

"So, once we had a break" Ronald Reagan said, "I sidled up to Margaret Thatcher and I said 'Excuse me, Margaret, but I just wanted you to know that I noticed how rude that fellow Pierre was being to you. If I hadn't been the 'new kid on the block', and if I'd known the rules, I'd have gotten up and given him a piece of my mind. But, as it's my first time here, it might be inappropriate for me to interject and chastise Pierre for his bad behavior. I just wanted you to know how angry I was about the way he spoke to you.'"

"And she just turned and looked straight back at me and replied,

'Oh, Ronnie, never mind that—we girls know when boys are boys.'"

By the way, one of the guests at my home actually had a video of Ronald Reagan telling this story. I got a copy of that video, and I played it for Lady Thatcher the next time I was with her. She almost cried.

A 72nd Birthday. When President Reagan took office, he set up a group of advisors, whom Bob Novak called "The Greybeards" but they operated under the official moniker of the "President's Economic Policy Advisory Board" (PEPAB for short). This group included people like George Shultz, Milton Friedman, Jack Kemp, Walter Wriston, and several others along with me.

Here we all were in the Roosevelt Room in the White House on, of all days, February 6, 1983. This was President Reagan's 72$^{nd}$ birthday. I had also spent a little bit of time with him close to his 65th birthday, during the 1976 campaign. Thus, this was the second birthday that I had spent with him—seven years later.

Now in the "olden days" when Reagan was President, prior to President Clinton's elimination of the "retirement test" for Social Security, turning 72 meant that you actually began collecting Social Security payments, no matter how much you earned. Before President Clinton signed into law his changes in Social Security, if a person was between the ages of 65-72, for every dollar he earned, he lost 50 cents in Social Security benefits. So, obviously due to the President's high income, he'd never received any Social Security checks because he was ineligible. This was called the "retirement test" on Social Security. At 72, the test went away, and Reagan started collecting Social Security no matter how much income he had.

So there we all were, wishing the President happy birthday, when he blurts out, "Isn't life wonderful? Here I am on my 72$^{nd}$ birthday, and can you believe it—I'm receiving welfare checks, and I'm living in public housing!" Never ever at a loss for a good quip. We all loved it (and him).

1983: Grenada. Perhaps the neatest story I have about President Reagan occurred shortly after the U.S. had invaded Grenada in October of 1983.

The President and Mrs. Reagan had a habit of visiting California every once in a while, and spending a few days with their old friends in Los Angeles. This usually included a little rest and relaxation time at their Rancho Cielo, near Santa Barbara, where the President would chop some wood and ride horses. As legend would have it, Mrs. Reagan was not nearly as enamored with Rancho Cielo as was the President, but she really did love her man and indulged him his idiosyncrasies.

After a few days at the ranch, Mrs. Reagan and the President would fly to LA, where they stayed in the Presidential suite (the top two floors) at the Century Plaza Hotel annex building. Often, before taking dinner with old friends at the mainstay restaurant, Chasen's, the President and Mrs. Reagan would host an hour's worth of cocktails with a few of the more junior colleagues such as me.

At one of these gatherings, right after the invasion and victory in Grenada, I cornered the President. I'm not very knowledgeable on military affairs, but I'm highly energized by them. Given that the Granada engagement was the first time in years and years where U.S. troops fought Communist troops "mano a mano" on foreign soil, I was very excited to find out just how the President had made his decision to go forward. I asked him point blank how had he made that decision.

With great seriousness, he looked right at me, raised his arms a little bit and said "I just asked myself, what would John Wayne have done?"

In retrospect, as funny as his answer was, it was the right answer. He did not go the pollster route, but instead did what he thought was right.

## 20

## DANA ROHRABACHER
Speech writer 1981-1988

first met Ronald Reagan, albeit briefly, when I had just turned 17 and was working with the 1964 Goldwater campaign. Then, a year and a half later, Reagan was running for the Republican California gubernatorial nomination (against former San Francisco mayor George Christopher) and I was the Los Angeles County high school chairman of "Youth for Reagan." We had hundreds of young people who walked the precincts, knocking on doors, handing out flyers, and talking up "Reagan."

All was not smooth, however. There was a lot of infighting between the Young Americans for Freedom, the Young Republicans, and "Youth for Reagan," each group competing to have the lead and win the laurels. Our state leader had no political experience whatsoever and let things get enough out of hand that, after the primary (which Reagan won handily) we were told that "Youth for Reagan" was to be disbanded and would not as a group participate in the general election—in which Reagan would be challenging the incumbent Governor Pat Brown. We could work under the control and guidance of the Young Republicans, if we wanted to..

I was crestfallen. We had put in so much effort—which I believed, of course, had been of great value—and now "Youth for Reagan" was being, well, demoted, treated as if it was insignificant. Well, I decided to make a plea to Ronald Reagan, himself. I found out where he lived—his home was in Pacific Palisades—and, lugging my sleeping bag, went out there at 2 o'clock in the morning, so I would be ready whenever he might arise. I walked up the long driveway, around to the back of the house—there was absolutely no security, which amazed me—and camped out on the lawn with a little sign that said, "Mr. Reagan, please speak to me."

So here I was about 6:30 or 7 in the morning when the lights started coming on—and Nancy Reagan stuck her head out the door and said. "Who are you?"

I said, "Well I'm with 'Youth for Reagan' and they are going to eliminate us and I need to talk to him for just 120 seconds, two minutes and that's it."

She said, "Look, I'm Mrs. Reagan, I have to watch out for him. If he comes out here he won't spend just two minutes with you, it will be 20 minutes and then he will either have to miss breakfast or be late for all of his appointments for the rest of the day. If you give me your name and telephone number, and leave right now, I will make sure that you get a meeting with the campaign manager."

Ok, if that was the best I could do, but as I was walking back down the driveway I hear footsteps coming up from behind. I turn around to see Ronald Reagan, his shirt hanging out and shaving cream on his face. He said, "If you can spend the night in my backyard, I can certainly spend a few minutes with you.. What's the problem?"

Sure enough, he spent 20 minutes with me—just as his wife had predicted—and in the event, "Youth for Reagan" was not disbanded, but remained active as a unit while Ronald Reagan went on to win the election by almost exactly one million votes.

He also won my heart. I went on to college and became a journalist, covering his last two years as governor—and he never let me down. He was always decisive, and strong . . . when it came to policy . . . but people came first.

It is his last year as governor, and I am a young reporter in Los Angeles for Radio News West-City News Service. I have been

covering him now for two years while establishing myself as a journalist—and I cultivated a reputation for asking tough questions
but in a totally respectful way. Reagan had a press conference to
announce the findings of a commission he had set up six months
earlier, to explore proposals on reducing crime in California.

I quickly went through a printed summary of the proposals,
and when I got a turn to ask a question I said, "Governor, you are
someone who has on many occasions expressed your strong Christian faith and how this impacts your decisions. I'd like to know how
this fits with the commission recommendation that calls for a more
extensive use of the death penalty. We're talking about a situation
where a person, yes, who has killed someone but is in permanent
custody and not a threat to anyone. How can you reconcile your
Christian principles with this recommendation and take the life of
another human being who is not threatening anyone?"

Reagan's tone was indeed serious. "That is a central question," he
said. He went on to explain that when he became governor he realized that he would have the power to grant some sort of clemency for
people who were about to be executed. Should he do so? He prayed
and he prayed and he prayed; he sought the advice of various theolo-
gians. And he came to this conclusion: if he was executing murderers
out of vengeance, that is not consistent with Christian principles.
"However," he said, "if you believe as I do that the death penalty may
have some deterrent effect in preventing a murder, even if just one
innocent person's life is thereby saved . . . then taking a life to save a
life is certainly within the boundaries of Christian principles."

And then—the state's attorney general grabbed the microphone.
"All this talk about morality and religion is irrelevant! The people of
this state voted for the death penalty and we're gonna give it to them!"

What a contrast—between Reagan, a thoughtful, caring conservative, and the thoughtless attorney general . . . who, by the way,
himself ran for governor four years later and pulled in less than 37
percent of the vote.

1976, I am now the assistant press secretary on Reagan's campaign staff and he is seeking the Republican nomination for president. We are in the parking lot of a large shopping center in North Carolina and, just before he was to begin speaking, I am walking around, making sure that the press contingent is all set up.

A lady grabbed me by the arm; "Do you work for Governor Reagan?" she asked. I said yes, I do, and she said, "I have a small group of blind children here. They are 10 or 11 years old and might it be possible for them to shake hands with the governor?"

I said, "Let me check, I'll be right back." I found Mike Deaver, who was running the show, so to speak, and as I was passing on the request, Reagan overheard me and stepped right in. "Dana . . . of course we are going to see those blind children." But, he added, that he didn't want anyone to think he might be exploiting blind children for political gain. "Here's what I want you to do," he said. "You tell the press we have a tight schedule and the minute I finish speaking they should immediately get back on the buses." Then, he pointed to the corner of a near-by building. "I'll meet the children over there, just around that corner and I will be happy to shake their hands."

He gave his speech, the press all ran to the buses, and Reagan moved quickly to the designated spot where about eight children were now waiting. He talked with them for a few minutes, then said, "I know you can't see me . . . would you like to touch my face to get an idea of what I look like?" So there he was with these eight kids putting their fingers on his face. When they were finished they all had big hugs—it sure brought tears to my eyes—and then we were off to the next stop.

Governor Reagan didn't want the press around because he didn't want this to be a "story" and especially because he didn't want anyone to take a picture. Can you imagine? Any candidate running for president I've ever met would give a million dollars to have a picture like that. It would have been on the front page of every newspaper and the cover of every magazine, probably with a caption, "Getting to know you!"

I knew that I was working for a very special human being.

PS: For the record, he won North Carolina in the primary but did not get the nomination. That year.

Some years later, I am now a speechwriter on the President's staff, and since he knew that I was from California, whenever he would make a trip out West my ever-thoughtful boss would invite me to ride along on Air Force One so I would have a chance to visit with my family. Also, as I learned, Reagan was not comfortable with flying and did not sleep very well on the plane, and we often spent hours just talking about almost anything except politics—Hollywood, Ireland, religion, his parents, what it was like being a lifeguard or being a movie star. For a speech-writer, such time is golden, a grand opportunity to actually get to know the man for whom you are creating things to say.

But, of course, these trips were not all, always, for chit-chat but provided an opportunity to get some work done. On one of those trips we were working on speeches he soon was going to give on a swing through South America. Judge Bill Clark, the National Security Advisor, came into the President's compartment and said, "I've got bad news." He had just learned that the leader of one of the countries we were scheduled to visit, with a joint press-conference on the agenda, planned to use that event to publicly belittle Ronald Reagan, to say nasty things, to put Reagan down to make himself appear, to his people, to be the fearless leader and thus the bigger man.

Forewarned is forearmed! I said, "Don't worry Mr. President. I'll work up some remarks for you and we're going to cut that guy's legs out from under him, we're gonna beat him up so badly he'll know that he can't get away with the insulting the President of the United States!"

Reagan sort of sighed, and said, "Well, now, Dana, that's exactly the wrong approach. I want you to find what we can say that's good about this man, learn a few of his policies that we can agree with; find some good things that he has done. I want to praise him, say what a wonderful leader he is, how lucky that country is to have a man like him in charge and he is such a good friend of the United States—and of mine—that I am going to work closely with him at every opportunity. Smother him with kindness. It'll work out a lot better."

Sure enough. I found good things for Reagan to say, and when our "host" heard Reagan talking about what a wonderful leader he was, how lucky that country was to have him in charge and what a great job he was doing, there was no way he could step in and criticize our President. We left that country on a high note and with greatly improved relations.

Reagan's creed: be tough on policy but nice to people. That person on the other side of the table is a human being, and should be treated as such. "Tough on policy, good to people," for example, is how he conducted himself with Gorbachev . . . which helped win the Cold War.


*Dana Rohrabacher was first elected to the Congress in 1988 . . . and is still so serving.*

**21**

## ALFRED H. KINGON

Assistant Secretary of Commerce for International Policy 1983-1984
Assistant to the President and Secretary of the Cabinet 1984-1985
Ambassador to the European Communities 1985-1989

After some event in the old executive office building the President and I are crossing over back to the West Wing of the White House. He is very agitated. "Did you see the Washington Post this morning?" he asks irritably. Of course I did. There was a story about how his aides were preventing Reagan from being Reagan and the chief culprit this morning was me.

"Yes, I saw it," I reply.

"What do they want from me ?" he continues very agitated. "Why don't they let me go one step at a time? Why do they insist I do everything at once?"

He is clearly very angry. And, I say, "Why are you yelling at me?"

He stops, and starts laughing, and says, "Because you're the only one here."

The President had given a political speech in New Jersey. We were headed back to the airport to return to Washington. On the side of the road a man held a sign that said, "Reagan is wrong—about everything." Then I heard the famous voice from the car up ahead saying "Put him down as undecided." We continued traveling and, as we approached a tolling station, I heard again from the front car, "Does anyone have seventy five quarters?"

I walk into the Oval Office and find the President holding a large bundle of papers and laughing intensely. I recognize the papers, which I have read, as the CIA's analysis of the future of the Soviet Union, which predicted major economic gains and a projection of it as perhaps an equal or greater economic power than us. I ask the President what was so funny? He says to me "It can't happen."

"Why?" I ask. He answers that that they did not have the economic system to make it happen. Guess what? The President was right—and the major CIA study was wrong. Again!

The President and I are in the lower level of the South Wing heading to Marine Helicopter One. He hasn't stopped talking about how intensely he feels against women having abortions. After awhile, I stop him and ask, "If you feel so strongly about this, why don't you do something about it?"

He stops dead in his tracks, turns to me and slowly and elaborately says, "Al, there's a limit to what you can do in politics." And so it was.

There was an unbreakable rule when working in the White House: Do not give the President any homework over the weekend. His Camp David time was supposed to be total relaxation. And, Nancy was adamant. There was an issue that concerned many departments in the government and I, as secretary of the cabinet, had a hard time collecting all the various departmental opinions and recommendations. Unfortunately, I finished the memo on a Friday afternoon and Congress had mandated a presidential decision and submission by the following Monday.

I had no choice. I entered the Oval Office to find the President, the Vice President, George H.W. Bush, and the Chief of Staff, Don Regan, preparing the President for his departure. The mood was light. Everyone was laughing. I said, "Mr. President, I am terribly sorry to do this but Congress demands an answer by Monday, and I could not get all the departments to give a timely submission until this afternoon. I hate to give you this but I feel I must."

There was an outcry with the President saying, "Aw, c'mon Al, it's the weekend. Give me a break" The Vice President echoed the president's wish and the Chief of Staff glared at me with looks that I thought were lethal. All three were yelling and pleading, "C'mon Al this can certainly wait till Monday."

"No, it can't" I replied. Then I heard the helicopter landing on the South lawn and I knew Nancy was waiting for the President. I was desperate, so I turned to the last page, where five options for the President were listed, and I said, "OK , OK. Pick a number from 1 to 5."

The President growled. "Give me those papers" and snatched them out of my hand.

He read them over the weekend and made his decision. Nancy made the following Monday very uncomfortable for Chief of Staff Don Regan.

The Oval Office was crowded. We were all there preparing for the President to meet with foreign editors who were waiting in the Roosevelt Room just across the hall. All of a sudden Pat Buchanan burst through the door and yelled, "The shuttle has exploded!"

This was the Challenger space mission that had just lifted off that morning. We all gasped and the President leaned over to me and asked, "Isn't that the one with the teacher on it?"

"Yes," I replied. Then the door burst open again and Vice President George H. W. Bush ran through the door with the same message. We all left our seats and retired to the small room adjoining the Oval Office that contained a television set. Everyone stood in tense silence. All of a sudden a parachute appeared and we let out a cheer. For a moment we thought the shuttle crew had been saved. But an announcer notified us that the parachute contained equipment from the exploded vehicle., and then slowly, we dispersed. A short time later Peggy Noonan came into the office and helped the President prepare his famous speech delivered that night when he told us all on board went to heaven and touched the hand of God.

*The "Loss of the Shuttle" speech will be found on page 339.*

# 22

# FREDERICK J. RYAN, JR.
## Chief of Staff 1989-1995

I had the honor of being President Reagan's chief of staff when he left office and went with him as he returned home to California. Soon after, we planned a rather ambitious trip—world leaders had expressed interest in hosting visits, to have an opportunity to recognize his great accomplishments in office.

The staff called it Ronald Reagan's "Victory Lap" (but we did not share that characterization with the boss). The first stop was Berlin, where Reagan went to the wall with a hammer and chisel and knocked off a souvenir piece of rock. Then, he went into East Berlin where the City Council held a meeting in his honor. Next, back to West Berlin for remarks to the German Parliament. Next, a visit to Warsaw to meet with Communist leader Jerry Osowski (soon to be out of office), then to Gdansk, then to Moscow for a meeting with Gorbachev—where people were lining the streets to pay their respects to President Reagan as his car went by. Last stop: Rome, for a meeting with Pope John Paul II, then back home to Los Angeles.

That's the bare-bones itinerary, but one of those stops was especially memorable: Gdansk, home of the shipyard where Lech Walesa was head of the shipyard workers union and a key player in the peaceful revolution that overthrew Communism in Poland. (Walesa would soon enough become the first popularly-elected president of the country, but at the time of this visit, he was not in government.)

The visit to Gdansk was especially memorable on two counts:

one, some 30,000 people were waiting to greet President Reagan, and, two, they were doing so in the middle of a torrential downpour. Everyone was soaked to the skin.

The visit started with a wonderful one-on-one meeting with Walesa which cemented a positive relationship that would last for the rest of his life, and then Reagan went out to greet the crowd—not a single person had left, despite the rain. But then, something truly strange: just as he walked out on a little stage that had been set up, the skies cleared and the rain stopped.

When Reagan started to speak, the crowd started to sing. He stopped, and the singing stopped. He started speaking again, the crowd started singing again. This happened three or four times; Reagan, obviously puzzled, stepped back from the microphone. Walesa came over and explained, the song they were singing was "May you live 100 years."

Reagan then let them finish the song, and then he finished his remarks.

*Fred Ryan became Chairman of Allbritton Communications and CEO of POLITICO. He serves as Chairman of the Board of Trustees for the Ronald Reagan Presidential Foundation'*

## 23

# PETER J. WALLISON
### White House Counsel to President Reagan 1986-1987

Weeks before the day that the diversion of funds to the Contras was publically disclosed in November 1986, I had organized a lunch for Reagan and the members of the Supreme Court. It was not something that could be cancelled without stirring up a lot of press chatter, and Reagan wanted to go through with it. Most of the Supreme Court was there, including Rehnquist, Whizzer White, Scalia and Thurgood Marshall. The lunch was in the private dining room, near the East room.

It is impossible to recreate the turmoil of that day. About 100 feet away, in the press room, Ed Meese was contending with a press corps that had gone completely bonkers, believing no doubt that they had a story that would actually bring down the Reagan presidency.

However, Reagan himself—who had fired both Poindexter and North that morning—seemed completely unperturbed. I concluded that it was because he was absolutely certain he had done nothing wrong and that would eventually be shown. At the lunch, he and Marshall traded funny stories about baseball, politics, their former lives, and just about everything else. These stories were hilarious and, as Shakespeare once said, "set the table on a roar." It was amazing to observe Reagan, on what should have been the worst day of his presidency, having a rollicking good time as though nothing at all was amiss.

In July 1986, I attended a lunch with the Board of Trustees of the Ronald Reagan Library Foundation. It included a few contributors, about 30 people, and Reagan attended. After the lunch he got up to make a speech, which of course he was always required to do. What he said, however, was vintage Reagan. My best recollection is this: "I hope you will all keep in mind that, when you are raising funds for this admirable project, that it is not for me that this library is being constructed. I am just a trustee of the office of the presidency for a few years and after me there will be many more presidents. This library is important because it will contain material that reflects a period in history that people in the future will want to study. That is what gives your efforts real significance."

During the fight over Rehnquist's nomination to be Chief Justice, the Senate Democrats asked to see his files when he was Assistant Attorney General in charge of the Office of Legal Counsel. I was outraged. Rehnquist had already been confirmed during the Nixon administration as an associate Justice of the Court, and his files in the distant past could no longer be relevant except as a source of invidious leaking to the media. I thought the President should claim executive privilege. The Office of Legal Counsel is the law firm for the whole government, and in that capacity they receive many requests for approval of actions, ordinarily after full disclosure of what they are trying to accomplish. If this didn't warrant a claim of privilege, I couldn't imagine what would. Ed Meese feared that this would mean the Rehnquist's nomination would be scuttled, and Don Regan set up a debate between Meese and me in the Oval Office. We each gave our views, and Reagan listened carefully.

After we'd finished, Reagan turned to me and said, "Peter, you made a fine argument, but I'm going to go with Ed on this one." He said this with such sympathy in his voice and manner that I remember thinking: I hope you *never* make a decision in my favor so as not to disappoint me; you're the president, and whether I am pleased or not with your decision is irrelevant. Incidentally, Meese turned out to be right; the files were made available, but nothing in them ever became an issue and Rehnquist was confirmed. Still, giving up these files set a bad precedent for future presidents.

After Reagan's refusal to give up the Strategic Defense Initiative at Reykjavik in late 1986, questions arose about what exactly Reagan had proposed to Gorbachev. At a meeting in the Oval Office to prepare Reagan for a press conference, Reagan noted that Gorbachev had referred repeatedly to "nuclear weapons" rather than "strategic weapons." Reagan, then, had asked Gorbachev what he had in mind, and was told that Gorbachev wanted to eliminate all nuclear weapons in 10 years. Reagan said he had told Gorbachev that this was a matter that could be discussed when Gorbachev came to Washington.

At this point John Poindexter suggested that Reagan tell the press that he only favored the elimination of strategic missiles, a policy that would be favorable to the U.S. because of our superiority in cruise stealth technology. Reagan responded sharply to Poindexter, telling him that he did indeed want to eliminate all nuclear weapons "eventually," and that he could not see how the Soviets would agree to something so one-sided as the elimination of only strategic missiles. This was the first time I had ever seen Reagan speak sharply to anyone on his staff. To me, this showed that he had his own strategic vision in mind, and was not relying on staff advice as to how he should pursue it.

## 24

# DONALD DEVINE
### Director, U.S. Office of Personnel Management 1981-1985

olling around the Oval Office after a presentation documenting how the Administration was back-filling bureaucratic slots we had cut during the first few years, someone was waiting patiently behind, just out of sight. Bragging to whomever would listen about the president's support for my plan to stop the backsliding, I figured he could wait. When I finally turned around, there was the President of the United States of America patiently waiting his turn to talk to the pompous personnel director!

Sensing my discomfort, he immediately put me at ease by saying: "Keep it up, fighting those bureaucrats, and don't give up." Smiling gently, he turned and went back to work. Here was the real Ronald Reagan—kind, considerate, polite, decent and letting you know that he appreciated the job you were doing. But he was also focused like a laser, keeping to the job at hand, here trying to keep his promise to cut government bureaucracy.

I saw him up close when he fired the air traffic controllers. As civil service head, I had expressed my displeasure with the concessions that the Federal Aeronautics Administration had made to the union, proposing pay and benefits well beyond the already higher rates controllers received compared to the remainder of the workforce. Since the union was gaining advantages through the threat of disruption and strike, the inevitable result would be more of the same throughout the government. Luckily, the union was greedy and rejected the offer. Then they crossed the line and the president made history. At the subsequent White House meeting, the president was insistent. The controllers had violated their no-strike oath as federal employees and they had to go. That was that.

The FAA head opposed the severity of the penalty and was dropped from the car on the way to the news conference by Transportation Secretary Drew Lewis, who had initially supported the concessions but said it was now time to support the boss. All three of us wanted to eventually hire back the controllers—on our terms—the penny-pinching personnel director because of the time it would take to train the thousands of replacements needed. Mr. Reagan, looking more broadly than we, would have none of it. As Secretary of State George Shultz wrote later, world leaders immediately became impressed with a president who would be so decisive. Chris Matthews reported that it was this one act that led Speaker Tip O'Neill to respect Reagan as a political leader who had to be dealt with. Business leaders told me for years that President Reagan's actions freezing employment, denying unnecessary pay and benefits increases, and—especially—firing the controllers steeled their resolve to slim their own bloated bureaucracies.

In early 1986, while I was advising Senate Majority Leader, Bob Dole, he took a piece of paper from his desk and lofted it over to me. "Look what your friend is trying to get me to do." "Do not forget about flattening the tax rates," it read, plus a few flattering words, and was signed Ronald Reagan. "He is the only person in Washington who thinks this has a ghost of a chance," said the Senator. "What does he expect me to do?" In less than a year, President Reagan signed a tax bill cutting the number of rates in half and reducing them to only 15, 28 and 33 percent, the lowest then or since. The top marginal rate went from seventy percent to one-third, the first substantial cut in a progressive tax system by a democratic government in recorded history. However alone, Ronald Reagan never gave up.

Everyone remembers his original supply side tax cut of 23 percent, a size most advisors thought was too large. Without it, total taxes would have been 23.8 percent of GNP, rather than the 19.3 percent he obtained. Fifty-five countries followed with tax reductions of their own. Even his admirers think President Reagan did not cut government spending. That is because he insisted on increasing defense. On non-defense outlays, spending did decline from 17.4 percent of GNP in fiscal 1982 to 15.6 percent in fiscal 1989. Soon after, his successor increased it to 19.8 percent so people, especially Republicans, tend to forget. He was even flexible enough to support two items originally opposed by his assistants—Dole's proposal to index tax rates for inflation and Sen. Phil Gramm's spending limits—that also helped promote limited government during his years in office.

Oh, yes, those higher defense expenditures and the technology and readiness they purchased convinced the Soviet leaders they could not compete. Then, there was no Soviet Union and he had defeated the "evil empire" too.

We miss him and will not soon see another of his stature.

*Donald Devine is Senior Scholar at The Fund for American Studies and a vice chairman of the American Conservative Union.*

# 25

# GILBERT A. ROBINSON
Deputy Director, USIA 1981-1983
Ambassador-Special Advisor to the Secretary of State 1983-1985

In the spring of 1979, California Governor Ronald Reagan was planning his (successful) run for the Presidency of the United States, and was coming to New York City to meet many of the people who could be helpful to him. As I had some valuable New York-area political experience as the field manager for John Lindsay's successful campaign for mayor and as the New York City manager for the re-election of Governor Nelson Rockefeller, Reagan's press secretary, Jim Lake, invited me to the meeting, to be held in a few weeks.

Well, Sunday, after church, I was waiting for my 13-year-old daughter Nancy when she came out with her Sunday school teacher, Joy Scheiss. I guess Nancy had said something about this up-coming meeting, because Joy said, "Nancy tells me you are going to meet the Governor of California this week; please give Dutch my very best regards."

I knew that anyone who would call him by his nickname "Dutch" must have known him from early on. "What's your connection?" I asked. And she told me a story—about how Reagan became a movie actor.

In 1937, Reagan was a radio broadcaster in Des Moines, Iowa, and once had worked with a singer named—at the time—Joy Hodges, who had moved to Hollywood and became a movie actress. One time, Joy was back home visiting friends, dropped by the station, and suggested that Reagan ought to try the movies; his immediate reply, he didn't know anyone in the movies, and she said, "Well, you know me."

Not too many months later, Reagan was assigned to cover spring training of the Chicago Cubs baseball team, in California, and when passing through Los Angeles, he got in touch with Joy. Could she really help? She said she would try to get her agent, George Ward, to arrange a screen test. Ward was well-connected—representing, among others, the well-established Myrna Loy and the newcomer William Holden. Ward set up a test at Warner Brothers for the following week, but Reagan—shall we say, a bit naive?—said he couldn't wait around in Los Angeles, he had to be back in Iowa and at work on Monday. Ward pulled some strings, the test was held on Saturday, and Reagan was on his way home before getting the results of the test.

Well, the studio called Ward and said Reagan was okay, they would put him on for three months at $100 dollars a week. Ward told the studio that Reagan couldn't quit his job and leave Iowa without some more substantial guarantee, and persuaded them to offer a seven-year contract, with one-year options, for $200 a week for the first year. Reagan said "Yes," and never looked back Skip ahead, to the 1979 meeting in New York with me and some 75 cautious Republicans; I do believe that some of them were rather skeptical, thinking this guy is an actor, somebody else writes all of his lines. But he won us over as he stood before the group for an hour, speaking in great detail and without notes, and then answered a lot of tough questions for another hour. And time had run out, he was off to another commitment.

But press secretary Jim Lake asked me for some advice: should Reagan accept an invitation to meet the next day with the editorial board at the *New York Post*, a liberal paper? I said, "Go . . . we Republicans spend too much time shaking hands with ourselves." The session with the *Post* editorial board was scheduled for 40 minutes but lasted two-and-a-half hours (and . . . the *Post* would endorse Reagan during the campaign).

Later that afternoon, Governor Reagan held a reception—he had not had the opportunity to shake many hands after his "presentation" the day before, and there were a few more people he wanted to meet. Naturally, I was in attendance—and arrived early, to ask Jim Lake about the meeting. Jim said "It was terrific," gave me some details, and added, "Come along, I'll introduce you to the Governor."

Reagan shook my hand and thanked me for my help. Then, to make conversation I brought up our "mutual friend," Joy Scheiss, "who sends you her very best regards."

He stepped back and took a long look at me, and said, "You and I wouldn't be talking here tonight and I wouldn't be running for President if it weren't for Joy. She got me started in Hollywood." And he told me the same story, about Joy and George Ward.

Some months later, I was proud to help stage the formal announcement of Reagan's candidacy—November 13, 1979—at a grand fund-raising banquet in a New York hotel.

Life has some interesting coincidences. I was head of a public relations firm in New York City. About six months after I talked with Joy Scheiss, I went to visit one of our clients in Boston. It was a large organization and we met in the conference room with several officials of the organization. One of the senior officials went around the table and introduced everyone there. He introduced a man named George Ward who was then in charge of their Film and Broadcasting Division. Of course, I kept wondering, "Could this be the same George Ward who got Reagan started in Hollywood?" No, it couldn't be; that George Ward was on the West Coast in Hollywood and here we were on the East Coast.

When a break came in the meeting I approached George Ward and said, "I was talking not long ago to Joy Schiess and she mentioned 'George Ward.' Could that be you?"

He gave a big smile and said "I am" and asked how Joy was. I could only think, what a small world.

A few years later I was in the Reagan Administration and in a meeting with the President and some others, in the White House Roosevelt Room. When the meeting broke up I caught up with the President and said, "I want to talk to you about George Ward."

He stopped and said, "Interesting that you should mention his name. I have just invited him and his wife to come visit me in Washington." The President was always so gracious and kind, always remembering those people who had helped him along the way.

When the time came for the visit George Ward called me and told me he had been in town for a few days. He said the President had given him a Park Ranger for several days to show them around Washington. Then he said on Friday morning he and his wife were invited to see the President in the Oval Office. He then asked my wife and me to join him and his wife Vera for lunch at a hotel around the corner from the White House, just after their visit with the President.

Of course, we did and were very interested in what they had to say. George said, first of all, they were blown away by the treatment the President gave them. He kept them for almost two hours and had the visit filmed and still pictures taken. They were elated. President Reagan never forgot who had helped him get where he was.

Then, George told us the rest of the story which I had first heard from Joy Scheiss. Reagan took the screen test, he said, and then hurried to get on the train to get home in time for his next scheduled broadcast. Then—as I noted above—the offer came from the studio. George Ward sent a telegram to Ronald Reagan with the offer. What he received back several days later in the mail was a very gracious and appreciative letter.

Reagan told Ward that he was so grateful and so excited that he kept folding and unfolding the telegram and showing it to his mother and father and brothers and friends. Just then Vera interrupted the narrative and said, "George, why don't you go up to the room and get the letter and show them" He did. We read the letter and it was very beautiful, filled with deep gratitude and disbelief that this was happening to him.

After I read it I said "George, I know that you want to keep your visit with the President private. However, it occurs to me that there is one man in town with the press who would handle this exactly the right way." I told him about a real gentleman named Hugh Sidey who was at that time writing the column each week on the Presidency for *Time* Magazine. I asked him if I could step out and call Hugh, whom I knew, and have him come down later that afternoon for a meeting. "And if you feel comfortable," I said, "show him this wonderful letter from Reagan." George thought for a moment and said if it would shine favorably on the President, he would do it. I called Hugh and the result was a beautiful column about President Reagan and George Ward. It appeared the next week in *Time* magazine.

George and Vera also said that Ronald Reagan came and lived with them a short while until he could find a place of his own.

June 6, 1944. The "D-Day" invasion of Normandy, France; the cliffs at Pointe du Hoc. Bill Petty and his team of Army Rangers scaled the cliffs hand-over-hand, while withering German fire was trying to stop them. The Rangers made it to the top, and took charge. Let me connect that event with President Reagan's memorable speech at Pointe du Hoc on the 40th Anniversary of D-Day, June 6th 1984.

This part of the story starts in 1974. Bill Petty was a friend and neighbor of mine in Carmel, NY. It was a Saturday and my wife and young daughter were off riding horses—a favorite week-end pastime—and at lunch time I went by myself to a nearby restaurant, where I spotted Bill Petty, and joined him.

He asked me how things were going and what's new . . . the usual conversations between good friends who hadn't seen each other for a while. I told him that, in a week, I was taking my wife, my daughter, and my mother to France for a visit. He asked if I was going to Normandy. I hadn't thought about it, so I asked, "Why?" He said if you go to the small town near there and mention my name you won't have to pay for a meal or a drink. Now I was really curious. And he told me his story.

He was a young Ranger on D-Day, landing in one of the first waves to hit Omaha Beach, just under the cliffs of Pointe du Hoc. The Germans had bunkers up there and were firing down at the beaches. The Rangers quickly got up under the cliffs and shot ropes with grappling hooks to the top. Then, as they tried to climb up, the Germans would try to cut the ropes. "If you could tell that your rope was being cut," he told me, "you would swing over to grab one of the others and keep climbing." He carried with him a Browning Automatic Rifle (BAR) He got to the top and they fought off the German counter attacks during the day.

At night during one counter attack he was separated from his unit. He was behind a stone wall stretched out and fell asleep. At day light he heard the sound of rifle bolts being readied. He peered over the short stone wall and saw a German firing squad and then realized right in front of him was a group of obviously French partisans about to be shot. Aiming between those about to be executed he took out the German firing squad with his BAR.

It was an amazing story. Of course, now we had to go to Normandy and Pointe du Hoc. We started our French visit in Paris, but a few days later we drove to Normandy. Our goal was to find the little town of Cricqueville-en-Bessin, the town nearest to Pointe du Hoc. As we came to the coast of France we followed the signs and the small road we were on dead-ended so that you could only turn right. Straight ahead was a big Catholic Church with people all dressed up. It was evidently a wedding. As I slowed down, a middle aged woman was coming past my car window. In my best French I said "Please may I talk to you?"

She stopped and came over. I said, I am looking for the Mayor of this town, Monsieur Villiers. She looked astonished and said, "I am Madame Villiers. Why are you looking for my husband?" I said I was a friend of Bill Petty. Without another word she yanked open the back door and slid in beside my young daughter and my mother and said "To my house. Follow my directions."

We were like long lost relatives. The Mayor of course was there.

I believe it was a Saturday. They feted us with lunch. The Mayor told us the exact same story that Bill Petty had told me and even more. Bill was a hero who had saved the lives of the Mayor and the other partisans. After lunch, the Mayor drove us over to the top of the cliffs at Pointe du Hoc, and used my camera to take a photo of me holding my 8-year-old daughter Nancy. We were looking out though the gun-slot in a cement blockhouse from which the German defenders had fired down on the Rangers.

Now, shift to 1984, ten years after my visit to Pointe du Hoc. Bill Petty had called to tell me there was to be a big reunion, the 40th Anniversary celebration, June 6, with him and the surviving Rangers. He knew I had access to the White House, and said, "President Reagan must be there!"

Needless to say, he got my attention. I regularly saw the confidential travel schedule of the President—and I knew he was going to be in Normandy on June 6, honoring the Anniversary. He would be at a cemetery about five miles from Pointe du Hoc.

As things turned out, a few days later I was at a big meeting in the White House Roosevelt Room with a number of people— including the President. After the meeting ended, I caught up with him and briefly suggested—with a quick explanation—that as long as he was going to be in the vicinity, it might be worth his time to visit Ponte du Hoc. He said, "Why don't you go over this with Mike Deaver?"

When I met with Mike, I brought along the picture of my daughter Nancy and me looking out through the slit of the German block house. I told him the story of Bill Petty and the other Rangers—and how Bill saved the partisans—and said I thought it would be a very appropriate venue for the President. Mike got it right away. He said "I think you have something here."

Reagan went, and met Bill Petty and the other survivors— perhaps five or six. The President shook their hands and Nancy gave each a big hug. Then he delivered one of the most memorable speeches of his career.

A few weeks after the anniversary, the White House sent me a note of thanks, and a photograph of the President and *his* Nancy looking through the same firing slit in the same block house at the top of the cliff at Pointe du Hoc.

*For President Reagan's speech at Pointe du Hoc, see page 333.*

I was invited to a party at the DC home of *New York Times* columnist Bill Safire—he and I had been business partners in New York, and remained close. It was quite a gathering; it seemed as if everyoneimportant wasthere: Barbara Walters, several Cabinet members, the Fed Chairman, and a bunch of major political players. I walked into the library and there was Bill talking with another man. Bill saw me and immediately introduced me to his other guest—Lane Kirkland head, of the AFL-CIO. We started to talk and another guest pulled Bill away. I was left alone with Lane Kirkland and didn't have much to say. I was only in the Administration about three months. I said to Lane, "Who is your contact in the Reagan White House?" There was dead silence for longer than usual so I said, "Ah . . . you don't have one."

"Right," he said.

I said, "That's not right. Do you mind if I try to do something about that?"

He replied, "Be my guest."

I had been working closely on some projects with Bill Clark, the National Security advisor at that time. Bill was very close to the President and had been with him when he was Governor. I called him and started to tell him the whole story. He repeated, "Lane Kirkland . . . Wait just a minute." Then the President came on the line with Bill on the line also; Bill said, "Tell thestory to thePresident." I did. Then the President said to me, "Gil, you remember that I was head of the Screen Actors Guild. We can't have him out there alone."

"OK," I said. "What should I tell him?"

There was a momentary pause. Then he said, "Tell him his official White House contact is George," meaning, of course Vice President George Bush.

My next call, of course,was to Lane Kirkland

Sometime later, Safire and I were having lunch . . . and he told me what had happened next. Kirkland was grateful for the contact, and was now enjoying a high-level back-channel access to the White House, where a mutual level of trust allowed for meaningful (and confidential) conversations.

# 26

# GERALD J. MOSSINGHOFF

Assistant Secretary of Commerce and Commissioner of Patents and
Trademarks 1981-1985

The Intellectual Property President. Prior to my nomination as
Commissioner of Patents and Trademarks in 1981, Commerce
Secretary Malcolm Baldridge and I met with President Reagan.
At that meeting, I was impressed with how much the President
knew about the importance of intellectual property and how
dedicated he was to strengthening intellectual property protection.
That included copyrights, of course—particularly important to the
motion picture industry—but also patents and trademarks.

`In a light vein, the President referred to a story he had heard
about Charles Holland Duell, Patent Commissioner at the turn of
the nineteenth century, who reportedly recommended to President
McKinley that he close the Patent Office because "Everything that
can be invented has been invented." President Reagan, tongue in
cheek, told me not to follow that example and not to make such a
recommendation to him while he was president.

Secretary Baldridge told me later that President Reagan viewed
intellectual property protection worldwide as the key to U.S. international competitiveness. The President rejected the idea—then
prevalent in some quarters—that the U.S. government should
pick "winners" and "losers" among U.S. industries to enhance our
international competitive positions. Secretary Baldridge reported
that the President saw protection of intellectual property as a far

more appropriate course for the U.S. government to pursue. And in fact, President Reagan's leadership in the field of intellectual property led to major and lasting contributions. Foremost among them follow below.

Government-Wide Attention to Intellectual Property. Early in his Administration, President Reagan established his Cabinet-Council structure, installing Commerce Secretary Baldridge as the Chair of the Cabinet Council on Commerce and Trade. In turn, to achieve President Reagan's goals on intellectual property, Secretary Baldridge established a government-wide Working Group on Intellectual Property, manned at the Assistant Secretary level, which I was honored to chair.

Adherence to the Berne Convention for the Protection of Literary and Artistic Works. On October 31, 1988, President Reagan had a Rose-Garden Signing Ceremony for the Berne Convention Implementation Act. He stated:

> Today we celebrate victory in the name of a right as old as the Union itself and as central to our Union as any: the right all Americans have to protect their property. We're here to sign into law the Berne Convention Implementation Act of 1988. It will enable the United States to adhere to the Berne Convention for the protection of literary and artistic works. The Berne convention, which was originally concluded in 1886 and approved by our Senate earlier this month, provides for the protection of copyrighted works from international pirates who make their living by stealing and then selling the creative accomplishments of others.
>
> With 77 countries as members, including most of our trading partners, the Berne convention features the highest internationally recognized standards for the protection of works of authorship. Our membership will automatically . . . secure the highest available level of international copyright protection for U.S. artists, authors, and copyright holders. This is especially significant because American works protected by copyright—books, recordings, movies, computer software prominent among them—have

been at risk because of differences between U.S. law and the Berne convention.

The cost to Americans has been substantial, not only in terms of the violation of the property rights of Americans but in terms of our trade balance as well. We've been running a trade surplus of over $1 billion annually in copyrighted goods, and it would have been much larger had it not been for the pirating of American copyright work. In 1986 alone, the entertainment industry may have lost more than $2 billion in potential revenue, and our computer and software industries more than $4 billion in potential revenue. That's why adherence to the Berne convention has been such an important goal of the administration and why this occasion marks a watershed for us.

* * *

Officials in our administration worked closely with many key Members of Congress, such as Senator Pete Wilson and Congressman Carlos Moorhead, to get this bill passed in Congress. And we must also remember our good friend and former Secretary of Commerce, the late Malcolm Baldridge, who led the charge on this legislation."

The Creation in 1982 of the Court of Appeals for the Federal Circuit. On April 2, 1982, President Reagan, in a Roosevelt Room ceremony that included Secretary Baldridge and Congressional leaders, signed the Federal Courts Improvement Act of 1982, among other things, establishing the Court of Appeals for the Federal Circuit. That court was empowered to hear appeals in all patent cases nationwide. This had the effect of assuring consistency and uniformity in patent cases among the 94 Federal district courts, the U.S. Court of Claims, the U.S. Patent and Trademark Office and the International Trade Commission. Prior to the creation of the Federal Circuit, the results in patent cases often depended more on *where* a case was filed rather than on the merits of the case.

Adding Intellectual Property Protection to the Agenda of the World Trade Organization. President Reagan decided to add intellectual property protection to the GATT (General Agreement on Tariffs and Trade) negotiations in the 1980s. That resulted ultimately in the creation of the World Trade Organization ("WTO") and the landmark Trade-Related Aspects of Intellectual Property Rights (TRIPS) international accord. That in turn forces "patent-pirate" nations to respect intellectual property worldwide if they choose to join the WTO.

A Firm Commitment to Reduce the Time it Takes to Acquire a U.S. Patent from the Patent and Trademark Office ("USPTO") to 18 Months from then-prevalent Protections of Four to Five Years. At the beginning of the Reagan Administration, the U.S. Patent and Trademark Office ("USPTO") was significantly underfunded and the backload of unexamined applications was growing at an alarming rate. High-technology industry was concerned that the resulting uncertainties about patent protection were adversely affecting their ability to fund research and development. President Reagan supported a two-way compromise. If the Congress would enact a meaningful increase in user fees, which the USPTO could retain, he would commit—through the Department of Commerce— to reduce the time it takes to acquire a U.S. patent to an average of 18 months. Congress agreed with the Reagan fee recommendation, and the goal of 18 months average time of patent pendency was achieved in 1989, the lowest the average pendency of patent applications has been in modern times, before or since.

A Firm Commitment to Replace the Enormous Paper Search System at the Patent and Trademark Office with a Fully Automated System. At the beginning of the Reagan Administration, the USPTO was using pre-World War II all paper search techniques to decide whether patents should be granted and trademarks should be registered. As part of the bargain on increasing user fees, the President committed to a fully automated search and retrieval system. That has now been achieved, resulting in one of the largest and most effective paperless automated search systems in the world.

Enactment of the Trademark Counterfeiting Act of 1984, 18 U.S.C. § 2320. This act established major fines up to $1,000,000 and provided for searches and seizures of counterfeit products without prior notice to suspected counterfeiters. As the chair of Intellectual Property Working Group, I testified before the House Judiciary Committee in 1983 in support of that act, which provided a clear model for subsequent anti-counterfeiting laws.

In a December 28, 1984, letter from President Reagan to me, he summarized briefly his Administration's successes in protecting intellectual property in these terms:

> You have served as Commissioner of the Patent and Trademark Office during one of its most eventful and productive periods. Through the enactment of realistic user fees, you have been able to greatly enhance your Office's service to industry and inventors. You have modernized operations at the Office through a far-reaching automation program. You have worked effectively to strengthen international intellectual property protection for U.S. industry. Your actions to accomplish these goals will be remembered for many years to come.

Since President Reagan's Administration, protection of intellectual property has moved from a somewhat sleepy esoteric form of law to where it now generates headlines daily in the lay press. Our internet economy depends heavily on the creation and protection of intellectual property. President Reagan saw that coming and personally led efforts in bringing about our dynamic high-technology society, dependent as it is on strong and effective intellectual property protection.

# 27

# P. X. KELLEY
General, USMC (Retired)
28th Commandant, United States Marine Corps 1983-1987
Assistant Commandant 1981-1983

A President salutes his Marines. Sunday, June 26, 1983 was a cool, moonlit evening. President and Mrs. Ronald Wilson Reagan cut short their weekend at Camp David to return to Washington so they could attend the traditional Change of Command Ceremony during which I proudly took my place as the 28th Commandant of the United States Marine Corps.

In his remarks, my Commander in Chief gave me my first order as Commandant:

> General, on behalf of all Americans, I want a message sent to every member of your Corps...to every clime or place where the words 'Semper Fidelis' are a way of life. General, tell it to the Marines, whether in dress blues, service greens, or combat camouflage...whether they serve in the air, on land, or at sea...tell them their countrymen are grateful...tell them we stand behind them...tell them that we are proud of the proudest.

During the parade, President Reagan reviewed the troops as they passed in review. He stood proud and tall—every inch the embodiment of a Commander-in-Chief.

At the conclusion of the ceremony, I escorted President Reagan from the parade ground. As we walked, we passed many members of Congress, the Diplomatic Corps, and members of the Armed Forces, both U.S. and foreign. Each member of the military saluted our nation's popular Commander-in-Chief. Many cheered him and applauded as he passed by.

Seeing this remarkable demonstration of respect, President Reagan said, "You know, P.X., I wish I could return their salutes." He said, when he joined the Army Reserves in 1935, he was told, that you "never salute when in civilian clothes." His humility was touching—after all, this was the President of our great United States and, in that role, the leader of our Armed Forces. He certainly could salute his troops any time he wished.

I replied, "That would be most appropriate, Mr. President, as you are our Commander-in-Chief."

From that night forward, whenever he was boarding one of the Presidential aircraft, reviewing U.S. troops at military bases across the world, or meeting with the Joint Chiefs of Staff, our 40th President returned each and every salute he received.

The President's exercise boy. Knowing of my love for horses, shortly after I became Commandant of the Marine Corps, President Reagan suggested that I might want to participate in the extensive equestrian course conducted for the training of the mounted U.S. Park Police who patrol the National Mall and other areas of Washington, D.C. Needless to say, I accepted this offer as it was a great honor to train with this exceptional mounted force.

When I arrived at the Park Police Barn on my first day, I was assigned to my instructor, Ralph Pfister, an exceptionally skilled rider and long-time member of the U.S. Park Police. A former drill instructor with the U.S. Army Airborne, Ralph was a gifted instructor and, during the progression of the course, we became great friends. I'm proud to say that we remain close friends.

After I graduated from the course, I often rode on the National Mall in the company of Park Police officers. It was thrilling to view our magnificent Federal City from the perspective of Washington, Jefferson and Lincoln—on horseback. One day, one of the officers suggested that I ride "Gym Crack," a magnificent black stallion whom President Reagan routinely rode when he was visiting Camp David.

Although I was flattered, I replied that Gym Crack was the President's horse and that it would be inappropriate for someone else to ride him. But, despite my protestations, my Park Police friends had Gym Crack saddled up and ready for my next ride. I rode him often in the ensuing months, each time amazed by both the magnificent stallion and the thought of his illustrious rider, the President.

One evening, while in my quarters, the phone rang. A voice at the other end said, "This is the White House Operator. President Reagan would like to speak with General Kelley." The next voice I heard was that of our 40th President, my Commander-in-Chief.

"P.X.," he said, "I heard that you want to ride Gym Crack in the Washington International Horse Show!" Tongue-tied, I responded, "Well, um, Mr. President, there has been some discussion, but I would never presume. But, yes, it would be a great honor."

My Commander-in-Chief replied, "I WANT you to ride him! Furthermore, I want you to consider yourself as my exercise boy!"

I not only rode Gym Crack in the show, we received a Blue Ribbon—and I have the photo to prove it!

Many years later, I was honored by President Reagan's alma mater, Eureka College, when they named me an Honorary Reagan Fellow. I joined the ranks of other Reagan Fellows—people named Mikhail Gorbachev, James Baker, Sandra Day O'Connor and Ed Meese. But of all the honors I have received in my 85 years, "exercise boy to President Reagan's horse" is the one I cherish most of all. Thank you, Mr. President.

# 28

# JOHN L. LOEB, JR.
## Ambassador to Denmark 1981-1983

1975. My friend Julian Gingold—an investment banker who had connections within the Reagan camp—asked me to help host a lunch for Ronald Reagan in New York City. His people wanted us to introduce him to a number of leading conservatives and notable Republicans who might further his plans to challenge President Ford for the Republican nomination in 1976.

I had been a Rockefeller Republican for many years, having had the distinction of being Governor Nelson Rockefeller's special assistant for the environment. Also, in 1970, after Earth Day, I became his New York State chairman of the Council of Environmental Advisors (a post I held for five years). However, during that time, I became disappointed with Rockefeller's fiscal policies of "tax and spend," especially because nothing was getting better. This was one of the reasons Governor Reagan's policies appealed to me. I understood our nation needed new leadership.

On Governor Reagan's first visit Julian and I ended up having lunch at the University Club alone with him and Mike Deaver (his number one consultant) as, at that time, no important political New Yorker was really interested in meeting a movie actor-turned-politician who was from the far right of the Republican Party. However, with a lot of persistence we were able at a subsequent dinner to bring together some prominent New Yorkers to meet with him.

In 1976, Julian and I went to the Republican convention in

Kansas City under the sponsorship of Governor Reagan's campaign manager John Sears. Sadly we all know what happened in Kansas City. *(Details, page 227.)*

In 1978, Governor Reagan and his secretary Helene von Damm came to my home in Purchase, New York. The governor was to be the guest speaker at a fundraiser I had been asked to give for Perry Duryea—the speaker of the state legislature now running for governor. I approached countless business executives throughout Westchester County to try to raise money for Perry, at $250 a ticket. With Governor Reagan as speaker, I thought it would be easy—some of the great corporations in America had headquarters only a few miles from my home and my next-door neighbor Peter Flanigan was a great friend of Donald Kendal, CEO of one of them, Pepsi-Cola.

Easy, it was not—until I lowered the ticket price to $100 and quickly sold more than 500 tickets to the public at large. When Governor Reagan arrived at the event, it was like Jesus Christ had come to my home. Once he began to speak, everyone was so quiet that you could hear the wind in the trees. That moment made me realize how Reagan and his ideas had already connected with the average citizen, whether Republican or Democrat. That had quite an impact on me.

Early in 1979, with the encouragement of Gingold and Max Rabb (a family friend and, later, Reagan's Ambassador to Italy) I assembled a group of important Republican leaders for a meeting in New York City to discuss the possibility of a Reagan campaign for the presidency—which, we believed, he should launch from New York City. Somewhat to our surprise, he did just that on November 13, 1979, to a packed ballroom at the New York Hilton hotel. Also to our very pleasant surprise Reagan went on to win the Democrat stronghold of New York state not once, but twice.

I was active during the first campaign—including hosting a successful fundraiser at my New York City townhouse with Nancy Reagan as the guest of honor. I met many times with Ronald Reagan during the campaign and served on Richard Allen's Foreign Policy

Advisory Committee. Following the election, I was most honored to be appointed United States ambassador to Denmark.

Just before leaving on that assignment, I took my parents and my six year old son Nicholas to Washington to meet with President Reagan in the Oval Office. The president told us a wonderful story about the King of Denmark during the Second World War. Once a week, the king would go for a very public ride on his horse, wearing a yellow star to show his support of the Danish Jews. Denmark was the only country in Europe that saved its entire Jewish population from the Nazis.

When I arrived in Denmark in the late summer of 1981, I found that Reagan was a very controversial figure. No one could believe that an actor had the experience and intelligence to be president of the United States. At that time, Radio Denmark (which was both a radio and television station) was controlled by the Socialist government, which would not allow footage of Reagan to be shown.

However, not long after I arrived Reagan gave what became known as the "Zero Option" speech" which called for the abolishment of all nuclear weapons. We received a video of the speech at the Embassy and, on a hunch, I went to see the head of Radio Denmark, Lauritz Brindslov. I was able to convince him that this speech was of such significance that the video should be broadcast on Radio Denmark and in prime time. This was truly a breakthrough: the next morning newspapers across Denmark trumpeted the headline, "Reagan: From Cowboy to Statesman!"

Soon thereafter I had a meeting with Prime Minister Ancer Jorgensen who told me he had been surprised to learn that Reagan had such a grasp of international relationships and foreign-policy, and was willing to abolish nuclear weapons. Not only was the Prime Minister impressed with the content of the "Zero Options Speech" but also with the fact that President Reagan seem to have the ability to speak for 35 to 40 minutes from memory and without a note. (The Danes had not yet learned about that wonderful machine known as a "Teleprompter.")

The last time I saw Reagan was in 1989, when, on behalf of the Winston Churchill Foundation of the United States (of which I am the chairman) the Duke of Edinburgh presented him the Winston Churchill Award. That Award has been given only four other times in the 50 year history of the Foundation: 1981 to Averell Harriman, 1983 to Margaret Thatcher, 1985 to Ross Perot (presented by Prince Charles), and, in 1991, to President George H. W. Bush (presented by the Queen of England).

*Some details about the 1976 Kansas City convention will be found on page 227 and The "Zero Option" speech is at page 319.*

## 29

## PETER J. MCPHERSON
Administrator, USAID 1981-1987

arly in the mid-1980s, famine threatened several African countries, but especially Ethiopia and Mozambique. Communist governments aligned with the Soviet bloc ran those two countries. There was some discussion within the Administration about how much should be done to help the Communist countries. USAID started providing some food to the two countries, but much more assistance was needed. Senator Jack Danforth of Missouri and Congressman Frank Wolf of Virginia separately went to Africa and then saw the President, to urge him to provide more food aid. Their involvement was very important.

I went to the countries where food was being provided and brought back pictures of desperately needy men, woman, and children. I showed the pictures to the President in the Oval Office. The President was deeply moved and clearly wanted to help, notwithstanding the Communist governments. He said, "A hungry child knows no politics." He told me to get as much food aid to the people as we could. Over the following 18 months, USAID delivered about 2 million tons of food to Africa, including huge amounts to Ethiopia and Mozambique. This represented about 50 percent of the donor food for the famine in Africa and clearly saved many lives. The U.S. led this international famine effort, yet President Reagan was not looking for credit. Nevertheless, people in Africa widely recognized what he and the U.S. did for them. In Sudan, another area hit hard, they called the delivered grain "Reagan."

A new U.S. humanitarian policy was established and generally followed thereafter. The President's words, "A hungry child knows no politics,"need no explanation.

President Reagan supported international family planning. In fact, during his years, more money was spent for that effort than during all previous administrations combined. He did not make a major issue of his support, but I always felt as USAID Administrator I had his support as long as no USAID resources were spent on abortion. Appropriately, he also strongly opposed China's one child per family policy.

The United Nations Fund for Population Activities (UNFPA) was an important player in international family planning. The U.S. provided about $30 million a year to UNFPA and that support helped get other countries to contribute to international family planning. The problem was that UNFPA provided $10 million each year to China and a large portion of that money went to support the one child program. On behalf of the U.S., I told the Executive Director of UNFPA, Rafael Salas of the Philippines, that the U.S. would withdraw from UNFPA if the $10 million to China continued to be used for the one child policy. It was absolutely clear that, as much as we wanted to, we could not get the Chinese to change their one child policy and so the question was how to deal with the problem without causing major harm to international family planning. Salas agreed to work with the Chinese to get them to use the $10 million from UNFPA only for children's health or perhaps only for the purchase of contraceptives. Of course, I needed President Reagan's support of this approach before we proceeded. Bud McFarlane, the National Security Advisor, reviewed the proposal with President Reagan. The President understood the situation and agreed. Mr. Salas then tried to reach an agreement with the Chinese. Unfortunately China would not agree to the compromise and the U.S. thereafter withdrew from UNFPA. Nevertheless, the situation serves as a clear example of the President's quiet practicality in pursuit of his policy goals.

As the law was written when I arrived at USAID, the agency returned to the Treasury any money saved when an existing project was cut out rather than allowing the agency to reprogram the money for a new and better project. Of course this meant that there was tremendous resistance within USAID to eliminating any programs that had a chance of someday being successful. I undertook a major effort to find the bad projects and give the money back. We did in fact find $28 million to give back to the Treasury for budget reduction. One of my staff members suggested that we publicly give a huge $28 million check to the President. This seemed a little over the top to me, being a new agency head. However, I agreed to take the idea to the White House. Almost immediately the President was told about the idea of the check and an event was scheduled. The President knew full well that this was a great opportunity to highlight his careful stewardship of taxpayers' money. There was an early spring Rose Garden event that resulted in front page pictures in a hundred papers across the country, including the *Washington Post* and *The New York Times*.

*Peter McPherson was also Deputy Secretary of U.S. Treasury, 1987-1988*

# 30

# JOHN HUGHES
Assistant Secretary of State for Public Affairs and State Department
Spokesman 1982-1986

had three assignments in the Reagan administration. First was Associate Director of the U.S. Information Agency. Second was Director of the Voice of America. Third was State Department Spokesman, and Assistant Secretary of State for Public Affairs.

Such jobs do not mean that you weekend at Camp David or sleep in the Lincoln bedroom. But they do mean that you see quite a bit of the president over time, in small meetings at the White House, traveling abroad with him, or at formal dinners and state functions.

My boss in the first two assignments was Charles Wick. He had been a member of Reagan's California "kitchen cabinet." As such he had considerable influence with the president. (When Charlie had interviewed me for my first Washington job he bemused me, a lifelong journalist, by declaring: "I don't know anything about journalism and I don't know anything about foreign policy. But I can make things happen." And he could, calling up his friend Ronnie, and slicing through the red tape and strangling bureaucracy of Washington).

My second Washington boss was George Shultz, not initially as familiar with Reagan, but who in time became his most trusted foreign policy advisor.

The closeness of these two men to the president gave me a window to observe Ronald Reagan. He was the same agreeable, friendly human being to almost everyone, whether riding horses with Queen Elizabeth, trading Irish jokes with Democratic Boston pol Top O'Neill, or bandying quips with janitors or Secret Service agents. Or simply performing backflips to impress Nancy at a private pool in Hawaii, en route to a heads-of-state meeting in Asia.

To each person he met, whether a waiter, elevator operator, or president or prime minister, he gave the impression he was completely interested in and focused upon them. And he was.

It was no act.

His manners were impeccable. Once, after two or three of us had been explaining a major new project plan to him at the White House, he stopped us gathering up our papers. "I know you fellows are busy," he said, then almost apologetically: "Can you stay for a few minutes?" We stayed while he told us a few amusing anecdotes. As we left, we marveled at a President of the United States who would ask our permission to tell a few stories.

But he had no lack of toughness when required to defend the principles he held paramount. When he thought US civil air controllers were wrong to strike, he fired them. When the Israelis kept on bombarding Beirut in defiance of a cease-fire agreement, an angry Reagan phoned Israeli Prime Minister Menachem Begin and demanded they stop. They did.

Reagan's loathing for communism's "evil empire" was manifest. He built up a retaliatory nuclear arsenal against Soviet attack. But he was visionary in proposing his Strategic Defense Initiative ("star wars") which, if successful, he saw as a path to world peace.

Reagan's firmness in military and diplomatic fields clearly led to the greatest triumph of his presidency, the end of the cold war.

He was a man who had a passionate belief in America as a "shining city upon a hill," and he had the words to translate that vision into reality for millions at home and abroad.

Not a bad record for a man some critics had dismissed as a second-rate actor.

*Former Pulitzer-prize winning Editor of The Christian Science Monitor; now a Professor at Brigham Young University in Utah*

## 31

## DONALD PAUL HODEL

Secretary of Energy 1982-1985 / Secretary of Interior 1986-1989

What's Right? When Secretary of the Interior James Watt was out of town on Cabinet meeting days, because I was the Under Secretary I attended in his place. I saw that the President was as genial and kind in person as he appeared to be in public. I remember marveling at some of the poor presentations he patiently sat through, when I would have thought that every presentation to the President would be sharp and precise. One time, however, he did something quite unusual. He interrupted the presenter. Then he said, "You're talking politics. I want to know what you think is right." What a powerful message that was to all of us, and I have never forgotten it.

Knowledge of Interior. Most issues in the Department of the Interior do not rise to presidential level. Some are very controversial, but the Secretary can usually keep them from becoming issues for the President. Secretary Watt was unusually knowledgeable about the department, having spent several years in positions in Interior during earlier administrations. Watt told me that when he was interviewed by the President prior to his nomination as secretary, he was astonished at the depth and breadth of President Reagan's knowledge of many key issues in the department. It turned out that in doing his numerous radio broadcasts over the years the President had researched and boiled down to their essential features a good many of the major Interior issues. Watt felt, and I personally saw it in my later service as secretary, that it is doubtful that any president knew as much or understood the significance of issues in the Department of the Interior as well as did President Reagan. Others who worked closely with him over the years attest to his excellent memory. Watt saw it in action in a way that he had not anticipated.

The Vote is 12 to 4, The Nays Have It. In 1987 an issue came to the Cabinet about whether or not to release western loggers from very high-priced federal timber contracts. They had bid for federal timber while there was a boom in prices and then the bottom fell out. Holding them to the contracts meant financial ruin for almost all of them. Secretary of Agriculture Dick Lyng (over the U.S. Forest Service) favored release. OMB and Treasury did not. After the issue was thoroughly discussed there were about a dozen members who thought we should enforce the contracts, as is, after all they had bid for them. Four of us from the West favored release because we knew that these small loggers had no assets to pay the government with and in many cases the only source of jobs in small western towns was the local logger/sawmill and bankrupting them would devastate those towns. The results would be a handful of large timber companies as the only survivors in the industry and numerous ghost towns. The President had been Governor of California. He knew what would happen if Uncle Sam enforced these contracts. It would get no money and the towns would be damaged. He decided in favor of release.

Tax Increase. In 1983 Dave Stockman and Don Regan made a presentation to the president at a full cabinet meeting in which they showed that we absolutely had to have a tax increase in order to cut the deficit. Stockman was one of the most able presenters I had ever seen. By the time he was done, I sat there wondering how the President could do anything other than approve pushing for a tax increase. I waited along with the rest of the cabinet for his reaction. Finally, with that little self-deprecating smile that was his trademark, he said, "Well, I understand what you've said, but the problem is that if we agree to a tax increase, the Congress won't use it to cut the deficit; they'll spend it." In one simple and accurate statement he demolished all the impressive and seemingly persuasive arguments that had been made to him. He did not take his eye off the ball.

*Don Hodel is Chairman Emeritus, Summit Power Group LLC*

# 32

# ROBERT "BUD" MCFARLANE
Counselor, Department of State 1981-1982
Deputy National Security Advisor 1982-1983
National Security Advisor 1983-1985

In the spring of 1982, roughly a year after the President was shot by John Hinckley outside the Hilton Hotel in Washington, we were headed west on Air Force One to spend the "Easter Recess" at Rancho del Cielo. Counselor Ed Meese, Chief of Staff Jim Baker, Mike Deaver and I were in the staff lounge talking about the challenges of the day. Once we reached altitude, President Reagan came back from his cabin and strolled in looking very casual and upbeat—as was always the case when he was going to spend a few days at the ranch in California.

After a few minutes of light banter, he remarked that he was bringing all of his suits with him on this trip to be altered. There was a somewhat awkward pause from our side since each of us separately imagined that he might be experiencing a little bulge in his waistline—as we were—and intended to ask his tailor to help deal with it. But immediately, he went on, saying, "Yeah, you know a year ago when I was trying to get back on my feet, the Doc gave me some tips for dealing with the deterioration in muscle tone. It involves a series of exercises, several weight-lifting protocols and one or two tips with my diet, but it's really helped. When he measured me last week, I had put three inches on to my biceps, added about four inches to my chest measurement, and taken about four inches off my waist, so I have to get my suits altered to fit."

That prompted a rowdy "Get out of here," in unison from the rest of us. What a man! How many 71 year-old presidents can you imagine would have the discipline to do that?

Political Courage and Nuclear Weapons. I'm often asked what quality distinguished President Reagan from other politicians. The answer comes easily; political courage—the will to do what would best serve the interests of the American people (and humankind), without regard for the possible impact on his own political fortunes. Asked for examples, two come to mind; his firing of the air traffic controllers in 1981 (which is treated elsewhere in this book) and his driven sense of mission to rid the world of nuclear weapons— against the advice of Prime Minister Thatcher, Chancellor Helmut Kohl, other European Allies, virtually every Democrat member of the House and Senate, even members of his own Cabinet, and of course Kremlin leaders (who were bent on building ever-larger stockpiles).

Most Americans have forgotten that throughout the Cold War with the Soviet Union the world lived in constant fear that—whether by accident or design—a nuclear attack could occur and the results would have been catastrophic for all of humankind. Nuclear Alert Drills required school children to crouch under their desks periodically, households built bomb shelters, hundreds of nuclear weapons were tested underground and in the air; such was the palpable climate of alarm in which all Americans lived for almost forty years. Our hopes for avoiding such a holocaust rested uneasily on the premise that if we maintained a staggering number of nuclear weapons on alert, able even to ride out an attack and then to respond with devastating power, that this capability—this "balance of terror"—would deter the Soviet Union from attacking in the first place. Any rational concept of "victory" under this doctrine had lost all meaning. And yet, the advocates of this strategy of "mutual assured destruction"—the so-called MAD doctrine—touted that it was working; nuclear war had not occurred, and therefore MAD ought to remain our strategy. President Reagan disagreed. He thought it outrageous to base the very survival of humankind on the fraught premise that accidents or misguided aggression won't happen.

He also believed it was immoral. Reagan was a very spiritual, God-fearing man who had been attentive to the scriptures, with a deep sense of personal accountability throughout his life. He had focused in particular on the passages in Revelation that portend mankind's violent extinction as a consequence of his competitive and aggressive instincts. He believed that that possibility was at hand as a consequence of the massive arsenals of nuclear weapons held—and growing—in the U.S. and the Soviet Union. And he believed with all his heart that it was his responsibility to prevent the cataclysm from occurring, and ultimately to begin the process of getting rid of all nuclear weapons.

To do so he planned to reverse the course of U.S. nuclear strategy by 180 degrees and instead of relying on *offense* (and the power to annihilate humankind), to rely on *defense* to defend us. Or as the then-Chief of Naval Operations, Admiral James D. Watkins, said, "Wouldn't it be better to protect Americans than to avenge them?"

Who could disagree with so noble an undertaking; what politician would have the nerve to challenge so sensible a course? Well, the answer was—plenty. Indeed, virtually every respected "strategic thinker" in our country was against it—Senator Sam Nunn, Chairman of the Senate Armed Services Committee, Congressmen Les Aspin (later a Secretary of Defense), Congressman (later Vice President) Al Gore, several former secretaries of defense, the Union of Concerned Scientists—all of them claiming that at least the bloodthirsty MAD doctrine had worked (even while acknowledging that it could easily fail). So the President had a major challenge ahead: to convince the American people, the Congress and our allies of the military soundness and moral virtue of his strategy.

Reagan tackled that challenge with a passion and over the next two years, through countless speeches, frequent meetings with the bipartisan leadership of the Congress, and further meetings and travel throughout the world to engage with foreign leaders, he made his case. The results were phenomenal. The American people got it; after all, what's not to like about a plan that will "…put a shield over my head and avoid having to go through a nuclear attack?" So did the Congress, albeit somewhat more slowly. Again, they were hearing from their constituents "…our president wants to protect us, so give him the money to do it." The allies were a little harder to convince. From their perspective, their safety in Europe—where Russian forces had always outnumbered theirs—had always rested on the commitment from the U.S. to use its nuclear weapons to compensate for the imbalance in conventional forces. Further, they saw Reagan's investment in his so-called Star Wars shield, as technologically risky, expensive, and even as appearing to signal that the U.S. was preparing its own "first strike" capability. Through patient listening and careful reasoning, the President was able to overcome their concerns. Indeed by the time that a Summit meeting was arranged with the new Soviet leader, Mikhail Gorbachev, in November, 1985, President Reagan enjoyed nationwide support for his national security policies by more than 70 percent of the American people, and received a ringing bipartisan endorsement from the Congress in a Joint Resolution that passed overwhelmingly. The frosting on the cake came in the form of a public press conference held at the United Nations in New York at which Prime Minister Thatcher of the UK, brought together the heads of state and government of Great Britain, Germany, France, Canada, Italy and Japan to announce their solid support for Reagan as he prepared to leave for his first summit with President Gorbachev. He had done it; in a little more than two years' time the President rallied the support of the American people, the Congress, and our allies and sat down with his Soviet counterpart in the strongest position of any president in modern history. The results were an historic breakthrough not only in arms control where he achieved the first reduction of nuclear weapons in history, but also in bringing on the end of the Cold War and victory in the 40-year ideological struggle between east and west. Truly, as he had foreshadowed years before, he had achieved the consignment of Marxism to "the ash heap of history." What had it taken to do that—political and moral courage to do the right thing, extraordinary communication skill, and determined leadership.

## 33

## TYRUS W. COBB

Special Assistant to the President for National Security Affairs 1983-1989

Beginning of the end of the Cold War. In his first meeting with a Soviet leader, President Ronald Reagan met with General Secretary Mikhail Gorbachev in Geneva Switzerland in November, 1985. That meeting produced three days of intensive, candid exchanges of views, difficult negotiations, near collapses of the Summit, and in the end, a historic agreement between two entrenched adversaries. In my opinion, the successful Summit in effect signaled the beginning of the end of forty years of the Cold War.

Many "experts" doubted that Reagan was up to the task of dealing with Gorbachev, the dynamic, young and globally popular new Soviet leader, who took over the ruling Politburo in 1985 following years of decrepit rule by aging and sick (Brezhnev, Andropov, and Cherenko) leaders in Moscow. If the truth be known, many of the top officials in *our own* government weren't so convinced that the President was ready to match wit and wisdom with Gorbachev.

Prior to Reagan's historic Summit meeting with Gorbachev we conducted extensive briefings and preparations for the President. Suddenly, just three weeks before the Summit, Reagan called a halt to all these interminable discussions. His advisors were perplexed, saying there were numerous topics to be covered in greater depth, from arms control to trade issues, to human rights. The President turned to all of us and said persuasively, "I have been preparing for this meeting for 40 years. If I'm not ready now, I'm never going to be." But was he?

Not to worry. Reagan took charge of the Summit in Geneva from the outset. Who can forget on that brilliantly blue but very cold November morning, when Reagan, wearing only his dark blue suit, bounded down the stairs of his villa to meet Gorby, who climbed out of his drab Russian-built Chaika limousine, wrapped from head to toe in his overcoat and oversized fur hat. Reagan had the psychological advantage and kept it throughout the Summit.

Although the negotiations were difficult and protracted, and Gorbachev proved to be as intelligent, knowledgeable and facile as we had anticipated, Reagan held firm to his principles. No more unverifiable treaties ("Trust but Verify" he loved to say in Russian), no more agreements codifying Soviet superiority in arms on the European continent, no more tolerating Moscow's refusal to grant its citizens basic human rights, and—perhaps most importantly to the President—no more reliance on *offensive* nuclear missiles to provide for our security.

Many times during the three days of the Summit it appeared that the negotiations would collapse. A failure would reinforce the image of Reagan as an aging cowboy-actor, unable to reach an agreement with the reform-minded Soviet leader. Reagan particularly would not compromise on his deep felt desire to *shift away from a dependence on the threat of annihilating each others' populations as a basis for maintaining our security.*

Gorbachev, too, hung firm, hoping that the President would "understand" that an agreement on Moscow's terms would ensure that the President emerged from the Summit as a popular and respected world leader and peacemaker. In the end, Gorbachev conceded on several key negotiating points, particularly relating to the America Strategic Defense Initiative. Gorbachev was undoubtedly aware of the deteriorating state of the Soviet economy and Moscow's inability to keep pace with American military and technological advances.

The Summit agreement was a signal triumph for Reagan. As the *New York Times* acknowledged, Reagan, "in great part through his own powers of leadership" was subsequently able to deliver "a historic series of agreements with Mikhail Gorbachev that led to the peaceful dismantling of the Soviet empire." Within seven years, the Warsaw Pact dissolved, Germany was reunited and joined NATO, and finally, the USSR itself disappeared.

Ronald Reagan ended the Cold War *on our terms,* an outcome that began that day in Geneva in 1985.

Reagan, John Paul and the End of the Cold War. Carl Bernstein called it "The Holy Alliance" (*Time* Magazine, Feb 24, 1992), the amazingly successful partnership between Pope John Paul II and President Ronald Reagan that accelerated, if not caused, the fall of Communism and led to the end of the Cold War. Reagan and the Polish-born Pope shared a spiritual unity, a common animosity toward communism, and an unshakeable commitment to bring down the Soviet domination of Eastern Europe.

President Reagan personally met with the Pope on three occasions—twice in Rome and once in Miami—but they maintained a vigorous exchange of ideas and plans aimed at ending, first and foremost, Moscow's domination of Poland, and ultimately, bringing about the collapse of the Soviet empire. The practical implementation of these plans was left to the President's and the Pope's principal aides. On the U.S. side that included, initially, Secretary of State Alexander Haig, Deputy Secretary and later National Security Advisor Bill Clark, and, especially, CIA Director Bill Casey, all strong Catholics. On the Vatican side these operations were coordinated principally by the Holy See's "Secretary of State," Agostino Cardinal Casaroli.

Pope John Paul himself caused the most serious crack in the Soviet Union's control over East Europe in 1979. His 9-day pilgrimage to his homeland drew enormous and enthusiastic crowds, marking, in George Will's words, "a national epiphany, a thunderous realization that Poland was of one mind" in rejecting the atheism of communism and restoring Polish national identity.

In the face of growing success by Lech Walesa and the Solidarity movement, the Polish government of Marshal Jaruzelski tried to salvage its authority by imposing martial law in 1981. That drastic measure only intensified American and Papal resolve to break the back of the empire. Washington provided extensive economic, communications, and organizational support to Solidarity, much of it distributed through Catholic Church networks. Ironically, the Reagan Administration also worked closely with two unusual allies in this cause, the Socialist International and the AFL-CIO (the former very anti-communist, the latter motivated to assist Solidarity).

Covert aid to Hungary and Czechoslovakia, as well as Poland, was accelerated. Radio Free Europe and Radio Liberty broadcasts were increased and became more direct and bold in encouraging resistance, and a plan to economically isolate the Soviet Union was developed. The twin pillars of the effort to bring about the economic collapse of the USSR were an accelerated defense buildup—propelled by the expectation that the Soviets could not keep pace (or if they tried, it might bankrupt their economy)—and a determined effort to deny Moscow access to advanced Western technology.

President Reagan valued his contacts with John Paul II, and held the Pontiff in great esteem. The meetings with the Pope included a number of advisors on both sides, but as was the practice with other leaders such as Margaret Thatcher and Helmut Kohl, Reagan and John Paul also conferred "one on one." A major difference was that the Pope preferred not to have any of us aides present, even as notetakers, in these private sessions. The President always emerged from these meetings animated and enthusiastic—clearly they shared a common vision and hope for the future of mankind.

These discussions were not completely free of friction, of course—the Pope and the President had different takes on the global role of capitalism and what needed to be done in the Third World. Pope John Paul pressed Reagan hard to ensure that capitalism took care to address the needs of the working class to share in the benefits generated by free markets. He also prodded the President to have the developed countries do more to eliminate the scourge of poverty in the lesser developed areas.

Pope John Paul returned to Poland in triumph in 1987, hailed by millions, and the cracks in the monolith further deepened. Under growing popular pressure, Soviet President Gorbachev finally conceded that Solidarity would be a full and legitimate partner in governing Poland, still essentially a satellite of the USSR. In December of 1990 Lech Walesa became the President of Poland and a year later the Soviet Union itself dissolved, to use the Marxist phrase, "on the ash heap of history."

The alliance and partnership between President Reagan and Pope John Paul II was a crucial element in bringing about these amazing changes.

## 34

# RICHARD PERLE
### Assistant Secretary of Defense for Global Strategic Affairs 1981-1987


From a meeting in the White House situation room, 1983: The subject of the meeting in October or November, 1983 was arms control with the Soviet Union and how the administration should deal with proposals to "freeze" the construction of nuclear weapons. The President was opposed to a "nuclear freeze" because it would take effect just as the Soviet Union completed a multi-year build-up of its nuclear weapons and just as the U.S. was about to replace its older weapons, some of them obsolete, with modernized replacements.

Near the end of the meeting someone brought a proposal by Senator William Cohen to the President's attention. "Mr. President," he said, "Senator Cohen, with the support of Senator Nunn, has suggested that, instead of a "freeze," we should "build-down."

"How would that work?" the President asked.

"As we understand it," he was told, "for every new, modernized nuclear weapon we build, we would retire two. In time, we would have many fewer weapons."

"Well," the President said, "I have a proposal. For every senator they elect, let's retire two."

At the Reagan-Gorbachev summit at Reykjavik: In the final hours of the Reykjavik summit on October 12, 1986, the delegation that had accompanied President Reagan to the Iceland meeting was clustered around him in a small room adjacent to the room where the meeting with Gorbachev was being held. After nearly two days of intense negotiation, the two leaders had taken a short break to confer with their advisors. Gorbachev had made his final offer: he would agree to American proposals sharply reducing offensive nuclear weapons if Reagan would accept limitations on the development of defensive weapons, especially the research and development program called SDI (strategic defense initiative) but widely referred to, especially by its critics, as "star wars."

The question the President wanted his advisors to answer was whether the restrictions Gorbachev was proposing—limiting the American program "within the four walls of a laboratory"—would allow the effort to develop a strategic defense against intercontinental missiles to go forward, or bring it to an end. The delegation gathered around the President consisted of Secretary of State George Shultz, Chief of Staff Don Regan, National Security Advisor John Poindexter, arms control negotiators Paul Nitze and Max Kampleman, arms control director Ken Adelman, and me, then an assistant secretary of defense. Reagan asked each of us whether SDI could go forward if he accepted Gorbachev's last offer. Others can speak for themselves. My advice was "No, there would be no way to continue SDI if it could not be tested outside a laboratory."

President Reagan listened to us all. Then he said, "If we agree to Gorbachev's conditions, won't we be doing so simply in order to leave here with an agreement? Well, we will not agree to that!" A minute later we were on our way down the stairs, headed back to Washington. I was never prouder of an American president.

The Oval Office, May 20, 1987. The President kindly invited me to the Oval Office for a farewell chat as I left the administration. We talked mostly about arms control, which had been one of my responsibilities at the Pentagon. I tried to discourage him from rhetoric about a world without nuclear weapons. Such talk alarmed our allies, especially the Europeans, and ran the risk of delegitimizing weapons on which we depended for deterrence.

"Mr. President," I argued, "can you imagine the day when our last nuclear weapon and the Soviets' last nuclear weapons are presented for destruction? Don't you think the Soviets would cheat—hide a cache of weapons? Margaret Thatcher told me she was sure they would cheat, and I agree."

"Of course," the President replied. "That is why successful completion of a ballistic missile defense is essential. It is the insurance against cheating that we would insist on having."

# 35

# SHEILA TATE
Press Secretary to Nancy Reagan 1091-1985

To truly appreciate his greatness, you need to know his heart. I was privileged to be in his company in informal and social situations over the years of his first term when I served as Nancy Reagan's press secretary.

I saw Ronald Reagan put awestruck, tongue-tied visitors to the White House at ease in a matter of moments; I saw moments when his deep seated modesty and lack of self-importance were stunning.

When his daughter, Patti, was getting married in Los Angeles, the parents of the groom-to-be walked into the Bel Air Hotel to meet the Reagans for the first time, just the day before the wedding. As they approached the President I could see shyness and nervous discomfort written all over their faces. The next thing I knew, in a matter of minutes, they were in a tight circle with the leader of the free world, all staring down into the President's cupped hands. I moved close enough to hear their obviously animated conversation. Ronald Reagan had taken his new tiny hearing aids out and was showing them to Patti's future in-laws. One of the relatives said, and I take a little poetic license here: "Wow, we have got to tell Aunt Madge about these."

He won my undying love in the first year of the administration when we were beleaguered by heavy criticism for purchasing new White House china. While it was actually a donation that did not involve taxpayer money, we could not get through the cacophony caused by the poor timing of the announcement on the same day ketchup was declared a vegetable for the school lunch program. Not to mention we were in a recession. Ronald Reagan was asked about the issue at a press conference and he expressed his annoyance that his wife was being criticized for accepting a private donation of new "dishes." His choice of the modest word "dishes" instead of china was important in putting the silliness of the press hysteria into context. He never lost that plain-spoken approach in his communications.

I saw President Reagan drop everything to take a call from Billy Graham, to put his feet up on his desk in his study in the upstairs residence and settle in for a serious conversation with one of his heroes. One day I arrived in the residence to pick up Nancy Reagan to go to some event lost to history; she was running late and he felt compelled to "entertain" me while I waited. He told me he had met an extraordinary woman that morning, a woman from Chicago, who had hidden a Jewish girl in Germany during WWII. He went on at some length about how this amazing woman had been recently reunited with the young woman she had sheltered, repeatedly expressing his awe at what she did. I kept thinking: how wonderful that the President of the United States is in awe of someone else. Our hero had heroes of his own.

He regularly out-Irished House Speaker Tip O'Neill on St. Patrick's Day. Our military office chief, Ed Hickey, used to host a St. Paddy's Day party in his office in the East Wing, and Tip and President Reagan used to come fully armed with Irish jokes and stories collected and rehearsed for the occasion. It was close but as my memory serves, our President always came out a little ahead.

Ronald Reagan loved jokes and remembered every joke he ever heard. Vice President George H. W. Bush used to come prepared with a new joke at every weekly luncheon with the President. And the Vice President canvassed all his friends for the best jokes before every luncheon.

Having been with Nancy Reagan during the ordeal and aftermath of the attempted assassination, watching him wheeled into the operating room and seeing his humor in the face of this crisis, nothing ever surprised me again about Ronald Reagan's strength of character. When he looked up from his gurney at the downturned faces of Mike Deaver, Ed Meese and Jim Baker on his way into surgery he put everyone at ease—all of America, in fact, with his humorous question: " Who's minding the store?"

The Reagans hosted an average of ten State Dinners a year at the White House, believing that tradition to be a strong component of diplomatic outreach. My job was to brief the press, escort reporters in to cover the toasts in the State Dining Room and other specific moments during the evening. Usually they went smoothly. But at one particular dinner there arose some confusion about exactly what President Reagan said during his toast. I asked him if I could borrow his "cards" ... the famous Reagan index cards which he liked to use ... to clarify for the press the precise Presidential language. He pulled them out of his pocket and said "Now, Sheila, you need to give these back to me when you are finished because I am required to turn them in for the archives. I would hate to have to tell them we lost them." This considerate man was thinking not of his important toast but of the folks who were counting on him to turn his remarks in the next day.

Reagan in China. We were, I think, in Shanghai, after a visit to Beijing, and Nancy Reagan called me up to their suite. We had been warned that our rooms were "bugged" and everyone was feeling a little bit paranoid. But nothing amused me more than when the Reagans handed me a pile of paperwork and Nancy whispered to me to please have them destroyed. I looked down at them and whispered back: "But these are just AP wire stories." She said, "Yes, please, just do it for us" or something to that effect. What an innocent age compared to today's data security issues.

Reagan Funeral. On the day Nancy Reagan escorted her husband's casket up the west steps of the Capitol Building to lay in state, I stood looking out of a holding room window with Margaret Thatcher and she shared some wonderful thoughts with me. We watched the Missing Man Formation of jets fly above the Capitol and as the one plane fell away she quietly said "You Americans have such wonderful traditions." She told me that the President himself had called her when he was planning his funeral—a task required of all Presidents while they were still in office—and he asked her to speak at his service. She said that since that day she never traveled anywhere without packing a black suit because she wanted to be prepared to get to his funeral no matter when, or where she was. Devoted friends.

# 36

# KENNETH L. ADELMAN

Ambassador to the United Nations
Deputy Permanent Representative to the U.N. 1981-1983
Director of the Arms Control and Disarmament Agency 1983-1987

Thirty-four years ago, Ronald Reagan showed us why he made a great president and leader, culminating in his epic performance at the Reykjavik summit which proved pivotal in ending the Cold War.

The background: it was February 23, 1980. The Nashua *Telegraph* offered to host a debate between Ronald Reagan and George H.W. Bush, three days before the New Hampshire primary election. However, the Federal Election Commission said that the newspaper- sponsored debate would violate election rules. Therefore . . . Reagan arranged to fund the event with his own campaign money, and—much to the distress of the newspaper's publisher, Jon Breen—invited other candidates to join in: Congressman John Anderson, Senators Howard Baker and Bob Dole, and Congressman Philip Crane.

Publisher Breen set the stage: "It is my privilege to welcome you tonight to the 1980 Nashua *Telegraph* Presidential Forum. On the right is former governor of California Ronald Reagan; on the left is the former ambassador of the UN, George Bush. In the rear are four other candidates who have not been invited by the Nashua *Telegraph*. At the end of the debate we will allow these four people to make statements."

Therefore, the other candidates would not be included in the debate, which provoked a reaction from Reagan. When he tried to protest, Breen said: "Would the sound man please turn Mr. Reagan's mic off for the moment?"

Whereupon Reagan grabbed another microphone, said, "Is this microphone on?" and exploded. "I am paying for this microphone, Mr. Green."

Reagan often had a problem with names, although "Green" was pretty close to "Breen"—but he had no problem in standing his ground. His rebuke brought the house down, as some 2000 people in the audience and even his GOP opponents cheered wildly.

Reagan later reflected back on it: "For some reason, my words hit the audience, whose emotions were already worked up, like a sledgehammer. The crowd roared and just went wild. I may have won the debate, the primary—and the nomination—right there." Ace *Washington Post* reporter David Broder sure thought so, as he often spoke of the electric effect of Reagan's stance. Here, he and others concluded, was a different kind of candidate.

And soon a different kind of President. When, in his initial months in office, the air controllers went on strike, against the contract each had signed, he fired the lot of them.

And when, at the critical summit in Reykjavik late on Sunday October 12, 1986, Soviet leader Mikhail Gorbachev wished to crimp SDI, Reagan staunchly refused. The meeting broke up and within minutes they were standing at curbside outside Hofdi House, where they had met. Gorbachev tried to soften the summit collapse by muttering, "I don't know what I could have done differently."

"Well," Reagan said according to the most sources, "you could have said 'yes!'" and turned away in Nashua, New Hampshire-like fury.

From that refusal, seemingly so disastrous as it helped end Reykjavik in utter failure, later proved so fortuitous as it helped end the Cold War in stellar success.

The nice coincidence in 2014 of Ronald Reagan's birthday and the opening of the Sochi Olympics reminded me of a wonderful story daughter Maureen Reagan told me in Reykjavik, Iceland. We were there in October 1996, on the tenth anniversary of the summit, which is the focus of my upcoming book *Reagan at Reykjavik.*

Sitting in the Hofdi House—the reputedly haunted house, which hosted the Reagan-Gorbachev sessions—I asked Maureen over a commemorative dinner whether she had any stories of her father, private stories, ones that hadn't already been told and retold.

At first, she couldn't think of any. So we listened instead to the Icelandic officials droning on. After they finished, after dessert and while second cups of coffee were being poured, she perked up and said she had remembered one.

It happened in the summer of 1984, when she was still living in the White House. Nancy was upstairs reading when Maureen heard her father call out that he was back, back from his LA trip.

After she greeted him—"Hi, dad. How did it go?"—he mentioned that he had been at the Olympic opening.

"Yes, I saw you on TV out there. How did you like it?"

He liked it just fine.

What, she wondered, did he like in particular?

After some shaking of that head, he said, "Oh, I know. It was the Opening Ceremonies."

What about *that* did he like in particular?

"Well, you see all the boys and girls marching behind the China flag, and they're all Chinese. And then boys and girls marching behind the German flag, and they're all Germans. And boys and girls from African countries marching behind their flags, and they're all Africans."

Okay, Maureen wondered. Where are we going on this?

"And then," Reagan said more excitedly, "you see the boys and girls marching behind the American flag. And they look like *all the others.* Our boys and girls look like the whole world!"

I thought then, as I do now, that if you had to summarize what

America is all about—why we're still what Reagan like to call "the city on the hill"—that's about as good a way as any I've heard.

*Ken Adelman is the author of* Reagan at Reykjavik—Forty-Eight Hours that Ended the Cold War *(HarperCollins, 2014)*

# 37

# ROGER W. ROBINSON, JR.

Senior Director of International Economic Affairs, National Security
Council 1982-1985

had the good fortune of sharing the same birthday and initials
with President Reagan and he was kind enough to invite me to a
joint birthday commemoration in the Oval Office that morning.
At the time, I was working for the President's close friend and
National Security Advisor, Judge William Clark, and asked him
if it might be possible to include my father (who, at least, had the
same initials). Judge Clark agreed, and suggested that I put together
a brief memo—standard practice for an Oval Office meeting—so
the President would have a sense of my father's background.

I knew that the President was a great sports enthusiast, and
thought he would like to know that my father had been a well-
known football player on the Duke team which, in 1938, enjoyed
an undefeated, untied season—indeed they had never been scored
upon—and then went on to challenge the University of Southern
California in the 1939 Rose Bowl. I also made reference to his 37
years as a special agent and supervisor in the FBI, a good part of
that time in the area of counterespionage.

When I introduced my father to the President, Reagan said,
"Well, we've met before."

Perhaps needless to say, my dad was a great admirer of the President but was now perplexed. "With all due respect Mr. President,"
he said "I daresay that if we had ever met before I would remember."

The President then told a little story: he reminded us that he had been for years "the voice of the Chicago Cubs," and as the 1939 Rose Bowl approached—to be played in Pasadena—he was working in the movies in nearby Los Angeles. On the Wednesday before the game he got an unexpected call: the scheduled announcer, Bill Stern, had developed laryngitis and might not be able to call the game. Might Reagan be able to come in as backup? Certainly. His first job in broadcasting had been covering football, back in 1932.

As it happened, Stern could handle the assignment, but Reagan was in the booth with him, spotting the plays and feeding him key comments. So, he said he spent part of the day talking about number 19, known as the "Blond Blizzard" —my father. (For the record: Duke held the lead at 3 to 0 until the last minute of the game when USC passed for a touchdown.) Reagan did acknowledge that they had not physically met, but after the game he felt as if he had known "Number 19" for a long time. The President then joked, "It's a good thing that we're not meeting in a locker room, as our monogrammed towels would get messed up."

We all laughed. The President next spoke of his great admiration for the FBI, and became quite serious. "You know," he said, "I was president of the Screen Actors Guild at a time when communist infiltration of Hollywood was a serious challenge and I was taking it on in every way I could. One day, a guy came to my door at home and threatened to throw acid in my face, disfigure me, so I could never act again if I continued these aggressive activities toward the Communist Party. And worse, if I continued to speak up, I'd be killed.

"Well, first thing I did was to call the FBI. Immediately, I was given self-defense training, I was given a gun and taught how to shoot. From that point forward, I carried it with me at all times. But the most valuable thing the FBI did for me was to provide regular intelligence briefings—especially about possible threats to me and the Hollywood community. These were invaluable and as a result I would often change my plans or modify the route I took to work."

At that, my dad chimed in and said, "Mr. President, my division in New York was preparing some of those briefings and communicating them to our LA office which, in turn, passed them on along to you."

The President was taken aback. "I guess I have to add my thanks to you and your team for saving my life!"

Needless to say, it all made for a most extraordinary father-son experience.

It was a pivotal moment in the roll-back, and ultimate take-down, of the Soviet Union, when President Reagan again demonstrated exemplary courage and resolve by sharply curtailing what he viewed as key forms of Western economic and financial life-support for the Soviet Union.

The story begins in December 1981. Poland was in turmoil; the Solidarity free-labor movement, led by shipyard worker Lech Walesa (and encompassing about one-third of the working population of Poland), was demanding systemic political and economic reforms and the Soviets were massing troops on the Polish border.

The combination of Solidarity's momentum and the active support of Pope John-Paul II caused great concern within the Kremlin: how to keep this political crisis contained? More than 90 percent of the Polish population was Catholic, and the Polish-born Pope was definitely viewed by Moscow as a trouble-maker. They ordered the Communist President of Poland, General Wojciech Jaruzelski, to declare martial law at once—and thus suppress the activities of Solidarity—or face Soviet invasion. He complied and the stand-off intensified.

President Reagan demanded that the Soviets permit the Polish authorities to reconcile peacefully with Solidarity and the Church, or face stiff sanctions (much like the March 2014 warnings from the U.S. and Europe for Russia not to venture beyond the Crimea into Eastern Ukraine). The Soviets refused to even consider reconciliation.

At this time, the largest project in East-West economic history was underway—the huge, two-strand Siberian gas pipeline project.

This unprecedented commercial endeavor consisted of two large-diameter pipes running some 3600 miles from the gas fields of Siberia into the Western European natural gas grid. Although there had been similar Soviet pipelines supplying Europe in the past, this was unique in its scale, at a cost of some $35 billion—an enormous sum in the early 1980s.

If both strands of the pipeline were built and fully subscribed by West European gas customers, it would have catapulted West European dependency on Soviet natural gas to as much as 70 percent or more of their total gas deliveries. In the process, total Soviet hard currency income (which was only about $32 billion a year at the time) would nearly double.

The stakes were particularly high for the integrity of NATO. President Reagan and his National Security Advisor and good friend William P. Clark believed that Germany and certain other European countries would likely be paralyzed and held hostage by the threat of interruptions in Soviet gas supplies (much like the inordinate dependency Western Europe presently has on Russian gas deliveries in the midst of the Ukrainian crisis unfolding at this writing). Moreover, the windfall hard currency revenue streams for Moscow would allow higher levels of defense spending, authoritarian control, technology theft, and Third World adventurism.

Accordingly, when martial law was declared in Poland, President Reagan labeled it "Soviet-sponsored repression" and, rather than sanctioning the Poles, immediately turned his attention to the anemic Soviet economy and financial structure, particularly the strategic and symbolic Siberian gas pipeline project.

Within a matter of days, the President announced unilateral U.S. oil and gas equipment and technology sanctions against the project to disrupt it, greatly increase the cost of construction of the already-contracted first strand of the pipeline and kill the second strand altogether. This was possible because the U.S. had a near monopoly on oil and gas equipment and technology for use in permafrost conditions, thanks to our experience on the North Slope of Alaska.

The President was aware that this project was being financed by European government loans with Western taxpayer-subsidized interest rates. He instructed Judge Clark (as he was known) to assemble, along with Admiral John Poindexter, a few of us on his staff, to move forward with a covert strategy designed to slow substantially completion the first strand of the pipeline and terminate the second strand, end subsidized interest rates on official loans to Moscow, tighten technology transfer controls, and seek to lower world oil prices to damage the Soviets' hard currency export earnings.

I had done a lot of thinking about such a strategy during the period before coming to the White House, when I served as a vice president in the International Department of the Chase Manhattan Bank, with responsibilities for the Soviet Union, Eastern and Central Europe, and Yugoslavia. I knew the territory quite well, particularly the sources and uses of Soviet hard currency cash and how the USSR financed itself (as it had an annual funding gap). I had also co-authored a *New York Times* editorial called "Europe's Big Gamble on Soviet Gas" in April 1981 while still at Chase, as well as a longer Washington Quarterly article that the President read entitled "Soviet Gas: Risk or Reward" in the Spring of that year that he used to help introduce this strategic issue at the Ottawa Economic Summit in July 1981.

The President had made it clear that, if after six months, there had been no reconciliation between the government of Poland, the Solidarity movement and the Church, Moscow could look forward to expanded sanctions. There was an effort led by the Treasury Department and NSC to negotiate with our European allies an end to those taxpayer-subsidized interest rates. At the June 6, 1982 G-7 Versailles Economic Summit . . . which occurred at the six-month deadline . . . there seemed to be allied agreement on this sensible measure which was included in the official Summit communiqué. Before the proverbial ink was dry, however, this understanding was publicly repudiated by German Chancellor Helmut Schmidt and French President Francois Mitterrand. They made clear that they had no intention of changing their existing credit arrangements with Moscow.

Immediately following the Versailles Summit, the President attended a NATO Summit in Bonn, West Germany. He made a final plea to Chancellor Schmidt—and to the German government officials attending—not to go forward with the two-strand pipeline project in favor of a more secure alternative supplier of natural gas. The President specifically called for the accelerated development of the massive Norwegian Troll gas field.

As it happened, while President Reagan was making this final argument, Chancellor Schmidt never even looked at him, but stared out the window at the garden (this according to the President himself in front of his Cabinet). The President returned to Washington disappointed and angry, and together with Bill Clark, called for an NSC meeting on, I believe, Friday, June 18, 1982. This was a meeting that some Europeans would come to call "Black Friday."

The meeting was to address three options for Presidential decision, outlined in a memo that I prepared.

> Option One: Lift the sanctions entirely and, in effect, declare the whole effort misbegotten and ineffective because of the disruption and estrangement the sanctions were causing to otherwise harmonious alliance relations.

> Option Two: Keep the original sanctions in place, which would mean that American companies would continue to be unilaterally penalized as they could not supply the pipeline project and had to watch as European suppliers snapped up their contracts, while operating under U.S. licensed technology.

> Option Three: Expand the sanctions to include U.S. licensees and subsidiaries abroad and apply U.S. law extraterritorially to block the deliveries of oil and gas equipment from Western Europe to the Soviets if it involved U.S. licenses.

During the discussion in the Cabinet room, the President went around the table to hear the views of all participants, as this was a crossroads in alliance relations with respect to the field of East-West economic and financial relations. Most Cabinet members were in favor of Option One and, as a fallback, Option Two. There were only perhaps 4 in the room in support of the escalatory approach represented by Option Three.

The President then shrugged with an air of frustration, and said, "They can have their damn pipeline..."

An audible sigh of relief swept through the Cabinet room—until the President slammed his fist on the table and continued, "...but not with American equipment and not with American technology!"

That sigh of relief was replaced by gasps. Judge Clark immediately said, "We have a presidential decision" and the meeting was adjourned. This was the real start of, arguably, the most acrimonious alliance dispute in NATO history. The allies were livid that American law was being imposed on what they felt to be their national companies and a few continued to ship equipment to Moscow over U.S. objections.

President Reagan responded to these instances of European defiance by imposing import controls against those companies that continued to supply the pipeline with banned U.S. technology, closing access to the U.S. market for their goods and services.

By November, 1982, there had been several important developments. There was new leadership at the State Department (precipitated primarily by the pipeline dispute), and the allied foreign ministers had assembled in Canada to resolve this bitter dispute. Encouraged by a seemingly new European attitude, the President signed National Security Decision Directive (NSDD) Number 66 (classified "Secret") and lifted the pipeline sanctions, but only under three specific conditions: that a ceiling be placed on Soviet gas deliveries to Western Europe at a 30 percent dependency level; the termination of taxpayer-subsidized interest rates on official loans to Moscow; and the strengthening of controls on technology transfers to the Kremlin.

The deadline for a written agreement among the allies on all three of these new measures was to be the May 1983 G-7 Economic Summit in Williamsburg, Virginia. By the time of the Summit, President Reagan had achieved his objectives—the first-strand of the pipeline was ultimately delayed by two to three years at debilitating expense to Moscow (about $10-12 billion annually in foregone earnings), and the second strand of the Siberian gas pipeline was never constructed. An International Energy Agency agreement limited future West European dependency on "any one supplier" (read: the Soviet Union), an agreement negotiated by NSC staffer Bill Martin. An OECD agreement had moved the USSR to a new developmental category that precluded subsidized interest rates on official loans. A high-level meeting of the Coordinating Committee on Multilateral Export Controls (COCOM) agreed to strengthen measures designed to keep militarily-relevant U.S. and Western technology out of the hands of the Soviet military. In short, these agreements ushered in a new era of genuinely security-minded East-West economic and financial policy that was universally adopted by the Western alliance.

Although "pipeline politics" is a commonly understood dimension of national security policy worldwide today, the Soviets had never before used natural gas as a geopolitical weapon. It was inconceivable to most, if not all, of our European allies that Moscow would ever leverage natural gas deliveries to the Continent as a strategic play, as it would be so counterproductive to its own interests and reputation as a "reliable supplier." (One need only observe Vladimir Putin in the context of the Ukraine crisis to put this issue in stark relief.) Ronald Reagan and Bill Clark, with the support of Cap Weinberger and Bill Casey. Ed Meese and Jean Kirkpatrick knew better.

There is also a bigger lesson here that refutes much of the revisionist history concerning why the Cold War ended and how it came about.

Some believe it was the more liberal vision of Mikhail Gorbachev. Some think it was an organic collapse born of the systemic rigidities of the Soviet economy. While there were a number of contributing factors, the fact is that the Soviet Union never recovered from this blow to its hard currency cash flow, and the limitations placed on the availability of Western government and commercial bank credits. In the days before the collapse of the Soviet Union in December 1991, Moscow defaulted on some $96 billion in Western hard currency debt. They simply could no longer sustain the costs of empire. Notwithstanding the engraved leather sign on his Oval Office desk along the lines that there is no limit to what can be accomplished if one's prepared not to take credit. Ronald Reagan and his friend Bill Clark deserve the lion's share of the credit for ending the Soviet blight on human freedom.

*NSDD 66 was signed by President Reagan November 29, 1982, and a companion directive NSDD 75 "U.S. Relations with the USSR" was signed January 17, 1983. Now declassified, they may be accessed at www.reagan.utexas.edu. They are fascinating windows into Reagan's vision for winning the Cold War.*

*Roger Robinson is President and CEO of RWR Advisory Group in Washington DC, and Chairman and Co-founder of the Prague Security Studies Institute.*

# 38

# WILLIAM BENNETT
## Secretary of Education 1985-1988

One of the great and untold qualities of President Reagan was his deep interest in education. If you inspect his diaries you will see how much he thought about education. Of course, his last public address was about the need to pass on our nation's history to the next generation of students.

During my tenure as his Secretary of Education, President Reagan would occasionally read an article about a particular school, school district, or school practice and ask me to look into it. Sometimes it would lead to a visit with President Reagan to that specific school or district.

On many occasions, these visits contained memorable encounters that illuminated President Reagan's charm and good nature. One such occasion was a visit to Suitland High School in Maryland. As our visit was winding to a close, the school principal invited the President to stay longer and visit with the students. With his usual good humor, considerateness, and sincerity, Reagan replied that he didn't want to interfere with the students' learning. The principal responded that it was fine; the students didn't get a lot of opportunities like that. So the President agreed to stay and speak with the students.

Perhaps the most memorable visit we took was a trip to Columbia, Missouri. As Secretary of Education, I paid particular attention to the award-winning schools around the country. I wanted to know what they were doing right and share that information with the country. I discovered that the community of Columbia, Missouri contained several award-winning schools so I decided to make a visit to speak with the superintendent. I asked President Reagan to go with me and he immediately agreed.

We landed in Missouri and hopped into the presidential limousine to drive to the school district. I sat in the limousine with President Reagan to do some last minute briefing on the district. Of course, this was no ordinary limousine. Along with the bulletproof glass, it was equipped with a special speaker system so that the president could sit in the car and greet the crowds that lined the side of the road as he passed by.

Before we arrived in Columbia, the President said that he wanted to test the speaker system. So he had the limo stop adjacent to a cornfield and asked me to get out of the limo so we could test the volume and reach of the speakers.

I walked several steps away from the limo into the cornfield and Reagan said over the loudspeaker, "Can you hear me?"

I said yes, and he told me to step further back into the cornfield.

"Can you hear me now?" he asked again.

I said yes and he told me to move even further back. I could barely see the limo at this point.

"Can you hear me now?" he yelled over the speaker.

Before I could even respond, the limo roared off, leaving me stranded in the middle of the cornfield.

After a few minutes, the limo turned around and came back to get me. In the backseat was President Reagan laughing so hard at his unoriginal but very funny practical joke.

# 39

# HELENE VON DAMM

Secretary to President Reagan 1981-1982
Director of Personnel 1981-1982
Ambassador to Austria 1984-1989

**DURING THE GUBERNATORIAL YEARS:**

I started out as Secretary to the Cabinet Secretary, Bill Clark. It was my privilege to take notes at Cabinet Meetings. At one of the first, and one I will never forget, Governor Reagan told the group, "For the record, I never want to hear at this table how many votes a decision will bring or lose me or we will start down a road from which there is no returning."

When I became the Governor's private secretary he mused one day and said, "I bet a lot of people are confused when they call me and get you with this strong German accent on the phone." When I assured him how hard I tried to lose it he said, "Don't you dare; you represent the American dream."

During the Vietnam protests a bunch of hippies camped outside the Capitol with a sign that said, "Make love, not war." Governor Reagan smiled and said, "I got a look at them and I am not sure they are capable of either."

During the Berkeley student protests Governor Reagan at one point insisted on addressing the group. When he returned from the Capitol steps with some of his aides and they filed by my desk I noticed a stranger marching with them at the end into the inner sanctum. I don't know why, but I alarmed the security. Sure enough, he was an intruder. The Governor's aides only noticed him when they all sat down. Just when they realized here is a person who doesn't belong, the security removed him. Thank God he was harmless, but it shows security can never be tight enough. The next day, the Governor conducted a mock ceremony, appointing me a sergeant and handing me a billy club. "Now I really feel secure," he said.

Governor Reagan was in principle against the withholding of state taxes. He felt that taxes should hurt, meaning that when the citizens pay their taxes once a year they are reminded how much their government costs them and they will pay attention to sneaky increases. Of course he was ridiculed for this, but he was adamant, saying his feet were in concrete on this issue. At the end, when the Finance Director convinced him that the State couldn't do without the cash-flow, he yielded. It was tough for him to admit this, so when he faced the press to announce his change in position, he said, "The sound you hear is the cracking of concrete around my feet."

## THE WHITE HOUSE

During the presidential campaign I was successful as NE Regional Finance Director. For the first time I held a line position and loved it. I started to think of a possible career instead of a job. When the President asked me to return to him as private secretary/assistant, I felt honored and privileged, but returned with mixed emotions. I knew that my time was now. If I didn't break away, it would never happen. So after six month of enjoying all the trimmings and glamour of being the President's secretary, I had a long talk with the President, essentially telling him I didn't want to die as a secretary. He started to laugh, "What's wrong if on your tombstone it reads, she was secretary to the president of the USA"? But he understood and sent me away with "O.K. eagle, try your wings. But remember, if it doesn't work out, I won't be able to help you. We all have to do our job or the people will send us home."

After proving myself in a deputy job I received the coveted position of Assistant to the President for Personnel. I was thrilled being one of 12 senior advisors to the President and intended to stay for the rest of the administration's term, providing the President would want to retain me in this position of course. For that reason I was stunned when relatively soon afterward he asked me to become Ambassador to Austria. You must be kidding, was all I could answer. I had no intention or desire to return to my native country. But the President didn't let go of the idea, and brought the subject up again and again. He finally prevailed by reminding me, "Helene, now that you have reached more than you ever dreamt of, it is time to go home. You left home at 16, your mother is now 80, if you don't go you will regret it the rest of your life." And so I left. He was right.

# 40

# LOUIS J. CORDIA

Special Assistant for Federal Activities, Office of the EPA
Administrator 1981-1983

Reagan's 80/20 Vision: At a meeting with President Reagan in his Century City office in Los Angeles a couple of years after his leaving the White House, I presented the President with his copy of the Reagan Alumni Directory that I publish annually through the Reagan Alumni Association. He expressed great appreciation of our Association's efforts to help keep the alumni of his administration and campaigns working together. He asked about several alumni, genuinely interested in how and what they were doing. I was aware of many current situations, as I told him, given conversations with alumni who would reminisce about the Reagan years as a very special time in their lives and in our country's history. His smiles and nods were heart-warming like those of a grandfather hearing about his grandchildren.

I tried thanking the President for all he had done in turning around our country from Carter's malaise to a thriving economy with 20 million new jobs, and winning the Cold War against the Soviet Union without losing men and women in battle. I brought up the 1981 Tax Cut, the Regulatory Reform Task Force, the Grace Commission on Waste-Fraud-Abuse, Peace Through Strength, Trust But Verify, among other initiatives; but the President seemed almost embarrassed by my doing so. He would often reference an administration official who was instrumental in each success. I probably should have caught on sooner that the President did not like taking credit. I should have remembered one of his humble sayings, "There is no limit to what a man can do or where he can go if he does not mind who gets the credit."

The President wanted to talk about the future—maintaining what had been accomplished and thinking about what more our country could do to advance freedom and opportunity, two words he repeated several times. He talked about an unfinished agenda. He talked about what the world should and could be, not what it was. One of the insightful observations he made that has come to mind on-and-off over the years was, and I paraphrase,

> Our citizens should determine what should be a reasonable percentage of an American's income that he should be able to keep; and let the rest go to government to provide its services. Without a clear understanding of what is an acceptable cost of government at the federal and state level, Americans will not only lose more and more of their money; but they will lose more and more of their liberty and individual freedom.

In this past year, I conducted surveys of tens of thousands of Americans to get an indication of what a reasonable percentage would be. I asked, "If we were forming our country today, how much of each dollar earned should American workers be allowed to keep; and how much should go to government?" 80/20 was the consensus; 80 percent said 80 cents would be fair to keep; and 20 percent said more than 20 cents could go to government. There were clarifications such as lower-middle-and-upper incomes paying different amounts up to 20 cents on a dollar; and there were variations on how the 20 cents should be split between federal and state government. The second question was "How much of the dollar you earn today are you allowed to keep; and how much is collected by governments?" Their answers averaged 50-to-60 cents of every dollar went to government. People were stunned to realize that government was taking 2-to-3 times more taxes and fees from them than they believed were "reasonable" and "acceptable."

I am not saying that Reagan knew the answer back then that people would want to keep 80 cents and give to government 20 cents of every dollar they earned; but I am confident that he believed in the American people, in that they would choose a "reasonable percentage," a percentage whereby government would be limited and freedom and opportunity would prevail.

*Louis Cordia is Executive Director and Co-Founder of the Reagan Alumni Association 1988–present*

## 41

# JOHN BLOCK
### Secretary of Agriculture 1981-1986

Ronald Reagan picked quite a few senior staffers and cabinet members right after the election. Of course, he selected a lot of people he already knew, people who had worked with him in California, people who were involved in his two earlier attempts (1968, 1976) to get the Republican nomination for president. However, there were some positions that remained open—including Secretary of Agriculture. Senator Bob Dole, who was from a farm state (Kansas) and was one of the agricultural experts in the Senate, sent Reagan a list of ten candidates for the job. Imagine my surprise when I picked up a copy of the *Wall Street Journal* one day to see my name mentioned—the first time I knew I was in "contention"—as a candidate for the post.

Why me? I grew up on a family farm in Illinois—corn, soybeans, and hogs—then went off to the military academy at West Point to get an education and see some of the rest of the world. (to add a bit of adventure, I became a paratrooper). In 1960, with my obligated service complete, I went back to the farm and, over-time, grew our holdings from 400 to 4000 acres. By 1980, I was Director of Agriculture for the state of Illinois.

But I wasn't active in politics and I didn't know Bob Dole. So I called him and suggested that perhaps we should meet. He agreed, and I went to DC, where Dole set up a joint meeting with Illinois Senator Chuck Percy, whom I knew slightly, and a few other senators from agricultural states. The meeting was cordial, and Bob Dole decided I was his man. He took a map of the United States and marked off the places from which the already-selected cabinet members had come . . . most from the West Coast or the East Coast and no one, as I recall, from the middle of the country. When he showed the map to Reagan, he made a clear recommendation: the President should appoint John Block, a hands-on farmer from the heartland.

Soon enough, I was on my way to California to meet with the Pesident-elect, in his home, not some left-over campaign office. I checked into a hotel, and headed out for Pacific Palisades. Nancy opened the door, and there he was, along with Ed Meese, Marty Anderson, and a couple of other people. We talked for about two hours; and then I went back to my hotel. I hadn't been in the room more than ten minutes when I got a phone call, "I want you to be my Secretary of Agriculture."

I moved to DC early in January, and attended Reagan's first cabinet meeting. Since he had not yet been inaugurated and was not in the White House, the meeting was held across the street at Blair House. Of course, I had met Reagan and Ed Meese, but I didn't know anyone else at the meeting. President Reagan, Secretary of State Alexander Haig, Secretary of Defense Caspar Weinberger, and a couple of other members made presentations, and then the President said, "Does anyone else have anything they would like to put on the table?

Naive me, I raised my hand, "Mr. President, in your campaign, you had promised to lift the embargo against selling grain to the Soviet Union. That's a big potential market for our struggling farmers, and I hope we can get that done soon."

Well, I just about had my head taken off by Weinberger and Haig. "Not until we get come concessions! The grain embargo gives us leverage!"

The President said he would "take it under advisement." And the meeting was over.

As I was about to leave the room, trade ambassador Bill Brock and several other cabinet officers came up to me; they agreed with the proposition that we had to help our farmers. Thus, I knew I had some friends and, collectively, we started to work the problem. Ed Meese was sympathetic.

By the end of March, we had made progress. I thought it was time for a one-on-one discussion with the President, so I called his scheduler and said, "I'd like to meet with the President tomorrow if I can. I need about 20 minutes."

"Well," she said, "he's pretty well booked . . . but he has to give a speech at the Hilton Hotel up on Connecticut Avenue. You could meet him there and ride back with him in the limo and talk about whatever you have on your mind."

That would work for me . . . but a few moments later, my secretary said I couldn't do that. She reminded me I already had a scheduled meeting with the ambassador from one of the European Community nations. So, I asked her to call the White House, apologize, and try to get me on the President's schedule sometime soon.

Thus, I missed being with the President on the day he and three others were shot, March 30, 1981, while walking out of the Hilton Hotel to get in the limo. I would have been in that group.

A footnote: after he had recovered enough to go back to routine activity, the President invited me over to the Oval Office, just before a scheduled cabinet meeting. Alexander Haig was there. The President looked me straight in the eye and said, "I'm lifting the grain embargo, today." I was elated. Haig was not so happy. Then, on to the cabinet meeting, where the President made that announcement to everyone. He knew that he had made a promise, and that he should keep it.

The President held Cabinet meetings about every other week, to make the members come together and talk with each other. At each meeting one or two cabinet officers would be asked to make a presentation on some topic of interest or import to them at the time. For example, Bill Brock might talk about a proposed trade agreement . . . the cabinet would discuss . . . some members might agree, some might not and raise objections. The President might support the idea, or he might veto it, but as a rule, he was supportive. Of most import: he was not an isolated executive, but had regular interaction with the members of his team . . . as did they, with each other.

At one meeting, we discussed a proposal to sell some farm machinery—harvesting combines—to the Soviet Union. Secretary Weinberger got up and said, in essence, he was opposed, that we must never sell them these machines, because they will be used as vehicles of war.

I thought to myself—having driven a lot of combines—his position didn't make any sense, and I said to the President: "With all due respect, I don't think Secretary Weinberger has ever ridden on a combine—or even seen one. A combine is not going to become a machine of war."

Eventually, we agreed; if the Soviet Union was willing to give us some money, we were willing to let them have some combines.

Right after the meeting, Al Haig—with whom I had disagreements on some other issues—came over to me, quietly, and said: "Here we are—the only two West Point graduates in the Cabinet, and we both realize that selling combines to the Soviet Union won't strengthen their military . . . but it's going to put some dollars in the till here at home."

# 42

# FAITH WHITTLESEY

Ambassador to Switzerland 1981-1983, 1985-1988;
Assistant for Public Liaison 1983-1985

The Choir needs Music. President Reagan was deeply committed to winning the Cold War, i.e., to the defeat of communism in general and the USSR and its satellites in particular. He understood that the struggle would be on multiple fronts—military, political, economic, cultural, and, most importantly for him, spiritual; thus, his strongly felt admiration for the heroic anti-communist Polish Pope, John Paul II.

One exchange I witnessed confirmed this for me. At the first Reagan-Gorbachev Summit in Geneva in 1985, President Reagan initially met with the then-President of the Swiss Confederation, Kurt Furgler (now deceased). As U.S. Ambassador to Switzerland, I was present at the historic meeting, sitting next to President Reagan (on his right). President Furgler, who was sitting directly across the small table, offered an opening observation that the Swiss, although politically (but not morally) neutral, shared the values of the West. President Reagan responded, stating without talking points (I paraphrase from memory): "Yes, we in the West believe human rights come from God. In their system [the communist-state system], human rights are privileges conferred by the state."

Throughout the Reagan Presidency in the closing days of the Cold War, Central America was one of the most hotly contested battlegrounds. The Soviets sought to displace existing, if sometimes admittedly seriously flawed, governments there by means of indirect aggression and to install Cuban/Soviet satellites in their place. President Reagan had no wish to risk the lives of U.S. soldiers in this struggle. He supported, instead, the policy of encouraging local opponents of Marxist-Leninist insurgencies to win the fight themselves. (The only exception to this policy was the very short U.S. military action in the island of Grenada to prevent Cuba from installing another communist beachhead in the Western hemisphere.)

However, in the first few years of the Reagan Administration, the valid arguments for the President's position regarding Latin America were nearly drowned out by a tidal wave of news stories portraying Marxist-Leninist insurgents in very favorable terms as "agrarian reformers," much as Fidel Castro had been described initially by another, earlier generation of gullible left-leaning Americans.

It was obvious to many of us in the Administration that traditional bureaucratic means being used to explain the President's policy both at home and abroad were proving ineffective to communicate the soundness of the Administration's position. For example, shortly before I returned to Washington to head the White House Office of Public Liaison in early 1983, a meeting of all U.S. ambassadors in Europe (of which I was one) was convened at which there was considerable lamentation about the barrage of anti-American press we were getting on the subject of Central America in Europe and how it was undermining U.S. diplomacy overall.

Shortly after I was asked to return and become a member of the White House Senior Staff in 1983, I was assigned to take on the task of better informing interest group leaders of the morally legitimate reasons justifying President Reagan's forceful opposition to Marxist-Leninist insurgencies in our hemisphere. The White House Outreach Group on Central America was established within my office as a result under the leadership first of Morton Blackwell and later Robert Reilly. It became a forum for the people of Central America to tell their stories of the systematic human rights abuses they had suffered from and witnessed. The meetings were held every week in Room 450 in the Old Executive Office Building (OEOB). Labor leaders, pastors, priests, newspaper publishers, businessmen, and ordinary citizens gave their firsthand accounts. Central America policy experts also spoke.

For instance, the Nicaraguan Native American Protestant preacher and farmer Prudencio Baltadano related his unprovoked torture and mutilation at the hands of the Sandinistas. U.S. Senator Jeremiah Denton from Alabama, who had served as a POW in Vietnam for 8 years, the longest of any American serviceman, recalled his mistreatment by communist "agrarian reformers" during his captivity. Religious leaders such as Bishop René H. Gracida of Corpus Christi, Texas, and Archbishop Roman Arietta, head of the Central American Bishops' Conference, gave witness to the systematic suppression of religion, another typical feature of Marxist-Leninist "revolution." The glamorous actor turned diplomat, then-U.S. Ambassador to Mexico, John Gavin spoke at one of the meetings. Juanita Castro, sister of the Cuban dictator, gave testimony at another meeting, as did Jaime Daremblum, the leader of the Jewish community in Costa Rica. The international legal specialist, John Norton Moore, addressed the group. A program, "Inside Nicaragua Today," with four panelists from Nicaragua, was the weekly feature another time. In all, more than 90 programs were given, week after week. We attempted to distribute accounts of these meetings to a wide audience of opinion makers.

On one occasion, one member of the White House career national security team spoke to me in the hall of the West Wing. After noting the continuing negative news, he offered the following criticism, "Faith, you are only preaching to the choir." But as I knew—and as Ronald Reagan had said to me, "the choir needs music." In short, President Reagan's long experience in persuading ordinary Americans of his positions had taught him that if relevant facts were communicated to ordinary Americans, they would make the right decision—act and vote accordingly. President Reagan also said to me, "Faith, members of Congress don't necessarily have to see the light; they just have to feel the heat." Firsthand accounts, i.e., facts, clearly turned up the heat.

What's barking? In his efforts to "win" the Cold War, not just to "contain" the USSR, President Reagan used humor extensively. Although he was Irish—quick with quips and one-liners (just like President Kennedy), he also understood instinctively that he could make political points more effectively if he could make his audience laugh. He frequently asked me if I had any new jokes for him. I did not think less of him for asking me; on the contrary, I knew jokes that had a telling point were among his best rhetorical weapons in the war of ideas and part of his political genius. One person I asked, in a moment of levity, was the very distinguished then Swiss State Secretary of Foreign Affairs. He smiled and offered me the following story which I later conveyed verbally to President Reagan, who used it:

> There are three dogs; one is French, one Polish, and one Soviet. The French dog puffed up and announced, "When I want meat from my master, I just bark." The Polish dog inquired, "What's meat?" The Soviet dog asked, "What's barking?"

President Reagan thus made one of his strongest arguments in favor of the free market system versus a socialist/communist system, that is, the free market expands the pie and brings prosperity and free expression. The other shrinks the pie and spreads misery and hopelessness.

The man truly was the Great Communicator!

# 43

## ELAINE L. CHAO
### Chairman, Federal Maritime Commission 1988-1989

I got my start in public service in President Reagan's administration. I was a White House Fellow, one of 12 who had been selected that year through a competitive process to serve as an aide to a high-level government official.

The White House Fellows program is nonpartisan; I was actually registered as an Independent when I was selected. Like many other Asian Americans at that time, I was not involved in politics because so few Asians had gone before me. Few Asian Americans served in either the political or career ranks of the federal government, so there were few role models in our community.

But being an immigrant to this country, I wanted to enter the White House Fellows program because I was curious about my new country and wanted to learn how the federal government functioned. At the time, I was working as a young banker living in New York City. I knew I did not agree with the political philosophy of many of those around me, and that there must be something better.

When I learned about President Reagan's positions on key issues and read his first inaugural address outlining his philosophy, I knew I had found my intellectual home: less taxation, less government regulation, a stable monetary policy, and peace through strength. I realized those were my values. I must be a Republican!

President Reagan was known for the power of his ideas, and for his success in reaching out to nontraditional groups and building new coalitions within the Republican Party. I count myself as among those who had been encouraged to join the Republican Party due to the power of his ideas. Previously, no one had been as persuasive and as strong in communicating what conservatives stood for.

President Reagan was supposedly quoted as saying personnel is policy! When I was appointed Secretary of Labor in President George W. Bush's administration, 18 years later, this was my guiding management principle. I knew I could not micromanage the Department, even if I worked 24 hours, 7 days a week. But, remembering President Reagan's mantra about personnel, I took care to choose strong conservatives to serve in the non-career ranks of the Department. I wanted to make sure that our team at the Department of Labor shared the same philosophy and would make the right decisions based on our shared principles.

The lessons and principles I learned in President Ronald Reagan's Administration helped me to become a better leader and to advance conservative ideals to build a better America. For example, during my tenure, the U.S. Department of Labor (which had more lawyers than any other department except Justice) concentrated on hiring lawyers who would be faithful to the Constitution, such as members of the Federalist Society. That's just one example of the kind of management principle I learned from President Reagan. As a result of this and other lessons learned, the Labor Department became known as a principled agency that was very effective in advancing conservative principles that helped strengthen America's workforce.

That's why I am so grateful to have had the opportunity to serve in President Reagan's Administration as a young staffer. I learned the power of ideas, and gained the experience that enabled me to understand how to lead.

*Elaine L. Chao became the 24th U.S. Secretary of Labor, serving from 2001-2009, the only member of President George W. Bush's cabinet to serve all eight years*

# 44

# MAX L. FRIEDERSDORF
Assistant to the President for Legislative Affairs 1981-1982, 1984-1986

Confined to the upstairs living quarters at the White House, President Reagan was recuperating from the near-fatal assassination attempt in the Spring of 1981. Rapidly regaining his robust vigor, the President, dressed in jeans and T-shirt, was anxious about the approaching Senate vote on his legislation to sell Saudi Arabia the AWACS surveillance aircraft.

A purely defensive early warning weapon, the sale, nevertheless, was strongly opposed by Israel and its aggressive and effective lobbying machine, AIPAC. (American Israeli Political Action Committee). Led by Senator Bob Packwood (R-Oregon) Chairman of the Republican Senate Campaign Committee, a handful of GOP Senators were threatening to vote against the sale, and hand the new President a stinging foreign policy rebuke.

Mrs. Reagan was still in her robe as the President, First Lady and I gathered early the morning before the vote to make some last minute "do or die" calls from the living quarters. High on the list of recalcitrants was Senator Mark Andrews (R-North Dakota), a hard case under the best of circumstances.

I could tell the phone conversation was not going well from the pained expression on the President's usually cheerful face. Mrs. Reagan was listening intently, and suddenly interrupted. The President put his hand over the mouthpiece, and the First Lady said:

"Ronnie, remind him of that trip to North Dakota in a bad snow storm for you to speak at one of his re-election rallies."

The President brightened up immediately and the conversation was now all about horrible snow storms and getting the Senator re-elected. When the President hung up, I felt sure North Dakota was solid for Reagan.

The President won the AWACS vote in a squeaker, one of the first of his many legislative victories. And the President gave all the credit to the First Lady who fortuitively remembered a difficult trip to the Dakotas that helped secure a Presidential legislative victory on an important foreign policy issue.

## 45

# E. PENDLETON JAMES
### Director, Presidential Personnel 1981-1982

We had just moved into the West Wing of the White House, the first couple of days of the Reagan administration. My office was on the second floor, a beautiful corner office. Of course, when you change Administrations, all the pictures and art come down and the new tenants get to pick their own decorations.

Clem Conger—the White House curator, whom I had first meet during the Nixon Administration—came in, and he said, Pen, what would you like on the walls? I knew that as one of the West Wing perks, you can draw upon the National Gallery for artwork to decorate your office.

I said, "Well, Clem, my hero in history is Benjamin Franklin and if you have something of Benjamin Franklin, that would be very nice. My wife's hero is Thomas Jefferson, so if you have something of Thomas Jefferson, that would be very nice, in keeping with the history of the place."

So he said, "That's good. Let's see what I can do." He left, and I got busy with my new job—finding top candidates for senior jobs in the Administration. Level of effort? We had already started with what we determined to be the 400 most critical positions, then would soon move on to the other 6,000 or so full-time and part-time openings—especially the cabinet, sub-cabinet, members of boards and commissions. Now, most of the positions were occupied, with the incumbents "serving at the pleasure" of the President, so the government was not about to collapse. Some of those folks would be kept on, some sent home once new appointees had been selected, and I had already received some 8,000 un-solicited resumes sent in by "hopefuls." It was going to be a busy couple of years.

A few days later I arrive for work, and Clem is standing in the doorway of my office.

I said, "Hi Clem."

He said, "Pen, come on in."

There, hanging on the wall, was a pen and ink drawing of Ben Franklin in a coonskin cap. There was also a nice oil portrait of Thomas Jefferson. And, to top it off, a huge oil portrait of President James A. Garfield. I'm trying to be very nice and I'm thanking Clem and I said, "Gee, that's swell," and so on, and finally I had to ask, "Why Garfield?"

He says, "Well, Pen, don't you know he was shot by a disappointed job seeker?"

He had his grand joke! Laughing, he took Garfield down and back to the National Gallery.

**46**

## MURRAY WEIDENBAUM
Chairman, President Reagan's Council of Economic Advisors 1981-
1982

O n my first day on the job as President Reagan's chief economic
advisor, he asked me to give him an off-the-cuff economic
briefing. My presentation was, I thought, a fairly decent response,
but admittedly over-simplified.

Before I got too far, the President gently reminded me that he had
been an economics major at Eureka College. Thus, I quickly learned
that Ronald Reagan possessed very effective economic as well as
management skills.

Those of us in the White House involved in preparing the initial
Reagan budgets in 1981 and 1982 used the substantial 5 percent
annual increase in real (after inflation) defense spending estimates
that were initially presented during the 1980 campaign. There were
no doves in Ronald Reagan's Administration. But when the Defense
Department urged much larger numbers, some of us advocated
staying with 5 percent.

I vividly remember the President patiently explaining to me,
"Murray, we don't want to send the wrong signal to the Russians."
I reluctantly dropped the matter although I was not convinced at
the time. In retrospect, the President made the right decision. The
Soviet leadership realized that their economy could not keep up
with a very large U.S. military buildup and thus began the thaw in
the Cold War.

Not all the meetings with President Reagan dealt with high policy. One lovely Spring day, Lyn Nofziger (the President's political advisor) and I were invited to join him for lunch in the Rose Garden. (We were told that the purpose was to express appreciation for the hard work we were doing in our respective areas.) While waiting for the meal to be served, I made a wisecrack. That prompted Lyn to respond with a real zinger. The President quickly matched Lyn and I became a fascinated observer watching two professionals display their talents. In the course of the meal, the President demonstrated his huge and diversified inventory of humor. In addition to a fine Irish brogue, he also displayed a very serviceable Italian accent. Ronald Reagan clearly was a man with an impressive array of talents!

The joy of working for Ronald Reagan was also accompanied by frequent reminders that you were not the President. When he was not using the presidential box at the Kennedy Center, he graciously let his associates use this valuable "perk."

On one occasion I wound up sitting in the President's seat. When the lights came on the audience did not suppress its disappointment. Despite the booing, my wife and I thoroughly enjoyed the evening.

On another occasion when I was enjoying that great perk, President Reagan called me, apologizing for interrupting my evening. When I told him where he reached me, we both enjoyed a good laugh.

One of the greatest Washington, DC, memories was my wife and I being invited to the White House family theatre. The movie was "Ragtime," starring James Cagney and Pat O'Brien. I don't remember much about the movie, but I have an indelible memory of the President entering the theatre with James Cagney in tow, while Nancy was wheeling in Pat O'Brien.

# 47

## JOSEPH WRIGHT

Deputy Director, Office of Management and the Budget (OMB)
1982–1989

n 1982, the President's pollster, Bob Teeter, was concerned that there was a 'generation gap' with the women voters. President Reagan asked me and Elizabeth Dole (Staff Assistant to the President) to review the situation and make recommendations on what should be done. After the presentation, President Reagan said to us "Well, Liddy and Joe—don't know how I did it, but I won the last election and I'll win the next one. Isn't that good enough?"

In 1983, President Reagan placed a priority on reducing the influence of the Soviet Union, both militarily and economically. David Stockman (Director of OMB), Dick Darman (Deputy Chief of Staff) and I conducted a six-month review of the U.S. Force structure and concluded that it could be maintained at much lower costs. We made a presentation to President Reagan in the Cabinet Room with the Secretary and Deputy Secretary of Defense attending. Stockman was never able to get through the presentation and left highly frustrated. Afterwards, President Reagan said to Darman and me: "What Dave doesn't understand is that the Soviets' will copy everything the U.S. does, but make it larger. They know what our budget is and they will ramp up their spending, but they can't afford to do that. Now do you understand?"

# 48

## FRANK FAHRENKOPF
Chairman, Republican National Committee 1983-1989

had been in politics for a long time; I was the youngest member
of the Republican National Committee in 1975 and moved up to
chairman in 1983. I had managed a number of political campaigns
and I thought I knew pretty much everything there was to know.

Well, soon after I became chairman, I was invited to the White
House for a "photo opportunity" with the President. The photographer decided we should be seated in front of the Oval Office
fireplace . . . but just the two of us sitting in chairs was too static.
The photographer suggested, "You should do something."

The President said, "I have an idea." He went to his desk and
brought back a sheet of paper. "Let's pretend to be discussing this."

I could see it was a page from a speech he had been working on . . .
typewritten in a large speechwriter font for easy reading . . . but the
words only occupied the top one-third of the sheet. The rest of the
page was empty. I asked him, "Why?"

"It's an old trick I learned in Hollywood, and I carried it over into
politics. If the words on the page go all the way to the bottom, well,
when you are standing in front of an audience delivering a speech,
as your eyes track down the page, soon the audience is looking at
the top of your head. If you only have to look at the top third of
the page, you don't even have to move your head . . . so your face
is always toward the audience."

I took that trick with me back into my RNC world and it was a lesson I shared with all our candidates.

Let me offer a salute to President Reagan's stamina. In 1983, he flew out in Air Force One to give a speech at the annual Cinco de Mayo celebration in San Antonio, Texas. Jim Baker, Mike Deaver and I went along for the ride. It was a warm day . . . no, call it hot. It was probably around 95, but out in the sun with heat bouncing off buildings and the pavement, I swear it felt like 120. It was so hot that, as I recall, in the middle of the speech at least one member of the audience—all of whom were standing—fainted, and the President called for his personal physician, Dan Ruge, to step in and help.

The President was in a black suit, under which was the bulletproof vest he always wore after the 1981 assassination attempt. He might as well have been wearing a snow suit. I was 45 and overwhelmed with the heat; I thought the 72-year-old President must be about ready to stroke out. But no, he soldiered on, gave his speech and shook a lot of hands. Eventually we were on our way.

I think he must have been in the best physical shape, ever, in his life. Back in 1981, after he had been released from the hospital, he was put on a heavy exercise regimen; a Nautilus machine was installed in the White House, and he used it daily whenever he was in residence. He once bragged to me about how much muscle mass he had gained!

So here we were, off again on Air Force One. Baker, Deaver, and I were soaked in sweat; a sympathetic steward brought us some cold beers. The President was unruffled. We were wiped out, he wanted to chat and tell us jokes.

# 49

# PETER H. DAILEY
## Ambassador to Ireland 1982-1984

joined the Reagan campaign in late March or early April 1980. The campaign team had been working together for years, back to the time when Reagan was governor of California. I—an outsider—became involved because of Bill Casey, who had taken over in mid-stream as manager of the Presidential campaign, and was unhappy with the established media strategy and message. He thought that I might be of some assistance.

I met Bill during Nixon's 1972 presidential campaign, where I was a media strategist—a role I revisited during the Ford campaign in 1976. The Reagan campaign team was packed with public officials and politicians, but was thin in folks with experience in business and advertising . . . my specialties.

But I hesitated. In 1976, when Ford and Reagan were fighting for the nomination, I was a member of the enemy camp, so to speak. Bill said stop worrying, we are all on the same team now. So I came aboard.

The first meeting I attended, along with Reagan and perhaps ten other members of the team, started out in a slow and plodding manner, people dealing with minutiae which—it was soon apparent—was not where Reagan wanted to be. He listened in silence for maybe ten or fifteen minutes, then pounded on the table and said, "Hold on. You guys all seem to want to go over here" and he pointed in one direction, "and I want to go over there," and pointed in the opposite direction. The whole discussion changed, more on concepts and less on schedules.

The last item up for discussion: should he participate in a televised debate with President Carter? The discussion was lively but undisciplined, with folks talking over each other, and Reagan finally said, "Let's have a round table. Everyone gets a say, in turn." Each gave his view—largely negative—and the reasons therefore; facts, statistics, they were well prepared. I knew nothing about such details, and all of a sudden it's my turn. "All right Peter, what about you?"

It just struck me. I said, "Well, the Gipper's gotta debate."

And he slammed his hand on the table, bang, and said "Right! The Gipper's gonna debate."

The Carter team agreed to debate, but there was a complicating factor: a third-party candidate, John Anderson. Carter would not debate with Anderson in the mix. Therefore, Reagan and Anderson debated alone on September 30 . . . which gave Reagan good practice for the Carter debate, October 28, one week before the election. That event may be remembered, yet today, for two things: President Carter reporting that his 12-year-old daughter Amy thought that "nuclear weaponry and the control of nuclear arms" was the most important issue of the day, and Reagan's throw-away line, in response to some misleading Carter comment: "There you go again!"

The winner, hands down: Reagan.

After the campaign, I went home and back to my normal life. Then I got a telephone call, "We'd like you to be our ambassador to Ireland." I was flattered but not sure that I should leave my business again so soon after the eight-month campaign . . . but in the end, I agreed to accept the assignment.

During my pre-deployment orientation, National Security advisor Bill Clark said it was important that I monitor talks then going on between British Prime Minister Margaret Thatcher and the Irish Teasoich (pronounced 'tee-shook.' the Irish equivalent of PM). Apparently, previous leaders of the two countries had never discussed the "problem" of Northern Ireland, as Britain and Ireland each claimed that Northern Ireland "belonged" to them and whatever was going on was no one else's business. At some point, President Reagan had stepped in and suggested to both, that no progress could ever be made unless both leaders worked the issue together. They agreed.

Skip ahead a few months . . . I settled in to the job, and at some point I scheduled a half-hour meeting with the Teasoich just for discussion of relations with Margaret Thatcher. His "report" was rather bland, yes they had been talking, yes it was a good idea, etc, etc.. That was fine, as far as it went, but I didn't think it went far enough. "Are there any," I asked, "personal issues between you and Mrs. Thatcher? President Reagan is a great believer in strong interpersonal relations."

The Teasoich mumbled something like, "Oh, can't really talk about that. Private." He was a former university professor, and in speech and manner, he was the exemplification of the typical parody of the fuddy-duddy academic.

I pressed him. He continued to duck the question. I said, "Please tell me, it is important to the President."

So, finally, he said: "I really can't stand the way that woman lectures me!"

Well, soon enough I was off to Washington for a home visit and consultations and at some point, I was in the Oval Office with Bill Clark and the President. I gave an overview: there had been some progress on the Northern Ireland issue, nothing definitive, but at least a first step. Then the President asked, "Well, Peter, what about the personal aspect? How are they getting along?"

I said, "Mr. President, the Teasoich didn't want to talk about that, but I managed to pull it out of him. He said, he just couldn't stand the way that woman lectures him."

President Reagan leaned back, laughing, and said, "You tell the Teasoich that I'm glad to see that she doesn't treat him any differently than she treats me!"

Well, the end of the story. I was back in Ireland, had another meeting with the Teasoich, and he asked, did I tell the President about that "personal issue"? I said, yes sir, I did. He asked, "What did he say?" I told him.

He perked up. "The President said that? Well, I don't feel so badly then!"

*From 1985 to 1988, Dailey served as Counselor to William Casey, then Director of Central Intelligence.*

# 50

## EDWARD ROWNY

Lt. General, U.S. Army (Retired)
Ambassador
Chief Negotiator, Strategic Arms Reduction Talks (START)
1981–1985
Special Advisor to the President and Secretary of State for Arms
Control Matters 1985-1989

SDI. During my first conversation with Governor Reagan in January 1980, I was impressed with his commitment to ballistic missile defense. "Let me see if I understand what you call mutual assured destruction," he said. "You tell me that we have a pistol aimed at the Soviets' head and they have a pistol aimed at ours. That's MAD," he said with wry smile. "Why don't we defend ourselves with a helmet."

"Because," I said, "We don't have the ability to defend against ballistic missiles."

"I have more confidence in our scientists than you., he said. "Go talk to Dr. Teller. He will tell you about developing a defense against a missile attack."

Peace Through Strength. I had a rear row seat at President Reagan's early cabinet sessions. Most cabinet members were complaining that the president was spending too much on defense. They said that in view of our double-digit inflation and unemployment we could not afford to spend money for defense. "Gentlemen," said the president, "As president of the United States my most important duty is to defend the United States, against all enemies, foreign and domestic. If we lose our freedom, all is lost. Through a policy of peace through strength everything is possible."

Martial Law. When Polish President Jaruzelski declared martial law in December 1981, Professor Richard Pipes, an assistant to the National Security Advisor, drafted a letter of protest to the Soviets. The president sent the letter despite strong opposition from the Department of State. He told the Soviet leader that if he deployed tanks to Warsaw there would be dire consequences.

First Summit with Gorbachev. At the meeting with President Gorbachev at their first summit in Geneva (November 19-20, 1985). President Reagan suggested to Gorbachev that they take a walk by the lake. During the walk Reagan suggested that they warm up in a boathouse. There was a fire in the fireplace and hot drinks were served. This opportunity for the two presidents to speak, along with only interpreters  present was cleverly staged in advance by President Reagan.

Reagan's Assessment of Pope John Paul II. During my series of briefings for the Pope he took great interest in learning about President Reagan's personality. After Reagan's assassination attempt the Pope said he admired Reagan's sense of humor when he told his surgeons he hoped they were all Republicans. When I reported this to the president he in turn commented on the Pope's actions after he was shot. "It's remarkable," said President Reagan, "that the Pope forgave his attacker; that man is a saint."

Berlin speech. The State Department expressed strong objections to the statement "Mr. Gorbachev, tear down this wall," believing it was too provocative. Nevertheless, the president, reviewing the speech shortly before delivering it, said, "I know it's gonna drive the State Department boys crazy, but I'm gonna leave it in." The speech played a significant role bringing down the wall two years later.

Reykjavik. At the overtime session of the Reykjavik Summit I was nervous that President Reagan might revert to his earlier discussions with Gorbachev about scrapping all nuclear weapons. However, my anxieties were relieved when President Reagan remarked that the United States would continue research and development on strategic ballistic missile defenses. An agititated Gorbachev snapped his book shut and stormed out of the room. I was greatly relieved that the Soviets' visceral fear of our SDI program saved us from possible disastrous agreement to scrap all nuclear weapons.

Reagan's final speech in Moscow. During the president's last visit to Moscow near the end of his second term he was scheduled to talk to the students at the University of Moscow. Scrapping his prepared remarks the president gave the students a 50-minute course in "Democracy 101." The spellbound students gave him a standing ovation. I believe this was one of the best speeches President Reagan gave during his career.

*The "Tear down this wall" speech starts on page 352.*

*A transcript of Reagan's "Moscow University" session begins at page 360.*

# 51

# SVEN F. KRAEMER
## NSC Director of Arms Control 1981-1987

Peace through strength / the "Zero" option. As Director of Arms Control on Reagan's National Security Council (NSC) from January 1981 until September 1987, and earlier working with Senator John Tower as a senior drafter of the "peace and freedom" section of Reagan's 1980 campaign platform and a member of Reagan's Defense Transition Team, I participated directly in the development and implementation of Reagan's revolutionary U.S. Cold War strategy of "peace through strength"—especially in its integration of national security-based U.S. defense and arms control strategies. During this period, Reagan rallied increasing bi-partisan support from Congress, the Committee on the Present Danger, "Team B" and other experts, and the American people. Yet he had to overcome strong opposition from Soviet leaders and American political, diplomatic, media, academic, and bureaucratic communities accustomed to the faltering U.S. Cold War strategies of "containment" and "détente." For his unyielding determination to roll back Soviet imperial momentum by rebuilding America's strengths—moral, military, economic, diplomatic, and in intelligence areas—Reagan was denounced as a "conservative ideologue" and "hawk" who was "provoking" the Soviet Union and "destroying arms control."

In this historical context, Reagan's dramatic "zero option" for Intermediate Nuclear Force (INF) arms control was a decisive early test, precedent, and turning point for arms control and for his wider

Cold War strategy to defeat the "evil empire." In the high-profile area of super-power arms control, the 1970s had featured "caps," "freezes," weak verification, and U.S. defense cuts. The Soviet Union, meanwhile, undertook unprecedented military buildups, treaty violations, propaganda, and international subversion through "active measures" deceptions and "liberation war" adventures. In INF, as for strategic systems in the Strategic Arms Limitations Talks (SALT) process, Soviet "peace" fronts and a Western "nuclear freeze" movement seriously eroded support for U.S. nuclear modernization efforts including NATO's "double track" INF decision of December 1979. The decision was that, absent an arms control agreement, NATO would make INF counter-deployments to begin in November 1983 for a total of 108 small U.S. Pershing II ballistic missiles and 364 slow-flying ground-launched cruise missiles (GLCMS), against massive Soviet deployments of new INF-oriented "first strike" systems.

The threatening new Soviet systems included SS-20 missiles, Backfire bombers, and submarines added to major existing Soviet/ Warsaw Pact advantages in conventional armor and artillery, chemical weapons, and "tactical" nuclear weapons. In 1977, the Soviets had responded to Jimmy Carter's weak policies by beginning deployment of a new SS-20 missile each week, to add to the existing 360 deployed Soviet SS-4 and SS-5 INF missiles, for which the U.S. had no counterparts. The mobile SS-20s were a particularly potent new "first-strike" threat, each with three warheads of 200+ kilotons of nuclear destructive power, capable of destroying cities or hardened silos and bunkers 3,500 to 5,000 kilometers away, i.e., in Europe, East Asia, the Middle East and on U.S. territory—attack threats for which the U.S. had no defenses..

NATO's 1979 decision was at once denounced by the Kremlin, much of the U.S. Congress and U.S. and Western "peace" and "arms control" groups that wanted traditional Soviet-style "moratorium" declarations or a "nuclear freeze," with the U.S./NATO to remain at zero counter deployments. The left's approach blocked U.S. modernization, legitimized the unilateral Soviet buildups, and eliminated

Soviet incentives for negotiating meaningful arms reductions and effective verification. Yet when Reagan became president in January 1981, the left's "zero" was predominant in the streets and parliaments of Europe and was getting stronger in the U.S.

Reagan's INF decisions were critical for arms control, diplomacy, and his presidency if he was to seize the moral and strategic high ground on a series of arms control, defense, and defense of freedom issues against the Soviet totalitarians. In March 1981, Reagan began by confounding Soviet and U.S. "freeze" supporters in reaffirming the 1979 NATO decision. In an April 30 NSC meeting (notes declassified), he overruled the State Department in deciding against starting INF negotiations soon, within Carter's deeply flawed SALT II framework, or without first getting a prior NATO assessment of the Soviet threat. In May 1981, he approved starting INF negotiations in the fall, but only if preceded by extensive prior NATO and Administration planning on INF defense requirements and negotiation options. In September 1981, Reagan approved five revolutionary "anti-freeze" arms control criteria to be applied to INF (but also a precedent for strategic weapons and other arms control) requiring: 1) equality of limits and rights; 2) strictly bilateral U.S.-Soviet focus; 3) global INF limitations; 4) no adverse effect on NATO's conventional defense; and 5) effective (i.e., high-confidence) verification.

At an October 13, 1981 NSC meeting (notes declassified), Reagan asked for the first time about a possible new U.S. version of an INF "zero option." This was understood as requiring dismantlement of all Soviet INF ballistic missiles (SS-20, SS-4, and SS-5, with a total of about 900 warheads) in exchange for all potential U.S. Pershing and GLCM missiles (totaling 572 warheads). Such a U.S. *double* "zero option" for *both* sides was first discussed in March 1981 by two NSC and Defense Department officials to whom it was clear that the Department of State and the U.S. arms control bureaucracy, as well as nervous Allied diplomats, considered the Soviet and "freeze" movement's "zero" as the inevitable "politically-correct" path to be taken. The two officials, in contrast, believed an alternative U.S. version could far better meet Reagan's national security and arms control requirements and gain effective diplomatic leverage. The option was kept outside the INF Arms Control Inter-agency Group (IG) process, was worked through separate channels, and was forwarded to Reagan in October.

Reagan's initial question about a U.S. zero option at the October 13 NSC meeting was answered negatively by Secretary of State Alexander Haig, who believed it would not be considered credible. It was supported by Secretary of Defense Caspar Weinberger, CIA Director William Casey, and Counselor Edwin Meese. Representatives of the Joint Chiefs and the Arms Control and Disarmament Agency preferred the ambiguous "lowest possible levels" formula that was the IG's lowest common denominator. When Reagan asked the JCS representative and Casey about verifying numbers of concealed *mobile* missiles, they, joined by Meese, indicated serious difficulties for numerical limits rather than zero. Later, U.S. military leaders at NATO expressed initial concern about the President's zero-zero, but like the proposal's supporters, came to understand that this was an innovative way to avoid legitimizing freeze asymmetries or bog down in endless "lowest common levels" talks. But it could instead incentivize effectively verifiable major asymmetric reductions of the entire class of SS-20s. At a November 12, 1981 NSC meeting (notes declassified), Reagan approved the option and on November 16 he issued an NSC directive (declassified) that formally established it as the official U.S. proposal.

On November 18, 1981 Reagan stunned the world in a national TV address setting forth his unprecedented proposal to dismantle the *planned* U.S. missiles (with 572 warheads) in exchange for dismantling all Soviet SS-20, SS-4, and SS-5 (then totaling more than 1,100 warheads). The speech became the first of many supported by moving color charts and maps provided by the NSC on U.S.-Soviet INF asymmetries and followed by a vigorous NSC-coordinated public diplomacy campaign that included the Pentagon's NSC-coordinated "Soviet Military Power" series and extensive briefings to Congress, Allies, and public policy institutions. Having established U.S. strategic modernization priorities in October 1981 (MX, B-2, D-5, etc.), Reagan in May 1982 made his innovative Strategic Arms *Reduction* Talks (START) proposal following his INF precedents, by replacing the ineffective SALT "caps" approach, and instead calling for deep reductions of one-half in missiles and one-third in warheads to equal levels of capability and with effective verification and with U.S. modernization permitted.

With INF and START arms control and modernization relatively harmonized, critical additional arms control leverage was gained from Reagan's Strategic Defense Initiative (SDI) of March 1983 to provide increasing anti-missile defenses that could help move the world away from the dubious U.S. nuclear deterrence doctrine of Mutual Assured Destruction (MAD). With Reagan friends Maggie Thatcher, Helmut Kohl and other European Allies supporting Reagan, the U.S. INF deployments began as scheduled in November 1983 in five European countries. At this point, the Soviets, still claiming an INF missile "balance" even as they deployed a new SS-20 each week, doubled down. They walked out on all U.S.-Soviet arms control negotiations, encouraged war-scares, and clearly thought Reagan would cave.

A year later, Reagan's overwhelming 1984 reelection victory, strengthened popular mandate, and continued tough Cold War policies (that some U.S. diplomats had sought to ease) caused the Soviets (under Konstantin Chernenko) to decide in January 1985 that they could not intimidate Reagan or force him off the moral high ground and should return to the arms control negotiations in the spring. Accordingly, a new team of U.S. ambassadors met them in the "umbrella talks" including INF, START, and Space issues. Each negotiation featured strong U.S. positions toward which the Soviet Union moved over the next months and which included "build-down" variants in START that permitted long overdue U.S. strategic modernization within Reagan's START reductions framework. At the same time, Reagan also increasingly linked the evidence of seven or more major Soviet treaty violations to the need for effective on-site verification beyond SALT's distant National Technical Means and to SDI as indispensible insurance against Soviet treaty breakouts and global proliferation. In December 1987, Mikhail Gorbachev, who had become head of the Communist Party and Soviet state in March 1985, joined Reagan in signing a "zero-zero" INF Treaty on the basis of Reagan's terms the Soviets had rejected for years. In May 1988, the U.S. Senate ratified the INF Treaty after further U.S.-Soviet discussions had strengthened data and on-site verification procedures. That summer Pershing I missiles held by West Germany (with warheads held by the U.S. were added to the mix to be dismantled.

Against much opposition and high odds, Reagan was the first and only president to have eliminated an entire class of nuclear weapons, although his nuclear modernization and testing policies make clear he was no nuclear abolitionist in a nuclear world. He established tough new arms control and defense criteria that set important precedents but were never matched by his successors. His INF "Zero-Option" is part of a great "Let Reagan be Reagan" story, as not yet fully told or documented, about Reagan's unique leadership and revolutionized U.S. Cold War strategy in defense, arms control, diplomacy, intelligence and support to anti-Communist resistance forces (from Afghanistan to Poland to Latin America. That story is about how Reagan's faith in America, "peace and freedom" and "peace through strength" overcame continuous strong opposition at home and abroad. It is about how he raised the Soviet Union's costs of empire to the point of exposing its founding myths and "active measures" deceptions and collapsing its totalitarian Communist ideology, regime, Iron Curtains and "Socialist Camp" of captive nations. Far more than any other person during the long Cold War, Reagan and his team provided for the common defense while reducing the risks and weapons of war. He secured the blessings of liberty on a path to Cold War victory for the forces of peace and freedom. Today, we and our posterity should be inspired to thank, think, and act on that extraordinary example in a world where leaders are few and dangers continue to increase.

*Reagan's "Zero Options" speech will be found at page 300.*

*Sven F. Kraemer was a member of the U.S. Civil Service from the Kennedy Administration to that of George W. Bush; his book,* Inside the Cold War from Karl Marx to Ronald Reagan, *will be published in 2014.*

## 52

# SIG ROGICH
### Director-Advertising, Reagan/Bush-'84

Convention Film/Santa Barbara. In August of 1984, I flew to Santa Barbara with Jim Lake while Phil Dusenberry, the Chairman of BBDO advertising agency, waited anxiously in New York to hear whether the President would approve our final edit for the 22 minute convention film or whether he was going to request changes. There was also a six-minute shorter film of the First Lady that needed approval and we were on a ridiculously tight timeline, as there were only two days before the convention.

Truth be told, we would be hard pressed to make any type of significant edits or changes as the technology of film at that time required cutting, splicing and more, and that was before you added sound. It wasn't yet the wonderful days of digital, and easier, instant editing. We had already used every good snippet of film and poured over every music edit to make certain that the sounds and the stills matched with the President's narration. We had it just perfect, the way we wanted, and we wanted the President to like it as much as we did.

Needless to say, the anticipation was a killer and should the President want changes, we would have been in a bad way to meet convention and network deadlines. The last words I got from Phil before heading to the Reagan's ranch in California was, "Ok Siggy, go sell this goddam thing. You can do it. Because, if you don't," then he paused. "Well, I don't have to tell you what that means."

Of course, I did know. For the first time in American Presidential history, we were able to buy air time on all three major networks for the film, so it would end up with a viewership in the tens of millions or not, depending on how things turned out on my trip to Santa Barbara. This was going to be a first, and probably a last if we couldn't make this work. So, not only did we have the convention deadline, we had network deadlines to deal with on top of every-thing. If the President wanted changes, there were no guarantees we would be able to make those deadlines and the pressure was on.

Jim and I drove up that long dusty road to the ranch and as we approached the entrance, there was the President, in a tee shirt, jeans and an old cowboy hat cutting logs for a fence he was building while some secret service agents circled in black suits. The late afternoon temperature was getting up there, and there was a tremendous dichotomy in that imagery and that memory. The movie star, the former Governor of California, the President of the United States and a man, cowboy hat and all, who loved his ranch, everything that made Ronald Reagan so unique was all there in this image. Whenever I think about him now, that image of him is what I recall. He was one of a kind.

Nancy was also working outside nearby, wearing casual clothes and a large sun hat. As we got out of the car and walked over to them, they couldn't have been more gracious, asking someone to bring us glasses of iced tea as we stood by the fence and chatted about his project and other things. While I was trying to remain calm, the entire time I am anxiously thinking, "Well, here we go," a quote many Americans heard from the President on occasion.

I finally said, "Mr. President, we are so sorry to bother you, but we have the film for the convention to show you and everyone is standing by in case you want to change anything."

"And Nancy, we have your film as well, so when it's convenient we'd like to show it to you to make sure you like it. Both films will be shown nationwide."

We knew they would have to go inside and while I was eager and we were really crunched for time, no one wants to be in the position of seeming to push the President. However, I can't say enough how gracious they were to us and to all the people that worked with them.

They took us inside to their modest bedroom, and the President stood beside the bed and offered me a seat at the end of the bed where Nancy sat beside me while we watched. At the point when Lee Greenwood starts to sing "God Bless the USA" with the opening lyrics of, "If tomorrow all the things were gone, I'd worked for all my life…"

The President and Nancy both misted up, but I just started sweating. I had a deadline and an entire studio standing by in New York waiting to hear from me.

We had spent the better part of four months finding the perfect locations and producing commercials and footage with shots of families, workers and all things that represent America. We shot in dozens of locations, worked tirelessly on the film to time it to Lee's song that we had selected for this short movie. I had talked to Lee about our idea and he ended up giving it to us to use in the film for the price of one dollar. Phil said it was much like filming a feature film, but on a lesser budget, with less manpower and significantly less time. As I mentioned earlier, there was no digital technology for us to work with per se, so it was tedious and arduous work both in the filming, editing and the post production.

There we were, watching the film together in silence in the President's bedroom. At the end of the film, there was a pause, and then The President looked at me and said, "That's just great Sig. I love it."

Overwhelming relief immediately set in for me, but Jim Lake, who was with me, glanced over at me in fear as if to say, "Please, Dear God, don't ask him anything Sig, just keep your mouth shut." So I just said, "Thank you Mr. President"

And with that, we had our convention film and he walked over to Nancy, bent down to give her a little hug and said "Why don't just you and Sig look at your film honey, and we'll see you outside." While there was a sense of relief that the President liked the longer convention film, now we had to go through the whole process again with the First Lady, and her film was much more personal. Her film included sweet memories about her father, Dr. Davis. Putting together a film about someone's life is a very personal process, and we wanted to make sure it captured her voice in telling her story and sharing private memories about her family.

So the First Lady and I sat at the end of their bed and watched her life story in what seemed like an eternity to me, and when it was finished, she turned to me, smiled, and said, "It was lovely, thank you Sig." And as she spoke, she teared up a little, so I knew we had captured the essence. Finally, I remember starting to breathe again.

What had started out as one of the most stressful days of my life and career became one of the more memorable days of my life. At the time though, all I could think was, "Let's get out of here now before anyone changes their minds!"

The film turned out to be a huge hit at the convention and it was a proud moment for all of the people who had worked so hard on that film from conceptualization, to filming, to editing, to sound and to production. Even today, when I see the film, it is a tremendous honor to know I played a small role in bringing it to reality. I still feel it captured the spirit, the feeling and the love that the American people had for their President and their country at that time in our history.

Oval Office Filming. Near the end of the 1984 campaign for re-election, we had planned a filming session with the President and the Vice President in the Oval Office. Filming in the Oval Office of the President of the United States is challenge because, as I indicated to my staff and crew, "there are no furniture knock offs or prints on the White House walls." They are all "the real McCoy," from the Russells, to the Remingtons, to the irreplaceable period pieces. So NO equipment, cameras, lighting or any other item we bring into that office can touch ANYTHING. And the curators were always hovering around to make sure all items were handled with the care required.

To prevent any of the furniture from being dinged or damaged, we removed it all from the office because more often than not, we laid down dolly tracks to get the perfect shots. It was an eerie experience to see the Oval Office empty of all items with the exception of the President's desk.

We set up for this particular shoot earlier in the day, knowing that we only had an hour of the President's precious time, and we wanted it to be all set and lit for him to just breeze in and do his read. At the end of the set-up, the Oval Office became a mini movie sound stage.

The video was going to run about 30 minutes with the President asking for America's vote at the close. Twenty five minutes of the show was for the President and five was for Vice President George H. W. Bush to speak about the President and their good work together.

When the President came in to do his read, he was terrific. He was such a natural behind the camera anyway, and so of course he gave us a perfect read. However, about 25 minutes into filming, I was looking at the monitor and noticed that as the camera moved on the dolly to a certain spot, there was a dark crease that appeared on the President's face. Panic!

We had not anticipated the sun going down and how much that would affect the lighting in the Oval Office. We had spent a great deal of time working with the lighting and adding gelled lenses to get the right warmth and texture, and now the sunset was wreaking havoc on our shot.

We had just taken up about an hour of the President's time with rehearsal and the actual filming, and his read was impeccable as always, but I couldn't let the crease go and so I had to yell "Cut." It got real quiet and the President looked at me and said, "Sorry Sig, did I screw up?"

I said, "No sir, we did. We didn't prepare for the sunset having such an effect on the office and you won't look right unless we do this again."

Always gracious, the President's reply was, "Well all right, let's just do it again."

It was about that time that Mike Deaver and Jim Baker came

in with the President's schedule and whispered in my ear in a not so pleasant tone, "What the hell is going on? We've got him tightly scheduled for meetings."

Before I could respond, President Reagan crossed the room and said "Say, Sig, can I borrow your comb? My hair was messed up for that take."

And that was that. Not another word was said, other than a few glares from his waiting staff. We finished filming and the President knocked it out of the park with his delivery. He never questioned the mistake and after the final take, he had that twinkle in his eye as he smiled at me and said in front of Mike Deaver, "Thanks for the comb."

The President had saved my bacon, and he knew it but never let on. Mike Deaver would later say to me on the way out, "Damit, you guys never stick to the schedule."

But on that occasion it didn't matter. I had been spared by The President of the United States.

First Lady in the Rose Garden. One afternoon we had planned a film shoot in the Rose Garden at the White House with First Lady Nancy Reagan. I had told Nancy to wear a red dress because that beautiful garden setting lent itself to it and I thought it would make her stand out. We had a host of dignified ladies there to participate with her, but of course, The First Lady was the star.

We set the cameras in position. At that time we were working with 35 mm cameras and big set lighting. We had selected a time in late afternoon when we knew the lighting would be perfect. It was that special time of day when filming takes on a life of its own. The sun is perfect, the clouds are just right, but as we only had one shot, we took the extra precaution of using silk overhead to give us an even cast of light that would eliminate shadows on faces and an evenness that made the Rose Garden look, well, like a Rose Garden from a perfect movie scene from old England.

We are all set up and have everyone seated, and we await Nancy who came down shortly afterwards and looked sensational. She took her seat, and I said, "Nancy, your script is loaded on the Tele-Prompter and I know you've gone over it, but this piece will receive a lot of play nationally as we are using it extensively. So I want you to be conversational if you can. Read it, but talk like you're telling a story to a bunch of friends.

She looked up and said, "I'm ready, Sig. Let's get it started."

So I went behind the camera and saw the worst clash of colors of red. Her beautiful red dress just didn't work with the red garden roses. You know how certain colors, the same certain colors, just clash together. It's like wearing two shades of yellow. It just didn't work.

At this point, I terrifyingly went to her and whispered, "Nancy, I hate to tell you this, but I can't film this shot because you are not going to look your best." And she said, "Is it my hair?"

I replied, "No, it's that beautiful dress you are wearing. It clashes with the roses."

She looked up and said, "Thank you, Sig. I'll be right back. But tell me what color should I wear?" I told her anything but red, maybe blue or yellow.

I should have known better. I should have checked the backdrop. But I hadn't. And worse, it was my recommendation to wear red to start.

She was so gracious and she smiled at me and said, "Thank you, Sig. Thank you."

And she went up and changed clothes.

It delayed things about half an hour, but it was just another example of working with someone of grace and decorum who understood that I wanted her to look her best and how image was such an important element in setting up the message being delivered.

No fanfare, no debate, just a "Thank you."

And a film that turned out wonderful because of a gracious First Lady.

But to this day I remember having to tell the First Lady of the United States to go change her clothes.

# JAMES H. BURNLEY, IV

Deputy Secretary of Transportation 1983-1987
Secretary of Transportation 1987-1989

Before the creation of the Department of Homeland Security, the Coast Guard was a part of the Department of Transportation. The Coast Guard Commandant and I invited President Reagan to deliver the commencement address in 1988 at the Coast Guard Academy in New London. The President agreed to do so.

I accompanied President Reagan on the flight to the Hartford airport, which was the closest airport at which Air Force One could land. Thus, the motorcade had to go approximately 60 miles to the Academy.

As we pulled out of the airport, President Reagan and I were engaged in a conversation. There was a crowd just outside the airport gate waiting to see him. He turned away from me to wave to them. As he did so, in his characteristically polite way, he said, "Jim, I don't mean to be rude, but many of these people have been waiting for a couple of hours to see their President. So we can continue to talk, but I need to acknowledge them."

We did continue to talk; and President Reagan also continued to wave to the onlookers throughout the entire drive. This was in the final months of his Presidency, yet he still felt that it was important to connect with the people at every opportunity, even if it was for a fleeting moment. It is one of many examples of how much respect he had for the American people and for the office of the Presidency.

## HALEY BARBOUR
Special Assistant to the President for Political Affairs
Deputy Assistant to the President and Director, White House Office of
Political Affairs 1985-1986

A "Maximum" Photo-Op, 1985: Presidents have egos, and I'm sure Ronald Reagan was not an exception. Yet he was as considerate as any man I've ever met. I learned this on my first political trip with the President after I got to the White House in 1985. I started work on April 19, and one of my first assignments was to plan and help manage a political trip to Florida, Oklahoma and Alabama for our three incumbent Republican senators up for reelection that year: Paula Hawkins, Don Nickles, and Admiral Jeremiah Denton. All were freshman and considered vulnerable.

I met with the staffs and campaign leaders of all three as well as with the National Senatorial Campaign Committee (NRSC) and the White House Advance Office to determine how to do the events to maximize the benefit to each senator. Nickles' Team had a special request. They asked if President Reagan would pose for photos with one hundred different couples . . . one hundred clicks.

Well, the White House rule was to limit photos to a maximum of forty; but the Oklahomans said they could raise $600,000 if the President would do a hundred: $2,000 per couple for the GOP primary campaign, $2,000 per couple for the general election campaign and $2,000 per couple for the State Republican Party.

I ran it by Ed Rollins, who was my boss, who said it couldn't be done unless Mike Deaver approved it; but I was welcome to run it by him. So I went to see Deaver, an old friend. Mike had decided he was leaving the White House, after a long career with the Reagans. I don't know if that affected his decision, but Deaver approved the hundred clicks.

The trip started in Florida, where we had a great event; then on to Oklahoma. After the motorcade got to the site, the President went to a holding room, and staffers like me went to the rooms where the events would take place. In my case, it was a rather small ballroom set up for the photo-op. A blue drape hung at one end of the room, the backdrop for the photos to be taken for maxed-out donors. Those donors were stretched back and forth across the room in a long serpentine line, waiting for us to start.

Besides Secret Service agents there were a handful of staff from the advance and/or political office, whose jobs were to manage the process.

The President arrived from behind the blue drape, smiling and speaking to those nearest to him. He took his place, and one of the most miserable twenty-five to thirty minutes of my life began.

After a staffer at the front of the line made sure we had the couples' names in the correct order, the next staffer, known as the "pusher," told the couple, "In order for us to have time to get everybody's picture, please don't talk. Don't try to strike up a conversation with the President as we're really pressed for time."

The couples would hustle up to stand by the President, who, of course, being a nice and cordial gentleman, would speak to them. Every couple was flustered and didn't know what to do. The photographer would ask everyone to look at the camera, then click.

On the opposite side from which the couple approached the President was another staffer, known as the "puller," who immediately started telling the couple, "Come this way, please. Clear the area for the next photo. This way. Here we go."

Most couples would hustle on past the "puller," while the process had already begun again with the next cycle. The President had to have hated it. It was so unlike him not to be cordial to everyone, and the couples had to have been confused and uncomfortable, which made it worse for Reagan.

About forty photos into the Oklahoma City event, Rollins found me and said, "Regan is so furious about this photo-op that he's red-faced," talking about Don Regan, the President's Chief of Staff.

I said, "Ed, tell him it's my fault, nobody else's. I got Deaver to approve it."

Deaver didn't make the trip, and, by God's grace, neither did Mrs. Reagan. She'd have had me shot on the spot.

The photo-op, with its massive, meandering line of couples, went on for almost a half hour. It seemed much longer than that to me.

After the dinner, which was very successful, though the lion's share of the money was raised at the photo-op, Senator Nickles was very pleased and thanked President Reagan profusely.

The next morning we flew from Oklahoma City to Birmingham for an enormous luncheon for Senator Denton. I hadn't slept much, worried about getting fired. As I sat on Air Force One, I felt a tap on my shoulder. It was the President, standing in the aisle next to my seat.

Of course, I jumped up.

He leaned over to speak to me quietly and said, "Haley, Don (Regan) says you're upset about the photo-op yesterday. Look, they're clumsy and uncomfortable, but you know I raised Senator Nickles $600,000 at the photo-op. There is nowhere else I can spend twenty or thirty minutes and help him that much. So don't worry about it. You're doing your job, and you're helping me do mine."

Obviously that minute or so really perked me up. And I've always remembered it, because he didn't have to do that. He was just that considerate and wanted the people who worked for him to know he recognized and appreciated their effort.

Operation Switch: President Reagan was not only considerate to the people who worked for him, he was every bit as considerate of virtual strangers. And as a staffer, that could catch you off-guard. While I was Political Director of the White House, a lot of Democrat elected officials switched to the GOP. A couple of times the President had events for the "switchers" at the White House, sponsored by the Republican National Committee. During the last of those, I was reminded of one of the reasons I loved Ronald Reagan.

There were thirty or forty party switchers invited to what amounted to a "clean up" event, as none of them had been able to come to the White House previously. So it was informal, with an appearance by the President in the Roosevelt Room to meet everyone, have a picture with each one and some brief remarks. The "switchers" then went out of the West Wing and did interviews with the media.

Nothing complicated here, but I was in charge.

We didn't take the big conference table out of the Roosevelt Room; we just moved it to the side, against the wall and put the chairs aside, too. The truth was, it was pretty crowded in there; but there was no way this large a group could be anywhere else. And they were in place before 1:00 for an event that started at 1:30 pm.

As the guests, some White House staffers and I stood around talking in the crammed full room, Jim Kuhn, the President's personal aide, came into the room and motioned for me to walk over. It was about ten after one, but when I got over to Jim, he said, "Let's start."

"Jim," I said, "We're not supposed to start until 1:30. It's only 1:10."

"No," Kuhn said, "We need to start."

"I don't even have a photographer here yet, Jim," I blurted out, "because we've got about twenty minutes according to the schedule."

Kuhn looked straight at me and said, "Haley, the President says 'Start.'"

Totally rattled, since scheduled events never started early at the Reagan White House, I said, "Give me two minutes to get a photographer up here. We're going, we're going."

I sent a staffer down to the White House photographer's office, and she ran into the photographer on the stairs, coming up. The video crew was just arriving as well.

Composing myself, I asked all the guests and staff to clear the doorway to the hall across from the Oval Office. Everybody got quiet. A few seconds later Kuhn stuck his head back in the Roosevelt Room door, nodded to me and turned around.

Within seconds the President crossed the hall and entered the crowded room to enthusiastic applause, smiling and shaking hands. He worked the crowd for a few minutes, and then the photos were taken in front of the mantle where Theodore Roosevelt's Nobel Peace Prize sits. He made a few minutes of remarks to the group, welcoming them to the Republican Party and telling how he, too, had been a party switcher.

It was a very special event for these elected officials who had made the switch and now were in the White House with the man who was the main reason most, if not all, of them had changed parties. Obviously, it was a wonderfully upbeat little crowd, but I was still agitated about what had happened, and why.

Soon we got all the "switchers" into the driveway, north of the West Wing, where they were being interviewed by a large number of reporters, including several who had come to Washington from the home area of one or another of the switchers to get the interview at the White House.

For me I confess to being impatient. As soon as the group left, I made a "bee line" to Jim Kuhn's little office off the Oval. I went in and said, "Jim, what in the world? I've never seen us start early, much less twenty minutes early."

Instead of pushing back, Jim laughed. He said, "The President was coming back from lunch in the Residence. When he got here, he saw the crowd of people packed in the Roosevelt Room and said, 'Jim, who are all those people?'

"I told him, and he never hesitated. He said, 'Jim, look how uncomfortable those people must be, standing up in that crowded room. I need to go on in there and not make them have to keep waiting.'"

Jim laughed and said, "Haley, you're lucky I got him to let

me tell you so you could get ready. He started to walk in the door without even telling anybody else."

That's the Ronald Reagan I admired and loved; being so considerate of a bunch of people he didn't even know that he disregarded the schedule and the staff preparations in order to be thoughtful and courteous of his guests.

Reagan's last public event in Washington, DC: After I was elected Chairman of the Republican National Committee in January, 1993, I went to California, and President Reagan graciously made time for me to visit him at his office in Century City.

My goal was to get him more involved in the RNC's efforts; but having been Political Director of the White House for the 1986 election cycle during his second term, I knew he wouldn't aggressively criticize the new president (Bill Clinton). So I asked him to help the RNC rebuild its small donor fundraising base, which was a stated goal in my plan for RNC Chairman. I explained to him that the RNC had more than one million donors in 1986, when I was with him at the White House; in 1992, however, the RNC had only 400,000 donors.

After twelve years in the White House, the Republican Party had become too reliant on big donors. With a Democrat in the White House, a lot of these big donors would reduce their contributions or not give to the RNC at all. Even though the RNC had raised a record amount (about $70 million) in 1992, the President agreed we needed a much broader donor base.

Over the course of the year he signed fundraising appeals that we sent mainly to small donors, especially those who hadn't given in the last year or two.

It worked. In 1993 the RNC had one million, two hundred thousand donors (1,200,000), triple the number of givers as in 1992; and we raised a record of $158,000,000 for the Committee, which was critical in helping save our new majorities in the Senate and House, as well as increasing the number of GOP governors to

31, where we had only 17 when I met with the President in Los Angeles that day.

In occasional phone conversations through the year, I could tell the President was pleased with the results, and I started thinking about how to ramp up his activity for 1994.

My first year as Chairman, 1993, was highly successful. The GOP elected Kay Bailey Hutchison as Senator from Texas; Mike Huckabee as Lt. Governor of President Clinton's home state of Arkansas; Dick Riordan, Mayor of Los Angeles; Rudy Giuliani, Mayor of New York City; Christy Todd Whitman, Governor of New Jersey; and George Allen, Governor of Virginia.

Things were looking up after a miserable performance in 1992, and there was a lot of optimism about further gains in 1994 (though I confess nobody thought at this stage it would be the tsunami that ensued.) The President seemed ready to do more.

Working through Fred Ryan, who had been President Reagan's scheduler when I was in the White House, I suggested to the President and Mrs. Reagan that the Republican Party was ready for a major event, that only he could headline. (At this point—late 1993 —President George H. W. Bush felt, correctly, it was too early for him to be doing public political events.)

Fred and I talked back and forth, and it *developed* we could get Margaret Thatcher to keynote this proposed event. We could do it as a giant birthday party honoring President Reagan. Slowly but surely Fred brought Mrs. Reagan around, and finally she agreed. Deep down I thought the President was dying to do it the whole time, but the Mrs. had to sign off. I'll never forget Fred's call to me, saying the event was approved. He said, "Haley, just know if anything goes wrong with this, Mrs. Reagan will never forget it. She is looking to you personally to make sure this isn't an embarrassment."

Talk about pressure, but I knew this could be a homerun; and it was.

On February 6, 1994, the President's 83$^{rd}$ birthday, some 2,200 of the faithful gathered at The National Building Museum (often referred to as The Pension Building) in Washington for a black tie gala, paying at least $1,000 each to be part of what turned out to be Reagan's last public event in D.C.

It was such a success we had to set up tables on the second and third floor balconies, raising some $2.5 million in the process.

As importantly, it was a hotbed of enthusiasm for the fall elections. People were starting to believe in the GOP again, and what a night to manifest that energy and optimism…with the two leaders of The Free World, who had brought down the Soviet Union and led an economic renaissance that not only brought renewed prosperity to their own economies but lifted hundreds of millions of people out of poverty across the globe.

It was a great day as well as evening. Several GOP groups had events in the city prior to the receptions that preceded the dinner itself. President and Mrs. Reagan attended two different receptions in the hall with Prime Minister Thatcher and her husband Denis in tow.

After many handshakes and photos, the main event began. As Chairman I got to be Emcee. I did have sense enough not to talk long.

Prime Minister Thatcher was magnificent, spell-binding. Everybody in the hall was familiar with her and her record, but few had ever heard her make a speech. She set a mighty high bar for the President.

As everyone would have expected, the President rose to the occasion; but there was a moment when my heart sank. President Reagan approached the podium, with multiple nods and "Thank yous." All as it should be.

Then he began his speech smoothly and comfortably.

All of a sudden he stopped, seemed like in mid-sentence. He seemed lost and confused, and then I saw he was reaching into his coat pockets, trying to find his speech cards.

"Oh (expletive deleted)," I thought. "The teleprompter's not working. What a screw up!"

I started looking for the advance man in charge, to see what had happened. We had checked all the equipment time and again, including the teleprompter that very evening. Before I could get out of the chair, Reagan started talking again...picked back up right where he left off. He got back in stride quickly, and soon was in perfect pitch timing and tone. Vintage Reagan. He peeled the paint off the walls.

Thirty minutes or so later the crowd was delivering its final standing ovation, after repeated interruptions of his great speech with thunderous applause and warm laughter. Reagan of yore!

About halfway through the speech, I conjured up enough courage to sneak a peek at Mrs. Reagan. She wasn't even staring at me, praise God.

When the event was over, and Marsha and I bid the President and Mrs. Reagan as well as the Thatchers adieu; the Mrs. was friendly and clearly thought the event was a positive for the Reagan legacy, and he seemed to have had a good time, seeing a lot of old friends.

The glitch or pause or whatever one terms the longest fifteen or twenty seconds of my life was not a mechanical or technological problem: The teleprompter operator, a Reagan devotee, was so excited as the President began his speech, he failed to turn on the teleprompter, so the speech did not roll across the panes. Another staffer grabbed him, and he started it after the brief, but terrifying pause.

It was a spectacular GOP night, made so by Ronald Reagan, as was so often the case. And it kicked off a spectacular GOP year. Republicans won a majority in the United States House of Representatives for the first time in 40 years, gaining fifty-four seats, including two in spring special elections. The GOP regained its Senate majority, lost in 1986. We also got up to 30 governors and won majorities in a number of state legislative chambers.

Three days before the election, President Reagan sent a farewell letter to the American people, November 5, announcing he had Alzheimer's disease.

Nine days later he sent me a note, to convey his pleasure and congratulations on the election outcome. Remember, he never had a GOP majority in the House during his entire presidency.

Dear Haley,

Congratulations on a great job for the Republican Party. I couldn't be happier with the results of the election. And please don't count me out! I'll be putting in my licks for Republicans as long as I'm able.

Sincerely,

Ronald Reagan

According to Kiron Skinner, Annelise Anderson and Marty Anderson in their book, *Reagan: A Life in Letters*, (Free Press, 2004) this was the last personal letter President Reagan would ever write.

*Haley Barbour served as Chairman, Republican National Committee 1993-1997 and was the 62nd Governor of Mississippi 2004-2012.*

# 55

# BECKY NORTON DUNLOP
### Deputy Assistant for Presidential Personnel 1981-1985

1984. It was a personnel meeting with the president on a day between the first and second debate with Democrat presidential candidate Walter Mondale. Circumstances of staff conflicts and the President's own schedule brought me to the weekly meeting with the president by myself. He had just returned that afternoon from a trip, and he asked that I bring the paperwork to him in the family quarters, rather than to the Oval Office.

I was escorted up the private elevator by the usher, and when I stepped out into the foyer, I was greeted by the president at what he called his "front door." He then ushered me to his private office—I quickly saw that I was in an office that was well and frequently used. Legal pads, pens and pencils were at the ready and a stack of books was on the desk. It was quite a contrast to the Oval Office desk—yes, he worked at that desk daily, but when he finished each day the desktop was clear.

Well, I wasn't there to gawk, so I got down to work.. Every week, the president is appointing someone—often, many "someones"—to major positions in the administration. In the 1980s, about 3000 were full-time and thousands more were part-time memberships on boards or commissions. Appointees come and go, so a president's work in this personnel area is never really done.

The routine: the Presidential Personnel Office interviews, clears, and recommends candidates to the troika of Meese, Deaver, and

Baker, who then pass along the top candidates to the President. Every Thursday, senior personnel officers meet with President Reagan to go over the nominees and record his decisions.

This week—at this meeting—I reviewed a rather short list of candidates—the jobs for which they were being considered, their resumes, and any other pertinent information. He asked some questions, considered my answers, and made his decisions. I was ready to take my leave but he asked another question: "Becky, have you ever seen the family quarters?"

"No, sir," I replied.

"Well," he responded, "I have a few minutes to spare. Let me give you a tour." The Reagan family living room with their furniture from California, the small dining room, the exercise room where he worked out daily following his recovery from the assassination attempt. He had stories about each room; for example, at the Lincoln bedroom he had a story about Lyndon Johnson hosting 1952-1956 presidential candidate Adlai Stevenson, a devoted admirer of Lincoln, as his overnight Lincoln bedroom guest.

When we came to the end of the "tour," I stopped and asked the President, might I talk to him about something that was on my mind?

Ever gracious, he said, "Of course."

I knew my time was basically over but I had to get in a few thoughts that were important to me . . . and plunged ahead. "Mr. President, I just want to really encourage you at this next debate to look straight into the camera and just tell us who are watching, your vision for our country. Don't throw out a lot of statistics to defend the work of your administration. We—the American people—trust you, we just want you to tell us where you want to take our nation."

He was listening. "Well," he said, "I actually look at the questioner because I think that is the polite thing to do."

"Mr. President," I said again, "you know best how you want to respond to the questions but I want you to know that all of my friends and I everyone watching just want you to look right at them through that camera."

As we walked back to his "front door," the President of the United States thanked *me* for sharing my thoughts. He promised me he would "look into that camera" and tell *us* where he wanted to take our country. "But," he said, "I am going to look at those reporters, too."

I went back to my office to finish up the personnel work of that day, with my heart moved by his graciousness, his sincerity, and his thoughtful consideration toward me—he actually listened to what I had to say.

In the event—the debate—the President did respond directly to his questioners but he also tried to look the audience in the eye. However, because of the position of the camera, it was a bit awkward. The camera was in front of Walter Mondale, who could look straight into the lens, and off to the side from Reagan, who had to turn to the camera.

There was a government shutdown, November 1981. "Presidential personnel" were considered to be "nonessential," and had to go home. We could not even volunteer (although we would have done so, of course). Before we left our office, I quickly drafted up a little note to present Reagan which was delivered by our boss Helene von Damm. This is the note November 23, 1981, signed by Helene, me, and about 20 members of the staff:

> Mr. President, we the undersigned members of the office of presidential personnel wholeheartedly and enthusiastically support you in this effort to establish a modicum of control over the federal budget. We stand prepared to take whatever action is required in to support your decision on this matter which is so crucial to the future of this country.

We were gratified to receive the following note, passed along by von Damm.

Dear Helene: Will you please tell all who joined you in signing the memo to me November 23 how very grateful I am. Believe me you brightened my day. Heartfelt thanks. Sincerely, Ronald Reagan.

After the president left office, my husband and I went out to California and visited him in his Century City office. We both had held subcabinet positions—George at Agriculture and me at Interior—so we talked about a lot of things, including some reminiscences of those positions.

At one point, we walked over to a window with a beautiful panoramic view from Angeles from Los Angeles to Santa Monica and the Pacific Ocean. The President pointed to a little forested area toward Santa Monica. "See those trees over there, with a blue mist rising above them? See—I was right: trees do pollute!"

*EDITOR'S NOTE: Back in 1981, Reagan was widely criticized for saying, "Trees pollute more than automobiles do." As it turned out, he was not all that far off the mark. As the* Guardian *newspaper noted (13 May 2004) "Environmental scientists ruefully confirmed he was partially right. In hot weather, trees release volatile organic hydrocarbons including terpenes and isoprenes—two molecules linked to photochemical smog. In very hot weather, the production of these begins to accelerate. America's Great Smoky Mountains are supposed to take their name from the photochemical smog released by millions of hectares of hardwoods."*

*Becky Dunlop is a vice president of the Heritage Foundation, Washington D.C.*

# 56

## J. WILLIAM MIDDENDORF II
Ambassador to the OAS 1981-1985
Ambassador to the European Community 1985-1987

n 1964, I was treasurer of the national "Goldwater for President" campaign, and as such was in daily contact with many of our surrogates in the field—including Ronald Reagan, who was co-chair of the California Goldwater campaign. I helped arrange his speaking schedule, wrote checks to cover his expenses, and sent him daily talking points.

Reagan pretty much stayed in California but delivered some one-hundred speeches on Barry Goldwater's behalf. "Speeches" were a large part of Reagan's kit: from 1954-62, he had a contract with General Electric which, among other duties (such as hosting the TV program "GE Theater"), required him to visit GE facilities around the nation at least ten weeks a year, speaking to employees and local civic organizations.

The best speech of the Goldwater campaign—perhaps of any campaign, ever—came on October 27, 1964, when Ronald Reagan stepped in front of a TV camera and onto the national political stage. This appearance was not scheduled or paid for by the Goldwater campaign, but by a group of friends and supporters in California—led by businessman and philanthropist Henry Salvatori—who had collected $100,000 to book the timeslot.

However, the speech almost didn't happen because of irrelevant objections by Goldwater's campaign managers. They told Barry that the speech was unacceptable and proposed using the booked timeslot for a rerun of some useless earlier Goldwater television program (in which he and former president Dwight Eisenhower took turns mumbling and looking uncomfortable). So Barry, accepting the guidance of his team leaders, called Reagan and asked him to step aside, to allow our own program to be run.

Reagan said it wasn't up to him, some other fellows were paying for the time out of their own pockets. Besides, he asked, what was wrong with the speech? Barry said he didn't know—he would have to go and listen to the tape. When he had done so, Barry looked at his campaign team and said, "What the hell's wrong with that?"

The managers would not give up; the speech was inflammatory, it was not "Goldwater," it would turn voters away, whatever. I told Barry quite the opposite: here was a fresh voice speaking truth, we were trailing in the polls, what did we have to lose? Barry agreed and said, "OK, let's go with it!"

I do believe the managers had been goaded by our ad agency, which had already complained to me of what they saw as "an obvious attempt to circumvent" their contract with the campaign, by a newly created "Reagan-Goldwater TV Committee" which was listed as sponsor for the forthcoming broadcast. This nullified the agency's right to claim a commission of perhaps $23,000. Within three hours of airtime, they were still trying to substitute a Goldwater rerun. However, as Reagan told Barry, the program was not being paid for out of the Goldwater campaign budget. The Californians who were funding it insisted that if Reagan didn't get the time, no one would.

The speech was called "A Time for Choosing." It began:

> Thank you, and good evening . . . Unlike most television programs, the performer hasn't been provided with the script. As a matter of fact, I have been permitted to choose my own words and discuss my own ideas regarding the choice that we face in the next few weeks.

A few excerpts:

> This is the issue of this election: whether we believe in our capacity for self-government or whether we abandon the American Revolution and confess that a little intellectual elite in a far distant capital can plan our lives for us better than we can plan them ourselves.

> No government ever voluntarily reduces itself in size, so government programs, once launched, never disappear. Actually, a government bureau is the nearest thing to eternal life we'll ever see on this earth.

> We were told a few days ago by the President [Lyndon Johnson], we must accept a greater government activity in the affairs of the people . . . [Another Democrat] voice says, "The profit motive has become outmoded. It must be replaced by the incentives of the welfare state." Or, "Our traditional system of individual freedom is incapable of solving the complex problems of the 20th century." . . . Another articulate spokesman defines liberalism as "meeting the material needs of the masses through the full power of centralized government"
>
> Well, I, for one, resent it when a representative of the people refers to you and me, the free men and women of this country, as "the masses". . . "The full power of centralized government"? This was the very thing the founding fathers sought to minimize.

> You and I have a rendezvous with destiny. We'll preserve for our children this, the last best hope of man on earth, or we'll sentence them to take the last step into a thousand years of darkness.

The impact was tangible. In one (admittedly limited) telephone-poll just after the speech, fully one-half of "undecided" voters (who made up 32 percent of the sample, just before the speech) had switched to Goldwater. We should have pulled Reagan into the national campaign a couple of months earlier; he might have made a difference.

Well, as the whole world knows, Goldwater lost the election but "A Time for Choosing" launched Reagan's political career. The first "Reagan for President" club was established soon after, and he was elected governor of California in 1966 with a plurality of one million votes.

*Bill Middendorf—who had been Ambassador to The Netherlands 1969-1973 and Secretary of the Navy 1974-1977—also served as Reagan's Ambassador to the European Community, 1985-1987.*

# 57

## PAUL LAXALT

National Chairman, Reagan's Presidential Campaigns 1980 and 1984
General Chairman of the Republican Party 1983-1987

1976. Ronald Reagan had finished his second term as governor of California and was making a run for the Republican presidential nomination against incumbent President Gerald Ford. Ron Reagan and I had long been friends—I had been governor of Nevada while he was so-serving in California, and we had cooperated on a number of cross-state issues—and I now was serving as his National Campaign Chairman.

By early summer, ahead of the Republican convention in Kansas City, each candidate had almost the same number of pledged or "leaning" delegates, somewhere between 900 and 1000. The magic number to assure the nomination was 1030. There were perhaps 100-200 uncommitted delegates. We knew that if the Reagan team could pick up the majority of those delegates, we might just win. Our campaign manager, John Sears—ever the tactician—came up with a brilliant but risky idea: Reagan could attract great media attention by announcing his choice for running mate before the national convention. It might also "freeze" those delegates thinking about siding with President Ford. Further, since some of the uncommitted delegates were from the northeast and generally more moderate in terms of ideology, we decided that it would be wise to select a running mate from that part of the country. Sears suggested Pennsylvania Senator Richard Schweiker.

Of course, I knew and liked Dick Schweiker a great deal—we sat next to each other on the Senate floor—but my first thought was "No way!" I thought that Ron Reagan, who didn't know Dick, would think he was too "liberal"—and might even "go into orbit."

Toward the end of July, John and I met with Dick in my Senate office to offer our proposal. He was, to put it mildly, surprised, but he was willing to consider it, pending a meeting with Reagan. Ron had previously approved the "plan" but to this point had no idea as to whom we would recommend for the slot. John and I flew out to Los Angeles ahead of Dick to brief Ron, particularly with regard to the "liberal" tag that was tied to Dick. Dick did have a pro-labor voting record, but that was understandable since he represented a state in which organized labor was a very strong force. And, after all, Ron had been the head of a union himself—the Screen Actor's Guild.

My apprehension vanished the moment Ron and Dick met; the chemistry could not have been better. They discovered that they were in basic agreement on many important issues, including fiscal discipline, national security, gun control, and the federal-state division of power. They had a deal.

The next step for me was to travel back to Washington and make the public announcement which I did in the Senate Caucus Room. It came as such a surprise—there had been absolutely no leaks—that the reporters could think of no difficult or contentious questions to ask.

Then I had to have some difficult "discussions" with some of my fellow Republicans, especially those from the more conservative Deep South who were not particularly pleased with the choice. However, they backed off after I explained our strategy, pointing out that we simply couldn't compete with the White House PR-apparatus, which was wooing delegates with rides on Air Force One and visits to the Oval Office.

Interestingly, our polling data showed that any time President Ford was matched with a potential running-mate, any of several possibilities, he would lose votes. Our new goal: to compel Ford to announce his running-mate in advance of the nomination.

This would require an "adjustment" in the governing rules of the convention, specifically Rule 16C which provided that the nomination of the vice presidential candidate would come *after* the presidential nomination. The rule could be changed by a majority vote of the delegates. Should we try? There was deep disagreement within our camp. But we eventually concluded that we had nothing to lose and really had no alternative. Ron agreed, and that was that.

As we began to court the various delegations, the excitement among the media was palpable—actual news was being created, and we were making progress. (I should add that this was the last convention where the candidates actually were battling it out for the nomination. Every convention since has been little more than a coronation and a television extravaganza.)

In the end, it all came down to the Mississippi delegation, many of whom supported Reagan, but many others could not accept the "too-liberal" Schweiker. The final Mississippi delegation vote: 31 against, 28 in favor. We had lost—by three measly votes.

It was now 24 hours from the nomination, and we had run out of ideas. Perhaps make another run on Mississippi? As we sat around gloomily in a hotel suite, Dick Schweiker suddenly came into the meeting. He said, in essence, that he knew he was the problem, and he offered to call a press conference to announce that he was withdrawing from the ticket.

Ron's reaction was immediate and unwavering. "Dick," he said, "we came into this together, and we're going out together." As Ron told some members of the press later that morning, he regarded his commitment to Dick to be a matter of principle. And so it was. Looking back, I've often wondered how many politicians would have reacted as Ronald Reagan did. It would have been easy to say, "Circumstances have changed" and then agree to Schweiker's offer. But that was not Ron Reagan's style. He was pure class. It was one of many reasons I was so proud to call myself a "Reaganaut."

Ron had previously asked me to place his name in nomination. I had been so busy trying to round up delegates that I hadn't had time to prepare my speech. So I wung it! In the end, it probably didn't matter what I said because the Reagan partisans in the arena were so fired up that every pro-Reagan statement that I uttered came close to bringing down the house!

The next night, after delivering his acceptance speech, President Ford graciously asked Ron to come up to the podium and say a few remarks. Ron was reluctant at first, but he finally acquiesced. Amazingly, off the cuff, he proceeded to deliver one of his most memorable speeches. As he concluded his remarks, a warm and thunderous ovation shook the arena. I remember thinking, contrary to the conventional wisdom at the time, that Ronald Reagan's political career was anything but finished.

*The final delegate count: Ford, 1087, Reagan 1070. Ford lost the general election to Democrat Jimmy Carter, who pulled 50.1 percent of the vote. Senator Laxalt went on to serve as Ronald Reagan's campaign chairman in the successful elections of 1980 and 1984.*

*Dick Schweiker served as Reagan's Secretary of Health and Human Services, 1981-1983.*

*Portions of Reagan's "concession" speech will be found on page 292.*

# 58

## BARBARA HAYWARD
### Personal Secretary to the Vice President

President Reagan really connected with people no matter who they were or where he went. On the first day I worked in the White House . . . I guess it was the first day for a lot of us . . . Reagan was walking around the halls, greeting people, and there I was in the vice president's office when the President walked in, unannounced and unexpected. He was carrying a tape measure that some high-ranking visitor—I don't know who—had just given him.

He said, without preamble, "I just received this measuring tape as a gift and I'd sure like to use it. Is there anything you'd like me to measure for you?"

Caught off-guard, I could only say, "Well, Mr. President, we're just getting set up here, I could get back to you later."

And he burst out laughing!

My brother and his wife came over from England, and the President wanted to meet them, so we set up an Oval Office visit. Now, you need to understand, my brother was the biggest English liberal you can imagine and he wasn't all that thrilled with the idea of meeting President Reagan. Well, nonetheless, I took them in and in a matter of moments he and the President were telling jokes, laughing, and getting along famously.

When the visit was over, the first thing my brother—who was his own man, you know, not a pushover by any manner of means—said to me, "I would vote for that man!"

*Barbara Hayward also served as assistant to Chiefs of Staff Jim Baker and Don Regan, and as Associate Director for Political Affairs.*

# 59

## EDWIN HARPER

Assistant to the President and Deputy Director of the Office of
Management and Budget 1981-1982
Assistant to the President for Domestic Policy Development 1982-1983

A couple of years into the Administration the President decided to have Monday Policy Lunches. They were held in the Cabinet Room every Monday when he was in town.

The Invitees included of course Meese, Baker and Deaver as well as the head of National Security Affairs (Bill Clark) and the head of Domestic Policy (yours truly) and Dave Gergen representing the Press Office.

The discussions were freewheeling and one could raise any topic they thought worthy of the President's time. For example, Japanese competitiveness was much talked of at the time. I showed a video of a Japanese machine tool plant that operated 24 hours a day, run by robots. As I suspected the President was very interested because of all of the exposure he had had to U.S. manufacturing in his work for General Electric touring their plants.

The President's Commission on Industrial Competitiveness was created as a result if this luncheon.

The lunches were served by the White House Mess Staff. The cabinet table was a beautiful specially made table by Kittinger and was, I believe, a gift to the White House by President Nixon. To protect the table's wood finish, place mats were put in front of each participant, on which were placed the plates and silverware. The iced tea glasses, which were fairly tall stemware, were also put on the place mats.

One day as I was speaking the unthinkable happened. My iced tea glass turned over, spilling all over the elegant table. In an instant all eyes focused on the pool of iced tea in front of me and then shot down the table to see what the President's reaction would be to my gaffe.

Without hesitation and with a big smile he reared back and threw his napkin to me. Immediately everyone else around the table did the same thing. After a brief laugh everyone went on with the discussion.

One more reason I thought Ronald Reagan was a great man. He did not worry about the small stuff but kept focused on the important issues of the day.

# 60

## GALE NORTON

Assistant to Deputy Secretary of Agriculture 1984-1985
Associate Solicitor of Interior 1985-1987

Ronald Reagan's inspiring vision permeated throughout his Administration in a way that no other modern leader has equaled. I was one of those in the lower levels of the Reagan Administration whose lives were affected by his leadership.

Every year the Administration held a "pep rally" for political appointees. One year I had a prior commitment that I knew would run late, and I would have little time before the gathering of 3000 people in Constitution Hall. I asked some of my friends in the Department of the Interior to save me a seat. They complied beautifully, and I ended up seated dead center, directly in front of the podium, in the first row of the balcony. From that marvelous vantage point, I could see not only the speakers, but also the multitude of enthusiastic political appointees.

Ed Meese and other opening speakers set the mood, preparing for the masterful performance by President Reagan. When the great man finally took the stage, he spoke with warmth, humor, and sincerity. I felt he was speaking directly to me, and all of us were spellbound. The president's message reminded each of us why we had devoted years of our lives, uprooting our careers, moving to Washington, trying to change the course of history. He gave us the ammunition to keep fighting our daily battles against bureaucracy and excessive regulation. He spoke in a heartfelt way about the importance of freedom and the greatness of America.

The Reagan administration served as a training ground for so many of my generation of political appointees. We understood and adopted, in a very deep way, Ronald Reagan's mission to rescue the American ideal. It became our own personal mission as well.

My friends from the administration became trusted allies, and we often had occasions to work together over the years. When I became Pres. George W. Bush's Secretary of the Interior, I was able to recruit several of those people to work in my department. I knew that they could draw upon the lessons we learned during the Reagan Administration and that we had a shared understanding of our goals. The network of Reagan appointees was bound not just by friendship, but by the enduring vision instilled by Ronald Reagan.

I had occasion to meet President Reagan personally, but it is always the Constitution Hall gathering that continues to endure in my mind. On so many other days, he shaped history. On that day, he shaped lives and inspired future leaders.

*Ms. Norton later served as Secretary of the Interior, 2001-2006.*

## 61

## KARNA SMALL BODMAN
White House Senior Deputy Press Secretary
Senior Director National Security Council 1981-1986

It was January 21, 2001—the "first day of business" in the Reagan White House. I was standing in front of Press Secretary Jim Brady's desk in the West Wing press office. I was his Deputy at the time. Jim turned to me and said that he had an idea for the "first story" of the day and asked me to go down to the press room and escort the reporters from the three magazines and their photographers up to his office.

So I went down and found the correspondents for *Time, Newsweek,* and *US News and World Report* along with their photographers and we all trooped back upstairs. Jim was standing there with about a dozen pages from a legal sized tablet in his hand. He fanned them out on the floor—like a bridge hand—and said, "OK, take a picture."

The photographers kneeled down and focused their cameras. No one knew what was on the pages filled with handwriting. Then Jim explained. "You are looking at President Reagan's draft of his Inaugural Address."

Jim's point, of course, was to dispel any notion that President Reagan was "a Hollywood actor who was always handed a script." No, these pages were a perfect example of Reagan's ideas, philosophies and dreams for our country as he outlined them the day before on Inauguration Day.

The Cabinet meeting convened. The subject was butter! Due to excessive farm price controls which would be difficult to reduce in a Democratic Congress, we had an excess supply of some 400 million pounds of butter stored throughout the country in warehouses, even caves and caverns. OMB Director David Stockman suggested selling half of it on the world market and putting the proceeds toward reducing the deficit. The Secretary of State countered that the world price was about a dollar a pound and the Soviets would be first to buy it. "How could we explain to the American housewife that the Soviets were getting cheap butter when the subsidized price here is about two dollars a pound?"

The President turned to Defense Secretary Cap Weinberger, "Couldn't the troops use more butter?" "No sir," Cap replied. We've got all we can handle." To Terrence Bell, the Secretary of Education, Reagan asked, "What about the school lunch program?" "Sorry," Terry said, "Can't use any more there either."

The President suggested giving it to African countries suffering from famine or malnutrition but the Trade Representative explained that we were working with those countries to develop their own dairy industries, and if we flooded their markets with cheap or free butter, it would wipe them out.

The President thought for a moment and said, "To get the attention of the Congress so they'll fix this ridiculous price support system, how about staging a photo op and dumping some of it in the ocean?" At this point, The Secretary of the Interior replied, "Sorry, Mr. President. That would cause a huge environmental mess. I get your point, but we just can't do that."

The President leaned back and mused, "We can't use it. We can't sell it. We can't give it away and we can't get Congress to change the rules." He turned to Advisor Ed Meese and quipped, "Four hundred million pounds of butter. Does anyone know where we can get four hundred million pounds of popcorn?" With that, he shook his head and walked out of the room.

# 62

## JAMES HOOLEY
Assistant to the President, Director of the Presidential Advance Office
1981-1981

One of the many great privileges accorded me as Director of the Presidential Advance Office was to be in close proximity to the President virtually every day, sometimes several times per day. This is because, in addition to designing and creating his public events, it was also my responsibility to brief him beforehand on the structure and theme of those events. These events ranged from overseas summits to domestic rallies, from factory tours to simple Rose Garden events. And I would accompany him through the events to act as the liaison between the advance staff and the President and his body man.

I was constantly struck by the President's keen self-awareness, always acting naturally and being totally true to himself; never trying to convince people that he was something he wasn't, the way it seemed Richard Nixon, Jimmy Carter, and others seemed to do. And one of the things that just came naturally to him was an instinctive ability to make people feel comfortable in his presence. He had to be keenly aware that most people tense up and feel awed when meeting a president. Yet, with a few kind words and perhaps an anecdote or two, he would get them to relax and feel comfortable.

He was also very humble, never acting like being President was anything less than a great honor bestowed on him by the people. In fact, he would express amazement that huge crowds would line his motorcade routes, some having waited hours with chairs, coolers and American flags, for a chance to see him as he travelled. And in response, he made sure to wave to every one of those people, often regardless of who was riding in the car with him. He would apologize to the governor, mayor, or other guest and explain that they should not take offense that he was turned away from them, toward the window. He was listening to them, he would tell them, but "those people wait out there to see me and I want to make sure they know that *I* see *them*."

He just didn't seem to see himself as the mythic, heroic figure that America saw. I recall one night early in his first term, when Senator Mark Hatfield hosted a dinner for the Reagans at his house in Georgetown, with about six Pulitzer Prize-winning historians, all of whom had written biographies of previous presidents, as the guests. Hatfield's goal was to instill in the President a sense of responsibility to future historians to be able to know what he was thinking, why he made certain decisions, what bearing the responsibility of being the leader of the free world was really like.

As I listened from the next room to the fascinating conversation, it became evident that President Reagan didn't put himself with the lionized subjects of the dinner guests' biographies: Jefferson, Lincoln, the Roosevelts, etc. For example, they were emphasizing the importance of keeping a diary to record his observations on the people and events around him every day. "Mr. President," one of them said, "just imagine if we had Lincoln's diary today! How much better we would know the real Lincoln!"

President Reagan's response was to express surprise that anyone would want to know his most intimate thoughts. It seemed he didn't think of himself as the "linear heir," as Charlton Heston once put it to him, of Washington, Jefferson, Lincoln, etc. (I might note here that the result of this discussion was the retaining of Edmund Morris, who had written "The Rise of Theodore Roosevelt" a few years earlier, as an "imbedded" biographer in the Reagan White House; and we all know how *that* turned out).

His humility would often be expressed in humor. I recall a backstage meeting with the senior faculty and administration of an Ivy League school, just prior to a commencement address. One of the smug and famously liberal academicians made too obvious a point of how honored the President should be to receive an honorary degree from such a prestigious school. President Reagan, I think mildly annoyed and tired of this arrogant self-proclaimed intellectual, said—with a twinkle in his eye and a wink toward us—"Gee, I never thought about it, but who knows how far I might have gone if I had gone to school here." I tried to contain my laughter and it came out through my nose!

There are so many stories that highlight his sense of responsibility to make others comfortable in his presence, but let me tell one more:

We were in a holding area off a gymnasium at Bowling Green State University waiting for the moment to go out into a huge rally during the 1984 re-election campaign. The holding room was actually the men's locker room, so we were literally under the bleachers as a raucous crowd stomped on the bleachers, waved signs, chanted "We Want Reagan" and almost literally brought the house down with their enthusiasm. It was perhaps the loudest, most enthusiastic crowd we had seen during that "Morning In America" campaign.

As we waited backstage for me to get the word from my advance men that the President should enter the arena, the excitement and noise was having an impact on all of us. I can remember feeling the hairs on my arm standing up and getting goose bumps. And I could tell that the others—Secret Service agents, staff, communications team—were having the same reaction. The only one who seemed to be taking it in stride was Ronald Reagan. The area's Congressman, who was going to walk in with the President, was visibly moved by the noise and the thunderous stomping on the bleachers. Finally, when it seemed like the crowd would come inside and carry the President out if he didn't come out on his own, I got the word and signaled the bandmaster to break into "Ruffles and Flourishes"(Ta-

ta-ta-ta-ta-ta-TAH! Ta-ta-ta-ta-ta-ta-TAH!) and on the first notes, the crowd went absolutely berserk! Pandemonium! Screaming adoration! The congressman was over the moon now; never had he been in such a wild scene. And President Reagan calmly turned to him, took a gentle hold on his arm, and said with a smile and a wink, "C'mon, Honey, they're playing our song!"—and out into a clamorous reception they walked together.

# 63

# JOHN S. HERRINGTON
Secretary of Energy 1985-1989

n one of my earlier postings, I was working as Director of Presidential Personnel—a job full of detail. In any given Administration, there are about 10,000 appointments—not just to cabinet, sub-cabinet, and senior staff positions but for judges, ambassadors, members of boards and commissions, and so forth. Some could be handled at the staff-level, but any senior, significant, or sensitive choice had to be made by the President.

Every Wednesday, the Personnel staff would meet to finalize the latest presentations for the President—we assembled data on the vetted candidates for his consideration (and there were often more than one for any given position). Then, we would meet with the President every Thursday afternoon; he would make his selections and sign the appointment documents.

At one Wednesday meeting, I think the "appointment" calendar was a bit thin, and we got into a friendly argument: what was the greatest Western movie ever made? Everyone had a favorite: Marlon Brando's "One-Eyed Jacks," or "Stagecoach" with John Wayne, or "Shane" with Alan Ladd. Since we could not agree, we decided to let the President make the decision during the next-day's personnel meeting.

Thus, after we finished our business that day, I posed the question and gave him the choices. He said, "Oh, no, no, John. The greatest Western movie is 'Red River' with Montgomery Clift and

John Wayne—clearly, the greatest Western ever made." I was a bit embarrassed, as that was one that we had not even considered.

But my embarrassment was quickly superseded.

Background: earlier that day, one of my young assistants, who had not yet met the President, asked, might she come along for the Thursday meeting? Sure, why not? There was nothing hyper-sensitive on the schedule and this would certainly be good opportunity for her—a hard-working but rather shy, straight-laced, devout Christian young lady.

Thus, imagine my surprise when just at this moment, she spoke out: "Mr. President did you really kiss all those women in all those movies?"

"Oh," he said. "We did it a different way. These were not the slobbery long kisses you see on television today and in the movies. It was much different. Here, stand up and I will show you."

So he got up from behind his desk and walked over to my assistant. She had gotten to her feet but was clearly very nervous. Reagan continued, "We did not kiss on the lips, we kissed on the cheek because it gave a better camera angle." He turned to me and said, "John, you pretend you're a camera and you get over here look at look at us . . . and you will see what I mean."

He took the young lady in his arms and kissed her on the cheek. Of course, by this time she had turned brilliant red and her legs were shaking. The president said, "Now, you see how it works?"

And I had to acknowledge, the "camera angle" was perfect.. And my young assistant survived . . . she probably could have made it on the silver screen!

We were at a cabinet meeting. The issue: should we control the export of raw logs from the state of Washington to Japan? It was one of the most contentious Cabinet meetings I had ever attended. Everyone had a passionate position—the Interior Department, the Labor Department, the Trade Representative, the Department of Defense (some of the wood was being used to build housing for U.S.

military personnel stationed in Japan). Few of them agreed with any other. What were the ramifications—should we be shipping vast quantities of raw materials overseas? But our troops needed housing. What about the issue of jobs in the Northwest. And—for that matter, what about the financial sector, the shipping companies? Each participant came prepared with talking points and the arguments might have gone on forever (or, at least until the scheduled hour was up) and the President finally said, "Thank you, very much"

He stood up, and we thought the meeting was over. Then, one of the cabinet officers couldn't stand it anymore. He asked, "Mr. President what do you think?

He sat back down, and said, "Well, I didn't hear the one thing that I wanted to hear." Everyone leaned forward, thinking, I am sure, 'My God, we have given him the economics, the environmental and foreign-policy issues, what is left?'

He said, "I was waiting to hear, if I decide one way or the other on this matter, what effect does this have on the price of houses for young couples starting a family?"

Oh, wow! We all knew that this should have been the issue, but nobody had even thought about it. The president added, "If anybody has any additional information on this I'd like to have it." And the meeting was adjourned.

Does the term "laser focus" have any meaning to you? Everyone went off to ponder. In the end, after several more meetings, a reasonable compromised was reached . . . and the President's policy-makers had learned an important lesson.

*John Herrington is currently a real estate developer and attorney in California. In addition, along with some other Reagan alumni and T. Boone Pickens, he is working with Clean Energy Fuels of North America to encourage the United States to become less dependent on foreign oil. Clean Energy is building the American Natural Gas Highway from coast to coast and border to border along with converting American trucking to natural gas instead of diesel fuel.*

# 64

## STANLEY SPORKIN
### General Counsel, Central Intelligence Agency (CIA) 1981-1985

There I was sitting at my desk at the CIA's General Counsel satellite office when I heard my secretary, Sue Nolen, who was on the phone, interrupting her call to respond to a new call with the following: "Hello, could you please hold on . . . . aah . . . what did you say . . . The White House is calling . . . Who in the White House is calling . . . . Did you say the President . . . ? One moment please." At that point, my secretary excitedly told me the President wanted to speak to me. She said she did not know what it was about. I replied that I thought someone was playing a practical joke on us. I nevertheless picked up the phone and played it straight. I said, "Hello, Mr. President."

The President said, "I called to ask whether you would be willing to serve as a judge on the United States District Court for the District of Columbia. I said, "Of course, it would be my pleasure" and thanked the President for the trust he was placing in me. He told me that the Attorney General's office would be contacting me to advise me on the next step in the process. There was another thank you and as the call ended, I felt that someone had to pinch me to make sure that I had not dreamed of what just happened. This was my dream job. My father had been a judge in Philadelphia for some thirty years and more than anything else, I had aspired to be appointed to the bench. While I had other experiences where President Reagan had a deep involvement, there is nothing that in any way, came close to this call from him.

I later learned that he was focused on appointees who adhered to Constitutional principles . . . and that it was his practice to call each, to offer congratulations.

With that one call, President Reagan not only made my day but also my entire career. I am forever indebted to President Reagan.

## KENNETH W. DAM
### Deputy Secretary of State 1982-1985

n 1984 or 1985 I attended a meeting chaired by President Reagan in a small White House room in the NSC area. (The Situation Room was in use for a larger interagency meeting.) I was substituting for Secretary of State George Shultz, who was out of town. Also present were Secretary of Defense Cap Weinberger and General Vernon Walters, whom the President used as a personal roving envoy. (Bill Casey, CIA Director, must have been there, though I do not recall specifically, and I do not recall who was there from the NSC staff.)

The problem before us was especially close to the President's heart as a former radio broadcaster of baseball games. The U.S. was about to launch Radio Marti aimed at Cuba, and the fear was that Cuba would retaliate by jamming the radio broadcasts of baseball games in the Eastern U.S., as they were quite capable of doing. The meeting was as contentious as any NSC meeting that I can recall, because the domestic political pressure to launch Radio Marti was intense, but the President certainly did not want domestic baseball games to be jammed.

President Reagan, who expected and appreciated well-run, orderly meetings, walked out of the meeting with me, grabbed my arm, and whispered in my ear: "This was the worst meeting I have ever been in."

# FRANK KEATING
## Associate Attorney General 1981-1983

He could tell a good story. During the second term of Ronald Reagan's presidency, I was in the Roosevelt Room chairing a group of federal law enforcement leaders from throughout the administration. I was still serving as Assistant Secretary of the Treasury for Enforcement, which assured that my direct reports, (the Director of the U.S. Secret Service, the Director of the Bureau of Alcohol, Tobacco and Firearms and the Commissioner of U.S. Customs) were in attendance. Also there were the heads of the FBI, the DEA, and the Marshal's Service. I don't recall the purpose of the meeting or what was said. I expect that Secret Service Director John Simpson thought that it would be dull so he invited President Reagan to step the few feet from the Oval Office to say hello.

We were in the midst of our discussion when the door opened. Reagan entered. To no one's surprise, he was lively and gracious.

"I didn't mean to disturb you fellas, but I have a confession to make. The first time that I had a run-in with law enforcement was as a boy in Dixon (Illinois). Several of us were hidden on a railroad overpass. When the trains came through we would throw stones on their roofs. You could hear them ping and pop as they hit the train. I don't think that we hurt anything, but we were having such fun that we didn't notice the cops sneaking up on our hiding place. Imagine our terror when they sprang on us. There was hell to pay at home but at least we didn't go to jail. I'm glad that it didn't get out during the campaign!"

*Keating served as the 25th Governor of Oklahoma, 1995-2003.*

## ANTHONY R. DOLAN
### Chief Speechwriter 1981-1989

Four Little Words. Ronald Reagan would embarrass himself and the country by asking Mikhail Gorbachev to tear down the Berlin Wall, which was going to be there for decades. So the National Security Council (NSC) staff and State Department had argued for many weeks to get Reagan's now famous line removed from his June 12, 1987, Berlin speech.

With a fervor and relentlessness I hadn't seen over the prior seven years even during disputes about "the ash-heap of history" or "evil empire," they kept up the pressure until the morning Reagan spoke the line. "Is that what I think it is?" I asked White House communications director Tom Griscom about a cable NSC Advisor Frank Carlucci had been nudging at us across the table during a White House senior staff meeting at the Cipriani Hotel in Venice. (Reagan had been attending a G-8 summit there and would shortly fly to the German capital.) With a shake of his head and a smile, Mr. Griscom confirmed the last-minute plea from State to drop the key sentence.

In the Reagan Library archives, similar documents chronicling the opposition's intensity surface from time to time. I was gratified though not surprised to hear a few years back about one NSC staffer's memo to Deputy National Security Advisor Colin Powell complaining that on multiple occasions, perhaps as many as five or six, I had declined as head of speechwriting—the writer talked about "a heated argument" between us—to remove the offending sentence.

And not only me. Shortly after the speech draft began making its review through the bureaucracy, the speechwriters, as Reagan true-believers, had deployed to do the interpersonal glad-handing that sometimes eases objections to speech passages. The Berlin event for us was the quintessential chance—in front of Communism's most evocative monument—to enunciate the anti-Soviet counterstrategy that Reagan had been putting in place since his first weeks in office.

Well before a draft was circulated, I called the writer who had the assignment, Peter Robinson, and told him I was going to an Oval Office meeting. Shortly before we walked to the West Wing, Peter told me what he wanted in the draft: "Tear down the wall." I pushed back in my chair from my desk and let loose "fantastic, wonderful, great, perfect" and other inadequate exclamations. The Oval Office meeting agenda went quickly, with little chance to pop the question. But the discussion ceased for a moment toward the end, and I crowded in: "Mr. President, it's still very early but we were just wondering if you had any thoughts at all yet on the Berlin speech?"

Pausing for only a moment, Reagan slipped into his imitation of impressionist Rich Little doing his imitation of Ronald Reagan—he made the well-known nod of the head, said the equally familiar "well," and then added in his soft but resonant intonation while lifting his hand and letting it fall: "Tear down the wall."

I had refused to talk to Peter until I was back in my office, such was my excitement. Slamming the door I shouted: "Can you believe it? He said just what you were thinking. He said it himself."

So it was "the president's line" now. And that made it easier, though not dispositively so, for the speechwriting department to fight off objections. But this is where the Berlin address was about more than the killer sentence.

As commentators have noticed, much of the rest of the speech is also memorable, with enduring ideas and stately cadences. Mr. Robinson, a Dartmouth and Oxford graduate, had been mentored in his career by such writer-luminaries as Dartmouth Prof. Jeffrey Hart and William F. Buckley Jr. This pedigree helped him understand how Reagan's own conservatism, while less formally instructed, was powerfully ideational. Closer historical scrutiny of Reagan's writings before the presidency, as well as the extent of his involvement in his presidential speeches, has revealed that he was more than merely a Great Communicator but also a man of ideas, a cerebral president.

And part of Reagan's caring about larger ideas had to do with the nature of his foreign policy and the often overlooked rubrics he adopted. Secretary of Defense Robert Gates has suggested that the Reagan years show that "containment" worked. In fact, Reagan explicitly and repeatedly rejected containment as too accommodationist, saying "containment is not enough."

As part of this strategy, Reagan established offensive-minded, victory-conscious rubrics like "forward strategy for freedom," "not just world peace but world freedom," and "expanding the frontiers of freedom."

Part of this was Reagan's attempt to codify while in office a Cold War narrative developed by the anti-communist conservative movement that formed him over three decades even as he helped form it. That narrative saw liberal notions about how to handle communist regimes as provoking aggression or causing catastrophe: Franklin Roosevelt's Stalin diplomacy, Harry Truman's Marshall mission to China, John Kennedy's offer of a "status quo" to Khrushchev in Vienna, Jimmy Carter's statement that we have an "inordinate fear of communism."

Reagan had the carefully arrived at view that criminal regimes were different, that their whole way of looking at the world was inverted, that they saw acts of conciliation as weakness, and that rather than making nice in return they felt an inner compulsion to exploit this perceived weakness by engaging in more acts of aggression. All this confirmed the criminal mind's abiding conviction in its own omniscience and sovereignty, and its right to rule and victimize others.

Accordingly, Reagan spoke formally and repeatedly of deploying against criminal regimes the one weapon they fear more than military or economic sanction: the publicly-spoken truth about their moral absurdity, their ontological weakness. This was the sort of moral confrontation, as countless dissidents and resisters have noted, that makes these regimes conciliatory, precisely because it heartens those whom they fear most—their own oppressed people. Reagan's understanding that rhetorical confrontation causes geopolitical conciliation led in no small part to the wall's collapse, 1989.

I am visiting in Ronald Reagan's post-presidential offices near Los Angeles. The security is there but unobtrusive, the sun comes into the offices easily and from all sides, and Selina Jackson, an assistant to Reagan chief of staff Fred Ryan, is the single replacement for what were once squads of official photographers. A change in from the White House days.

A photo with the former President is *de rigueur* for visiting former staff members, so Selina does her thing. Then I step aside. Reagan wants a shot of himself next to a painting he has just hung in his office. It is of a horse—skillfully done. The photo will be his gift back, he explains with some delight, to the precocious nine-year-old artist, the daughter of a lady who works in his barbershop.

Which reminds me of Elizabeth. During his first term, Reagan was well down the West Wing driveway when the girl's father, a visitor, yelled, "Mr. President, Elizabeth came to the White House today just to see you." Reagan turned back. Ribbon in her hair, white gloves and pocketbook, holding a stuffed animal, six-year-old Elizabeth looked up. The septuagenarian President looked down. They shook hands. The photographers moved in. For a few moments, the Reagan of the evening news—the cold warrior and budget battler with Congress—faded from view.

Or the teenaged girl at the rally in Missouri. Her ninety-year-old grandfather had heard Reagan was in town and wanted to shake hands with him—couldn't this, she asked straight-forwardedly, be arranged? It seemed simple enough to her; which was sad, because the chances were slim. But Reagan heard about her request and after his speech made his way over. He left and I followed; but before running for the motorcade I stopped for a moment to watch them. I can still see the girl's face.

It wasn't just kids or teenagers, though. Confronted with contending factions within the Administration, all of whom wanted their views represented exclusively, a woefully inexperienced, 33-year-old speechwriter tried in 1981 to produce a draft for Reagan's first major foreign-policy address. He worked long nights. The draft went in. Word came back a day later: the President was writing his own draft. Failure, big time.

The next day I was called to the phone with words that are a fair piece of magic in any White House: "The President wants to speak with you." Reagan wanted to say he appreciated my work and the "many fine things" in the draft, some of which he was keeping. It's just that his view of the speech was different from some other people's. He talked about the pressure of working at the White House. "I hear they had a committee helping you write this." He chuckled.

Awfully nice of you, I said later to my bosses, having the President bolster staff morale with a phone call. One of them told me, in a way that made it clear he was not all that happy with Reagan reaching down to one of his subordinates, "Reagan's calling was Reagan's idea."

The speech, to the graduating class at Notre Dame, which in fact Reagan rewrote entirely, went well. Something I would see happen over the years. When he didn't like the drafts sent him for the "Gang of 17" budget negotiations in 1983, he sat down the day of his nationwide broadcast and—with a visit from the prime minister of someplace squeezed in—rolled his own. Or after the exhausting three days with Gorbachev in Reykjavik, the yellow sheets with the distinctive handwriting came down from the residence for the speech that night. It was better than what we had come up with. This, from the President who was supposed to need imagemakers and scriptwriters to look good.

It was not just the writing. Reagan simply had different ideas from most of his resident geniuses. Particularly the celebrated pragmatists who advised him against most of what worked: Reaganomics—the tax cuts and supply-side theory responsible for the biggest economic boom in history. Not to mention high defense budgets, SDI, the zero-option formula, and, most especially, Reagan's insistence on talking candidly about the Soviets while trying to negotiate with them—the very step that may have caused a legitimacy crisis in the Soviet Union and led to the rise of Gorbachev.

Still, the suggestion that a kind of moral force generated by Reagan's will and words brought about the current crisis of Communism is, for adherents to the conventional wisdom, a long way to go. A thesis obviously needing book-length treatment, which, come to think of it, in something called *Undoing the Evil Empire: How Reagan Won the Cold War*, I am completing.

On the day I visit him, Reagan knows this. But it doesn't come up. As ever, I am more interested in getting him to talk about Hollywood. In the old days on Air Force One, I would ask a question or two and start the stories going. In his office now he has me over by the window, showing me the old 20th Century studio lot. I mention I was at a dinner party given by a former actress, Dani Janssen, and met a fellow named Lew Wasserman, whom I guess he knows of. This amuses Reagan, since Wasserman is the Hollywood demigod who runs the behemoth MCA and was once Reagan's agent. He is off then on Reagan and Wasserman stories and other incidents from the early years, while I am thinking that if somebody doesn't get about thirty or forty hours of this on tape it will be a loss of artful storytelling, if not valuable history.

But there won't be hours of it today; there are other visitors. On the way out, I am telling him again what I have already said several times: how well he looks. This is probably dumb, since one of Reagan's jokes is: "There are three ages of mankind: youth, middle age, and 'gee, you look terrific.'" But I say it again; and he points to the sun pouring in the window and says: "It's California."

Later, I am recounting this to the maitre d' at the Beverly Hills

Hotel Polo Lounge, Nino Osti, and wondering out loud why I made such a fuss about how well Reagan looked. I blurt out: "It's just, you know, I love the guy and it's great to see him so happy"—which, while hardly elegant, would probably also be the sentiment of not a few million other Americans, were they to see him today. It was David Broder, I think, who used to write about the unusual warmth of the crowds that came to see Reagan and the strange profusion of "We love you, Ron" signs.

Which is part of the reason why when I'm asked what I remember most about nine years with Ronald Reagan, it isn't sitting near him and Gorbachev at the Bolshoi Ballet or the fact that he may have led us successfully through one of the epic struggles for human freedom. Mostly I find myself telling the story about Elizabeth, or the teen-aged girl at the Missouri rally, or the phone call to the speechwriter who was so miserable. It's improbable—and corny, of course—but so were Reagan and his era. Which is why when I'm asked what I remember most about him personally, the same words keep popping out: "his kindness."

The Gipper was alive and well and living in California. Mellow out, Mr. President.


*The "Tear Down This Wall" speech begins at page 352.*

*Reagan's speech to the graduating class at Notre Dame will be found at page 309.*

*"Four Little Words" is from the* Wall Street Journal, *November 6, 2009.*

*The "visit" is adapted, with permission, from the November 24, 1989, issue of* National Review.

*Mr. Dolan also served in the George W. Bush administration as special advisor in the offices of the secretary of State and the secretary of Defense.*

# 68

## EDWIN J. FEULNER

Public Delegate to the United Nations
Chairman U.S. Advisory Commission on Public Diplomacy
Consultant to Counselor to the President
Advisor to the Chief of Staff 1982-1987

onday, November 30, 1987 was a very special day for everyone at The Heritage Foundation and especially for the Feulner family. We would be attending a Heritage luncheon at Washington's fabled Willard Hotel where our guest of honor was to be President Ronald Reagan.

As Heritage's president, I was in charge of the luncheon seating plan. So, I used my presidential authority and decided that, as a treat for the family, our children would be seated together with Linda and me and President Reagan at the round center table.

It was a very happy group of Heritage key supporters who gathered that day. The Secret Service motorcade arrived at the side door, I met the President and we passed through the kitchen entrance into one of the anterooms to the ballroom where the President had agreed to greet our guests and pose for the usual "photo op."

After these preliminary activities, we moved into the ballroom where the salad had been preset and the wait staff was unusually attentive even by the Willard's high standards. The President was in a relaxed and friendly mood, and he would make very generous remarks about Heritage, about the work I had recently done for him as a "dollar a year" advisor to Senator Howard Baker, his new Chief of Staff, and about his old friend, Joe Coors, Heritage's founder, who was in the audience.

As we enjoyed the first course, President Reagan engaged our two children, Emily age 14, and our son EJ, age 16, in conversation. He was particularly interested in EJ's soccer and lacrosse teamsatSt. James, his boarding school in rural Maryland. And when EJ told the President that he was the play-by-play announcer for St. James's basketball team, the President recounted his own background as a radio announcer for major league baseball games many years earlier.

The main course was served: a perfectly prepared filet mignon with baked potato and mixed vegetables. We continued our conversation and the President was very engaged with all of us.

After just a few minutes, the President noticed that EJ, "a growing boy of 16," had rapidly devoured his entire steak. President Reagan, conscious of EJ's appetite, and always in control of his own disciplined eating habits, asked EJ, in front of all of us at the table: "EJ would you like to switch plates with me and eat my steak?"

Our son was a bit embarrassed, but only a little bit! He nodded in agreement, and the two discreetly switched plates, much to everyone's delight.

Ronald Reagan's willingness to ignore protocol, and to show personal kindness to a young person, will certainly never be forgotten by our son, our family, or anyone at that table those many years ago. The speech that day is recounted in the collected speeches of President Reagan. It centered on the issue of US-Soviet relations, and he included a strong plea for the pending nomination of Judge Anthony Kennedy to the U.S. Supreme Court.

Some would remember those significant comments. But those of us who saw the human side of Ronald Reagan will remember that lunch for a very different reason.

# 69

## SELWA "LUCKY" ROOSEVELT
### Chief of Protocol 1982-1989

During my seven years as President Reagan's Chief of Protocol, I took hundreds of foreign leaders and VIPs to the Oval Office to meet with him. I saw the empathy and charm he manifested with every visitor—the sensitivity and understanding of various cultures. He also had a great sense of humor, as the following story illustrates:

I escorted the new Ambassador from Saudi Arabia, Prince Bandar, who was young and rather brash, to present his credentials.

The President shook hands with him and said, "Prince Bandar, I remember the first time we met in 1978. You led a Saudi team sent to me, a former governor, to marshal support for the sale of the F-15s to Saudi Arabia. You were then an air force major. You've really come up in the world!"

And Prince Bandar shot right back, "You haven't done so badly yourself, sir. When we first met, you were an unemployed former governor." The President loved it!

I should add: Bandar stayed in the post long enough to become Dean of the Diplomatic Corps and is today head of Saudi intelligence.

I suppose my happiest moment in the Oval Office was when the President sent for me—not with a VIP visitor—but on my own. This was at the end of his first term and many of his appointees were wondering if they would be asked to continue in the second term.

I thought I would probably leave.

When I entered the Oval Office, the President was seated behind his desk and Secretary of State Shultz, smiling broadly, was seated at the side. The President rose as I walked toward him. Placing his hands on my shoulders he said, "Lucky, the Secretary and I think you have done a marvelous job as Chief of Protocol, and I would like you to continue in that position during my second term. You see," he added, half-singing. "I've grown accustomed to your face!"

That tune from "My Fair Lady" never sounded sweeter. And the four years that followed gave me the opportunity to observe first hand the President and Russia's Michael Gorbachev working together to end the Cold War.

# 70

## ALLEN SHERWOOD
### Governor Reagan's Personal Staff 1973-1975

972. I was a young naval officer, just home to California from a three-year deployment in Asia. All I knew about our Governor was what I'd read in old magazines that the USO delivered. All that was about to change.

I landed a job at the California Office of Emergency Services. This was the Governor's command post in the event of natural or man-made disasters befalling California. It was ably run by the governor's former military aide, Colomel Herb Temple. (Herb went on to four stars and command of the entire National Guard program under President Reagan.)

One of my first assignments was to prepare a flyer for distribution to California schools on natural disaster preparedness. I was handed an ancient Speed Graflex camera and put on a plane to Hollywood, where I was to meet up with the Governor and Charlton Heston, who was doing the narration for the film accompanying the flyer. Upon arrival I was taken to the studio set where the Governor and "Moses" were sitting, engaged in an animated conversation with a professor from Cal Tech who was providing the technical background about earthquakes.

With the help of technical staff, I got the set lighted and the pictures taken. Earlier, my secretary had handed me her own small Kodak camera and asked me to try to get her a photo of the Governor and Charlton Heston. Mustering up some courage, I asked if they would consent, and told them where the request had originated. Both smiled and posed as I clicked away. This was my first of many encounters with Ronald Reagan's sincere charm.

Time passed, and I moved up to the Governor's personal staff in 1973. I was the Deputy Appointments Secretary, responsible for briefing the Governor weekly on nominations to all the State's boards and commissions. Many of these had strong political ties to certain organizations or businesses. When I discussed this with Ed Meese, the Chief of Staff, he advised me to make my recommendations based on merit, and that the Governor wanted it that way. This is what I did. I never saw an appointment made that I didn't think was justified. One of Reagan's favorite sayings was, "There is no end of the good you can do if you don't care who gets the credit." He practiced what he preached.

Fast forward . . . It's Christmas 1974 and the Governor's Office staff gather for the last annual Christmas party. The staff was small and informal—about 40 of us total—and Nancy Reagan distributed small gifts that had been given to her and the Governor at official functions throughout the year. There was also a drawing for a 26 lb frozen Butterball turkey, and by great good fortune, I won it. I stepped forward to claim my prize from Nancy, who was not that much bigger than the turkey she was struggling to pick up. The Governor, lifting the turkey into my arms, asked how I would be getting the turkey home that night, and he smiled when I replied "riding on my lap on the bus." With that he responded, with a twinkle in his eye, "Nobody will ever believe you when you tell them who gave you this bird." He was right. Nobody ever did—including my spouse!

In 1976, when Ronald Reagan was seeking the Republican nomination for President, he attended a party fundraiser at the Roosevelt Hotel in downtown Los Angeles. I had gotten there early, seen the large crowd in the lobby, and decided to hike up the stairs to the ballroom via the inside fire escape. I was on the second set of stairs when I became aware of footsteps behind me. When I walked, they walked. When I stopped, they stopped. My concern was rising in this unused, dimly lit stairwell so when I stopped the next time, I spun around to confront my "stalker."

A smiling Ronald Reagan casually asked where we were headed. I was as lost as he was, I admitted. We tried various doors until eventually we came to the Ballroom and when he stuck his head in, he was greeted by thunderous cheers and applause. He calmly entered and waved to the crowd as if he did it this way every day.

Part way through Reagan's first term as President (1983), he and Nancy hosted a State Dinner for Queen Elizabeth and Prince Philip. Most State Dinners are held in the White House, but the Reagans wanted the Queen to see the ranch in Santa Barbara, and then travel to San Francisco for a formal State Dinner. I was by that time back on active Navy duty, and was asked by the White House to help with the military arrangements for the Royal Yacht Britannia and the arrival ceremonies. The original plan of sailing in under the Golden Gate Bridge was scrapped at the last minute due to weather, and the President and the Queen flew instead on Air Force One to San Francisco.

A State Visit is all pomp and ceremony. I had a U.S. Marine Corps contingent to act as honor guard with the arrival of Air Force One. We hand-picked 12 young Marines, and with the Royal red carpet in the back of the van, rushed to the airport to meet the plane.

It was not raining, it was pouring. Air Force One landed, and taxied to the Coast Guard Air Station at SFO where we stood at sodden attention, red carpet at the ready, for the lowering of the ramp and the arrival of the President and the Queen. When Air Force One swung around to the ramp, the jet blast hit us in the face with cold water from the ramp and the Royal red carpet was swamped with two inches of oily water. Hats blew off, flags toppled, and flowers shredded. The Reagans and the Royals deplaned and bravely sloshed through the squishy carpet to the waiting cars. When the dignitaries were safely in the limousines, and departing, I stood at sodden attention and caught Ronald Reagan's eye. He smiled, raised his arm in a broad gesture of greeting. I was supposed to have saluted him, but in the wet confusion committed a breach of protocol. I managed to regain my composure and salute Prince Philip as the motorcade departed. That act of respect for his Marines and military was classic Reagan.

My Marines rolled up the sodden carpet, and headed back to the barracks. I am sure they had a lot to write home about that night. It is rumored that they dried out the carpet, cut it into squares and sold it to their buddies as souvenirs, but I could be mistaken . . .

My last meeting with Ronald Reagan occurred the week after he left the Presidency. He had a transition office set up at the Fox Plaza in downtown LA. I stopped by to see a long-time acquaintance who was acting as Reagan's transition aide. Reagan was in the office, having the finishing touches done on his official oil portrait that hangs in the White House. I was ushered in, and Reagan motioned me to sit down. He was most cordial and spoke of his accomplishments in eight years as President. He seemed most proud of ending the Cold War, and the bringing down of the Berlin Wall. He spoke of admiration of Margaret Thatcher and other heads of state he had known. Our conversation was interrupted and he had to leave. I never saw him again.

On the airplane back to San Francisco, I mused about my personal experiences with Ronald Reagan, which spanned sixteen years. I admired him as a great American and I always will. He made us all walk a little taller. When I got back to the office, nobody thought to ask me how my day went.

Too bad, as I had quite a story to tell.

*Allen Sherwood is a retired Commander in the U.S. Navy, served as a University Administrator at San Francisco State University, and 15 years as city and county Commissioner in Butte County, CA*

# 71

# PETER D. HANNAFORD
## Assistant to the President and Advisor 1981-1989

I n his first campaign for governor of California, Ronald Reagan said that once there were budget surpluses they'd be sent back to the taxpayers. Late in his first fiscal year, State Director of Finance Casper "Cap" Weinberger gave Governor Reagan the surprising news that they would have a surplus for the year, not huge, but a surplus nonetheless—all the more remarkable after his predecessor's accounting maneuvers to mask deficits.

Cap said, "The legislature will learn about this in 15 minutes or so. What do you want to do with it?

Reagan said, "Give it back."

"Give it back?" Cap, replied. "But that's never been done before."

"No," he said, "but then you've never had an actor for Governor before, either."

In summer 1932, after his graduation from Eureka College, Reagan set his sights on becoming a radio sports announcer. He hitchhiked to Chicago and called on the big regional stations. None would give him an interview. At the last one, a kindly receptionist told him these stations only wanted experienced announcers. Instead, she said he should try small cities and town that were anxious to get talented people, even if they had no experience. Back home, he made a list of towns and stations within a 100-mile radius of Dixon, Illinois, his home. He borrowed his father's car to call on the first one, WAC in Davenport, Iowa, just on the other side of the Mississippi River.

He asked to see Peter MacArthur, a crusty Scot with arthritis so bad he walked with two canes. MacArthur told him he'd been advertising for an announcer for a month and after interviewing 94 applicants, had just hired one. Thinking he was being dismissed, Reagan got up to leave.

MacArthur clamored after him, shouting, "Not so fast, ye big bastard." Reagan stopped by the elevator and MacArthur said, "Do ye perhaps know football?" Reagan told him about his high school and college football experience. "Do ye think ye could tell me about a game and make me see it?" Reagan said he could.

MacArthur led him to a sound studio and told him to start when the red light came on. When it did, he recounted the fourth quarter of a Eureka game the previous season, his voice rose and the play became more exciting and he even described the "chill wind."

When the "game" was finished, MacArthur burst through the door and said, "Ye did great, ye big SOB." He offered to have Reagan broadcast a college game at Iowa City the next Saturday for $5 and car fare.

Thus began a successful career in radio, followed by one in films and, ultimately in politics and governing.

*During the Reagan White House years Peter Hannaford served on the USIA's Public Relations Advisory Committee, as a trustee of the White House Preservation Fund and as consultant to the President's Privatization Commission. He is the author of six books about Ronald Reagan, the latest being* Reagan's Roots. *(Images from the Past, 2011.)*

# 72

## MORTON C. BLACKWELL
Special Assistant for Public Liaison 1981-1984

The Navajo rug. For the first three years of the Reagan Administration, my role as a Special Assistant to the President for Public
Liaison included managing the White House relationship with a
number of different categories of groups: the conservative organizations, the veterans' organizations, the religious groups, and the
civic and fraternal groups.For the first two years, I also served as the
President's liaison to all 500 federally recognized American Indian
tribes and organizations.

All requests for scheduling meetings with the President went
through the office of Deputy Chief of Staff Michael Deaver. Early in
1981, Mike called me and instructed me not to propose any meetings for President Reagan with Indian tribal leaders. I asked why not.

He asked me if I had seen the widely circulated old photograph of
President Calvin Coolidge in a full Sioux Indian headdress. I had. He
said that was a ridiculous pose and that he would never put President
Reagan in a situation like that. Well, you might imagine my surprise
when, just a year later, Mike Deaver directed me to prepare a schedule
proposal for a meeting at the White House between President Reagan
and Peter MacDonald. the Chairman of the Navajo tribe.

"Why," I asked, "do you want to have the President meet with
MacDonald?"

It seems that Mrs. Reagan had been travelling out west with
a friend, and along the way they happened to see a hand-woven

Indian rug, beautifully patterned in a traditional Navajo design. Mrs. Reagan's friend had told Mike how much Nancy admired that rug. The friend suggested to Mike that he arrange a meeting for the President with the Navajo tribal Chairman, whom she knew. Once the meeting was set up, she would suggest to the tribal Chairman that, at the meeting, he present to the President a nice Navajo rug.

So I prepared a schedule proposal and sent it to Mike. He approved it in record time, and I called Chairman MacDonald to tell him he had an Oval Office meeting with the President. I made no mention of Mrs. Reagan or a rug.

On the appointed day, Peter MacDonald and his wife arrived at the West Wing with two young Navajo men who were carrying a long, wrapped cylinder. Obviously a rug, I thought. I escorted them into the Oval Office. The two young men put the wrapped cylinder in the center of the Oval Office and left. As always with visitors, President Reagan was the soul of grace. He and Chairman Mac-Donald exchanged several pleasant comments, and then Chairman MacDonald said, "Mr. President, I have brought you a present."

Chairman MacDonald got up, removed the wrapping, and unrolled the rug across the Oval Office floor. Sure enough, it was a hand-woven Navajo rug, but I was certainly surprised to see it was woven in red, white, and blue as an American flag, not a traditional Navajo pattern! The President got up, walked over to the gift, and picked up a corner of it. He commented on the fine workmanship and warmly thanked Chairman and Mrs. MacDonald for the fine gift. After another exchange of pleasant comments, the meeting was over.

After the MacDonalds had left the room, the President had a question. "Morton," he said, "what can I do with this? I can't use our flag for a rug. I don't have a wall big enough to hang it on."

He paused for a moment and said with a smile, "It will have to go to the Library." If they are of any value, gifts to the President of the United States are the property of the U.S. government. If a President wants to keep a gift personally, he must pay the government the fair market value of the gift. Otherwise, such gifts usually wind up after the presidency in the official Presidential library.

I have checked. That hand-woven Navajo rug in the design of the American flag is now in the collection of the Ronald Reagan Presidential Library in Simi Valley, California.

*Morton Blackwell is Founder and President of the Leadership Institute, Arlington VA.*

**73**

## ANNE COLLINS WALKER
Deputy Director of Congressional Relations
Consumer Product Safety Commission 1981-1984
Deputy Director, Public Affairs, Department of Commerce 1984-1989

"Happy Birthday, Mr. President." It was the summer of 1980 when the wall phone (remember those?) rang in the kitchen of our Dallas home. "This is Mike Deaver calling for Ron Walker." Wow, I knew who Mike Deaver was, Governor Ronald Reagan's right hand man. He told Ron that it looked like the Governor was going to get his party's nomination for President of the United States, and they needed help. Could Ron come to the convention in Detroit and help?"

I, of course, wanted to go too. I'd never been to Detroit.

The first morning we were there, a bunch of us were standing in the lobby of the Detroit Plaza Hotel. Ron was waiting to go to a meeting. Chuck Tyson, the Governor's scheduling chief, asked me what I was going to do that day. I told him I was available for any assignment that needed a volunteer. Well, as a matter of fact, they needed someone to do a special favor for the Governor.

It seems that this very day was former President Gerald R. Ford's sixty-seventh birthday. The two men had experienced both private and public differences over the years, and Governor Reagan wanted to make a gesture of friendship. In the summer of 1980, there was lots of talk about a Reagan-Ford ticket, and the Governor had gone to Ford's desert home right after the California primary to discuss the idea. Ford declined the offer of the second spot on the ticket, but said he would support him. You probably remember, too, that rumors were flying that a co-presidency was being talked about.

My assignment was to find a peace-pipe. Have a plaque engraved and have it framed, in time for the Governor to present to President Ford at their meeting scheduled for 3:45 THAT AFTERNOON. (Gulp)

Now, I've already told you I had never been to Detroit, so how in the world was I going to pull this off inside of a few hours? Chuck assured me that they would provide me with a car and volunteer driver. That was a help.

A short time later, a very nice young woman introduced herself to me. (I deeply regret I don't remember her name.) We were sworn to secrecy as we jumped in her car and began our mission. She knew Detroit. She saved the day. I was soon going to learn that Detroit had a huge Polish population. She was Polish. She saved much more than just the day.

Our first goal was to find a peace pipe. She took me to a section of Detroit that was full of little store fronts, filled with antiques and treasures of various vintage and design. We would pop in, find a sales person, and ask if they had any peace pipes. We got lots of surprised looks, smart alec answers, and my favorite retort, "What do you think this is, the Navajo Nation?" Just about the time we were getting really discouraged, and even talking about finding a place to eat lunch, an amazing thing happened. "Yeah, do you want one with a tobacco pouch, or without it?"

Well, I figured, if you give a guy a peace pipe, shouldn't you provide something to smoke in it, too? We bought the one with the tobacco pouch. Next stop: an engraver.

As we waited for the little brass plaque to be engraved, we paced the floor of the tiny shop. It seemed like the guy took forever to put a few words on a piece of metal. The minutes were flying by and we still had to get the thing mounted and framed. Next stop: find a framer.

My wheel lady, heroine and Detroit expert, knew right where to go. Now, it really wasn't a huge secret anymore, because anybody could read the plaque and put two and two together.

Mission accomplished: We flew back to the hotel with a very few minutes to spare, and delivered the precious present to the security desk on the floor of the Governor's hotel room.

Then we hurried down to the Lobby Bar and I was proud and happy to buy my new friend a congratulatory glass of wine, or beer, or something. Honestly, I don't remember what we actually drank; I just remember how happy we were. Hats off to you, dear wheel lady and miracle worker. I hope you think as fondly of this day that we shared and take pride in it, as I often do. If you happen to read this someday, please get in touch.

The 50th Presidential Inaugural. After running the 1984 Republican National Convention that nominated Ronald Reagan and George Herbert Walker Bush for a second term, Ron Walker was asked to be a Co-chair of the 50th Presidential Inauguration, along with Michael Deaver. As it turned out, Mike got sick and wound up in the hospital and Ron wore both of their hats. The week-end before the swearing in was a gorgeous, sunny day. Ron and I walked the entire length of the parade route, from the Capitol to the White House to check things out. Then an arctic blast moved in and by the next weekend, Ron was being advised to cancel the parade. The bitter cold would be unsafe for horses and band members in polyester uniforms.

The extreme weather forced the swearing-in to take place in the Capitol Rotunda and the parade was moved to the Cap Center. The morning church service at St. John's Episcopal Church was so memorable because a shaft of light highlighted only one person in the whole church, President Reagan. It was a sight I will never forget. It seemed to me that God was shining his light on him because of the place he would forever hold in our history.

## 74

## JAMES BUCKLEY
Under Secretary of State for Security Assistance, Science and
Technology 1981-1982

As a member of his administration, I never had that personal contact that would have enabled me to have those illuminating insights, but I can assert that I am probably the only person alive who can claim him as having been a member of my team rather than the other way around. My brother Bill [William F. Buckley] was a close family friend of Reagan, and brought him to our mother's home in Connecticut for our Thanksgiving dinner in 1976. As was our family habit, we had a touch football game after the meal. I was the captain of one team and Bill of the other. Reagan was on my team, and scored the winning touchdown. He was very modest about it and attributed his success to the skill of whoever it was who passed the ball to him. (There is now a plaque on the field noting the fact that he played touch football there in 1976.)

I can also report that after I left the administration and moved to Munich as president of Radio Free Europe and Radio Liberty, I came in possession of a "samisdat" (a document smuggled out of Soviet controlled areas) that was written in tiny script on flimsy paper by women in a Soviet prison congratulating Reagan on his reelection. I gave it to him personally on a visit to Washington. His comment was a muttered "It *is* an evil empire!"

In the meantime, another RR encounter comes to mind. I first met him shortly after I had been elected to the Senate in a three-way race as the candidate of New York's Conservative Party. Reagan was attending a governors' conference in DC or VA and stopped by my office to say hello. Two days later, I attended a meeting of the New York congressional delegation called by our governor, Nelson Rockefeller, whose brand of Republicanism the Conservative Party had been organized to oppose. To my astonishment and delight, Rockefeller opened the meeting by telling us how impressed he had been by Reagan's description of the success of his California campaign reforms.

# 75

## NANCY ROBINSON-SHAFFER
### White House Intern 1983 and 1989

was 16 years old, still in high school, and was honored to be given a summer post as a White House intern. The interns did a lot of things that involved the President but rarely did they involve actually *meeting* the President. I worked in both the Press and the Radio Actualities offices, and they were preparing for Spanish Heritage Week.

The speechwriting team down the hall put together remarks for the President, and then came to our office for review and discussion—especially on the proper pronunciation of the Spanish phrases. Someone asked if anyone in the office knew Spanish; I raised my hand. Suddenly the fast forward button was pressed; I was given a copy of the speech to read and asked to repeat the Spanish phrases. What they didn't realize was that when I indicated that I *"KNEW* Spanish" I meant that I knew what it was, having studied Spanish in middle and high school—thanks to my dad, who once offered me a bike if I took Spanish instead of French.

When you worked in the halls of the EOB or White House, time flew! From the time I raised my hand to the time I stood eye to eye with the President might have been a total of 30 minutes, which included traversing the black and white hallways, across to the "real" White House, through many doors with security guards checking my badge and being vouched for by my director, who always impressed me with the speed in which she could move in stiletto heels.

I was taken to a part of the White House near the Oval Office where press was set up, with a small group that included President Reagan. My director walked up to him, said something and I was introduced. The President extended a hand to me, pulled me in closer to him and flashes went off as a quick photo-op documented my moment. Then, as I stood next to him, not quite sure what to say or do, he was handed the speech, and rehearsed some of the Spanish words with me. He gave me a warm sideways smile and said in that voice that will always be recognized, "Did that sound ok?" I smiled and said, "Yes, sir," and he continued to read, glancing up here and there to ask questions, give a wink and even to make some joke that made us all laugh. He was warm and didn't rush anyone, although the entire room rushed around him.

Next, the staff called him to come over to the microphone and do the speech. He gave me a nod and a smile and said "Thanks!" I smiled in embarrassment and felt my arm taken as I was shuttled over to stand with my boss. The President did the speech in one take, perfectly, the staff applauded, he gave that famous smile to the small group, gave a humble head bow and a wink, and followed his entourage out the door.

His ability to give this speech flawlessly, in one take, was remarkable . . . but what stays with me most was the warmth and comfort that walked in and out of the room along with President Reagan.

# 76

# CHARLES L. GRIZZLE
Deputy Assistant Secretary for Administration, Department of
Agriculture, 1983 - 1988

The term "Reagan Revolution" has become part of our political lexicon over the course of the past 30 years. However, I'm not sure if there is a general understanding of the inherent genius President Reagan exhibited for strong interpersonal relationships among the appointees in his Administration. No matter how low one might have been on the political totem pole, you were made to feel you had an important role to play and that you were part of something much bigger than your day-to-day duties. The President knew he needed his foot soldiers working together if he had any hope of harnessing the bureaucracy to implement his agenda.

I can think of no better example of how the President promoted this esprit de corps than the annual Executive Forum held each year on the anniversary of his inauguration. The events were held at Constitution Hall and the traditional security precaution of having a cabinet member designated to "stand down" to preserve the continuity of government in the event of a catastrophic event was waived. Of course, other normal security precautions were in place and everyone except those on dais had to arrive sufficiently early for security processing. The early arrival in advance of the program afforded us the opportunity to roam freely within the auditorium and visit with our friends and colleagues from other agencies and departments, while we were entertained by the Marine Band. It had the atmosphere of a family reunion.

The Executive Forum was a command performance, attended by all Reagan appointees of every station. While it was part family reunion and part pep rally, there was an important substantive element to the event since we were briefed on the major challenges faced by the President and his team during the preceding year. The Forum was typically convened by the President's Chief of Staff and featured remarks from two members of the cabinet, one to review domestic accomplishments and another focused on national security. Those remarks were followed the introduction of Vice President Bush for his remarks.

As the applause for the Vice President abated, the Marine Band struck up "Hail to the Chief" and the President took the stage. As President Reagan approached the podium a large American flag suspended from the ceiling was unfurled above our heads. More than 30 years later, I can scarcely recall any messages conveyed by the President, Vice President or any other speakers at those events, but I will never forget the pageantry and the feeling that I was playing a role in a larger production to restore and reshape America. I think I can speak for many of my former colleagues in saying that each year when we left the Executive Forum we had a sense of renewed purpose and commitment.

*Charles L. Grizzle was appointed Assistant Administrator of the Environmental Protection Agency (Administration and Resource Management) at the end of the Reagan Administration, and continued in the post under President G. H. W. Bush., 1989-1991.*

# 77

## KENNETH KHACHIGIAN
White House Speech Writer 1981-1989

On February 5, 1981, the President gave his first report to the nation on the state of the economy—a report card on the situation he inherited when he came into office. He realized, of course, that getting something done required the Congress to act on critical elements of the economy, taxes and the budget. So we scheduled an economic speech to a joint session of Congress for Wednesday, February 18th, just a few days after the first one. In reality, the speech before Congress was his first, unofficial, State of the Union Address. The President was headed up to Camp David for the weekend before the speech, and I was told he would like to work on it while he was there. I completed a draft and faxed it to the President late Friday night.

I hadn't heard anything back until the military aide called the following Monday morning to say that the President had completed his edits and would be sending them along. As the President helicoptered back from Camp David, the speech was being faxed back to our office, page by page, over the Signal Corps' secure communication line. As always, I viewed the President's edits with a mixture of admiration and trepidation—the latter in case I had not faithfully struck the right chords. But just a few paragraphs into the speech, a statistic caught my eye. The President always felt that illustrations often told his story better than a mere narrative. In this case, his goal was to dramatize how dire the impending one trillion dollar national debt was (a number now dwarfed by $17 trillion of debt). In his handwriting, he penned a paragraph saying you could visualize a trillion dollars by stacking $1000 bills on top of each other—rising to a height of something over 80 miles high. Alarm bells went off. I needed a source for that number.

Shortly thereafter, the White House operator called to say the President was on the line. "Ken, just wanted to make sure you got my edits and that you're able to read all of them." I replied, of course. Then, I asked: "Mr. President, if you'll excuse the question, where on earth did you come up with the number for the $1000 bills reaching up to the sky?" There was a slight pause at the end of the line, and he said: "I did it by long division." I stifled a laugh, picturing the President with his yellow pad and dividing some mysterious factor into 1,000,000,000,000.

I knew the President had scores of his old note cards filled with facts and figures, but I knew that this number would be scoured by reporters and had to be confirmed. I figured the only source we had was the Bureau of Engraving and Printing—remembering there is usually at least one person in the vast federal bureaucracy who specialized in obscure factoids. Our crack research team called over there and after a few hours the answer came back. "It depends on whether your stack the bills loosely on top of each other, or if you use bound bundles of bills."

Well, we had our answer—loosely stacked, they would reach 67 miles high and, bound, 63 miles high. Naturally the President chose the former. So no more than a few minutes into speech he said: "Our national debt is approaching $1 trillion. A few weeks ago I called such a figure, a trillion dollars, incomprehensible, and I've been trying ever since to think of a way to illustrate how big a trillion really is. And the best I could come up with is that if you had a stack of thousand-dollar bills in your hand only 4 inches high, you'd be a millionaire. A trillion dollars would be a stack of thousand-dollar bills 67 miles high."

The full speech was well received—putting pressure on the

Congress to act to end what the President called an economic "calamity." But I'll never forget the President's confidence in his math skills or the fascinating way in which the bureaucracy mastered the minutiae of government.

# 78

# HENRY R. NAU
## Senior Staff Member, National Security Council 1981-1983

ersonal Memories. Ronald Reagan had many of the character-
istics of a great leader but three stand out from my personal
interactions with him: humor, self-confidence, and strategic
vision. I illustrate each with snapshots from the time I served
President Reagan as senior staff member of the National Security
Council responsible for international economic affairs from January
1981-Auust 1983.

Humor was the note on which I met Ronald Reagan for the first
time in a private gathering on Pennsylvania Avenue in spring 1980.
Reagan listened attentively as the assembled policy advisors gave
him their counsel. At the end of the session, he looked at us and
said: "I do not want you to focus on the politics of the campaign. I
have other advisors doing that. I want you to focus on the policies
I intend to pursue to straighten this country out once I move into
that little White House down the street." Then he sat back pensively
for a moment and continued with a big grin on his face: "And if I
don't get into that little White House down the street, who needs it
at my age?" The room broke up. It was a great leader's way of saying,
"Look, I'm not in this for me; I'm in this for the country."

Humor often portrayed the quickness and cleverness of Reagan's
mind. At the first cabinet meeting after George Shultz became secretary of State, Reagan took a moment to introduce Shultz. Shultz

thanked him and then noted that his name on the White House place card was misspelled. He said that happened so often when he was a Marine that he got into the habit of replying, "Sir, Shultz without the C." Without missing a beat, Reagan interrupted and said "George, I know what you mean; right across the table from me is Reagan without the A." He was referring of course to Don Regan, the secretary of the Treasury.

Reagan often communicated through stories. At one cabinet meeting where exchange rates were discussed, Reagan told a story about a book he picked up in the 1930s that had all of the major exchange rates listed. One economic advisor, a professor at a marquis American university, said to me afterwards, "What was that story all about?" I replied, "Maybe he's telling us that exchange rates should be less volatile and more stable, like the rates he could look up in that printed book."

Reagan often scribbled or doodled during meetings. I was the note taker at one of the sessions of the Versailles Summit when Francois Mitterrand, the French president, sharply criticized Reagan's economic policies. After the session, the President handed me a blue sheet of paper and told me to dispose of it. He had written on it numerous observations, the most telling of which was: "Does he [Mitterrand] really believe all this socialist crap?"

Reagan's self-confidence was not appreciated by many people, including some of his closest advisors. I recall one incident in particular that illustrates this fact graphically. Reagan hosted the G-7 Summit in Williamsburg, Virginia in May 1983. I was the White House Sherpa preparing for that and other G-7 summits. For three months before the summit, we had briefed the President, once every two weeks or so, on the issues likely to arise at that summit. The world was in a deep recession, and the summit was expected to be contentious. When we arrived in Williamsburg, we held a final briefing session over dinner at the restored colonial house where the president was staying. After the session ended, Reagan sat at the end of the table and reviewed with me one final time the issues covered in the briefing book. He was very familiar with the material, even commenting at one point that it all seemed in order. As he got up from the table and entered the foyer to ascend the stairs to the bedroom, my boss Judge William Clark asked him if he wanted to take the briefing book with him to the bedroom. "No, Bill," the President replied, "I'm going to spend the evening with Julie Andrews." He smiled mischievously and went up the steps to relax watching the movie, *Sound of Music*. He knew he was ready; and the Williamsburg Summit that followed was one of the most successful meetings in G-7 history, laying out the free market economic policies, dubbed the "Washington Consensus," that guided global growth for thirty years and confirming the NATO commitment to deploy intermediate range nuclear missiles, which occurred in November 1983 and, according to George Shultz, marked a turning point in the Cold War.

A senior advisor, however, doubted the President's preparations and self-confidence. He reported the incident differently to Lou Cannon, who subsequently included the anecdote in his biography of Reagan. The advisor said the president left his briefing book on the table that evening and "hadn't even glanced at it," even though this senior advisor knew that the president had received multiple briefings over previous months. No doubt, the advisor's comments were part of a public relations strategy to play down expectations in case results were less favorable than anticipated. But it also reflected a tendency to underestimate Reagan's grasp of the issues, even among his closest advisors. Much later, another close advisor to Reagan confided to me at a luncheon meeting shortly before he died that he was one of those people closest to Ronald Reagan who did not fully trust his policies, especially toward the Soviet Union. This advisor admirably acknowledged that he had been wrong. Why the President, so supremely confident and knowledgeable about what he was doing, allowed himself to be so underestimated is one of the intriguing riddles of the still unfinished history of Reagan's presidency.

The last quality—of greatest, strategic vision, is perhaps the most important. And it may explain why Reagan was so humorously self-confident. As declassified and other records are making increasingly clear, Reagan had a vision of where he wanted to move the country and how his policies would accomplish that. He needed help from advisors on the details, which may have led them to think they were his tutors. But he did not need any help from them on the overall strategy. In fact none of his principal advisors supported *all* the elements of his strategy. The soft liners opposed the defense initiatives, especially the Strategic Defense Initiative. The hard liners opposed negotiations with the Soviet Union. Only Reagan embraced all of the elements and integrated them into a strategy that John Lewis Gaddis, the noted historian, credits with ending the Cold War.

The anecdote that best illustrates Reagan's vision occurred in November 1982. The U.S. and world economy were still deep in the doldrums, and daily street protests in Europe threatened to undermine NATO missile deployments to counter Soviet missiles. My boss, Judge Bill Clark, the National Security Advisor, visited Reagan privately. "Mr. President, what should we do? Do we need a Plan B?" After some discussion and thought, Reagan replied: "No, Bill, we're on the right track. Our policies are in place, and I think the economy is going to turn around soon and the Soviet Union will too once they have an effective leader." Then he looked wryly at Judge Clark and said, "And what's the worst thing that can happen to you and me if things don't turn around? You and I go back to the ranch in 1984. What can be so bad about that?" The self-confidence wrapped in humor that filled the room at that moment, I will never forget. Here was a great leader, granite-like and completely at peace with himself and his policies.

And Reagan was right. Within six months the U.S. economy started to roll, and within a year NATO deployed intermediate range missiles in Europe. Reagan's policies, without doubt, had more to do with ending the Cold War than any other single factor, including Gorbachev. Indeed, Gorbachev may not have come along in the Soviet Union at all if the United States had continued along the path of stagflation and military weakness that characterized its situation in the late 1970s.

*Henry R. Nau is a professor at the Elliott School of International Affairs, The George Washington University.*

# EPILOGUE

## JAMES A. BAKER, III
Chief of Staff 1981-1985 / Secretary of the Treasury 1985-1988

This compilation of personal anecdotes written by those who worked for Ronald Reagan provides keen insight about the Gipper's strong character and many skills as a leader. It is a tribute to his enduring legacy. Gale Norton's memories of Ronald Reagan's inspirational vision are a reminder that lofty ideals accentuated with strong rhetoric can change the world. Frank Carlucci's tale of President Reagan's desire to rid the world of nuclear weapons is a testament to his dedication to peace.

After reading these anecdotes, it is easy to understand why most Americans consider Ronald Reagan to have been one of our nation's best presidents. He restored our confidence in the country following the Vietnam War, Watergate and the Iran Hostage Crisis. He brought us through a tough recession and helped establish one of the greatest periods of peace and prosperity in America's history. He put in place tax and budget policies that lead to eighteen years of sustained, non-inflationary economic growth. And as a man from humble beginnings, he proved that the American Dream was alive and well. Any American can not only rise to the pinnacle of leadership, but can also succeed once in that position. These anecdotes also demonstrate that Ronald Reagan believed in the principle of "loyalty up—loyalty down."

But if there is a single Ronald Reagan trait that deserves emphasis three decades after he left office, it would be his ability to govern and get things done. He was simply masterful at reaching bi-partisan consensus. As such, he should continue to serve as a model for elected officials in Washington who are so deeply wedded to a zero-sum game of politics that is leaving our country bereft of problem-solving for the American people.

President Reagan knew how to look his adversaries in the eye and not back down. Nevertheless, at the end of the day he could find a solution. After all, this was the president who stood at the Brandenburg Gate and challenged Soviet leader Mikhail Gorbachev to tear down the Berlin Wall. And yet, this was also the president who negotiated arms control with the very same man. This was the president who heard Democrats launch sharp verbal barbs against him night after night on the evening news. And then, he worked with those same Democrats to achieve tax and budget legislation, trade agreements, Social Security reform and many other laws that benefitted both parties, and more importantly, the entire country.

As President Reagan's White House chief of staff for the first four years and then his Secretary of the Treasury for three-and-a-half years, I was fortunate to have closely observed how he did what he did to become a very successful two-term president. His meetings with House Speaker Tip O'Neill were particularly tough because the Democrat was a cagey adversary. He was as liberal as Reagan was conservative. And both of them had stubborn streaks. Budget battles between the two helped spark eight government shutdowns during Reagan's two terms in office.

Nevertheless, President Reagan knew something about the American people—that we judge our presidents on their ability to implement their policy goals. More often than not, that means working with Congress to turn those goals into law. No one ever doubted that Ronald Reagan had strong convictions. They were always four-square. But he was not unwilling to compromise. "Jim," he would often tell me, "I'd rather get 80 percent of what I want than to go over the cliff with my flag flying."

Many of the president's strongest supporters sometimes seemed to feel that it was better to lose everything than to give an inch. I don't think they fully understood what President Reagan knew: Pragmatism without principles is cynicism. But principles without pragmatism are often powerless.

Tax policy is a good example. We hadn't reformed our tax code in 100 years, and it took a lot of hard work to do it. It also took both Republican and Democratic votes. The president was able ultimately to bring the top marginal tax rate down from 70 percent to 28 percent—which Republicans loved. And he eliminated many loopholes and deductions—which Democrats loved. Along the way, he took six million Americans off the tax rolls and simplified the tax code. If these efforts had not been bi-partisan, they would not have happened. President Reagan knew how important it was for the economic health of the country and he made it happen.

I always considered Ronald Reagan's approach to be what I would call "pragmatic idealism." He was a master at turning policy goals into law. He was willing to fight hard, and he was very good at it. But he also knew how to accept victory in terms that could be won.

That lesson from Ronald Reagan is one that Washington would be wise to follow today . . . and in the future.


*James A. Baker also served as Secretary of State under President G. H. W. Bush, 1989-1992.*

# APPENDIX

## SELECTED REAGAN SPEECHES MENTIONED IN THE TEXT

All, from the Reagan archives at the Univeristy of Texas

Mr. President, Mrs. Ford, Mr. Vice President, Mr. Vice President-to-be, the distinguished guests here, you ladies and gentlemen. I was going to say fellow Republicans here but those who are watching from a distance (including) all those millions of Democrats and independents who I know are looking for a cause around which to rally and which I believe we can give them. Mr. President, before you arrived tonight, these wonderful people, here, when we came in, gave Nancy and myself a welcome. That, plus this, plus your kindness and generosity in honoring us by bringing us down here will give us a memory that will live in our hearts forever.

Watching on television these last few nights I've seen also the warmth with which you greeted Nancy and you also filled my heart with joy when you did that. May I say some words? There are cynics who say that a party platform is something that no one bothers to read and it doesn't very often amount to much. Whether it is different this time than it has ever been before, I believe the Republican party has a platform that is a banner of bold, unmistakable colors with no pale pastel shades. We have just heard a call to arms, based on that platform.

And a call to us to really be successful in communicating and reveal to the American people the difference between this platform and the platform of the opposing party which is nothing but a revamp and a reissue and a rerunning of a late, late show of the thing that we have been hearing from them for the last 40 years.

If I could just take a moment, I had an assignment the other day. Someone asked me to write a letter for a time capsule that is going to be opened in Los Angeles a hundred years from now, on our Tricentennial.

It sounded like an easy assignment. They suggested I write about the problems and issues of the day. And I set out to do so, riding down the coast in an automobile, looking at the blue Pacific out on one side and the Santa Ynez Mountains on the other, and I couldn't help but wonder if it was going to be that beautiful a hundred years from now as it was on that summer day.

And then as I tried to write-let your own minds turn to that task. You're going to write for people a hundred years from now who know all about us; we know nothing about them. We don't know what kind of world they'll be living in. And suddenly I thought to myself, "If I write of the problems, they'll be the domestic problems of which the President spoke here tonight; the challenges confronting us, the erosion of freedom taken place under Democratic rule in this country, the invasion of private rights, the controls and restrictions on the vitality of the great free economy that we enjoy." These are the challenges that we must meet and then again there is that challenge of which he spoke, that we live in a world in which the great powers have aimed and poised at each other horrible missiles of destruction, nuclear weapons that can in a matter of minutes arrive at each other's country and destroy virtually the civilized world we live in.

And suddenly it dawned on me; those who would read this letter a hundred years from now will know whether those missiles were fired. They will know whether we met our challenge.

Whether they will have the freedom that we have known up until now will depend on what we do here. Will they look back with appreciation and say, "Thank God for those people in 1976 who headed off that loss of freedom? Who kept us now a hundred years later free? Who kept our world from nuclear destruction?"

And if we fail they probably won't get to read the letter at all because it spoke of individual freedom and they won't be allowed to talk of that or read of it.

This is our challenge and this is why we're here in this hall tonight. Better than we've ever done before, we've got to quit talking to each other and about each other and go out and communicate to the world that we may be fewer in numbers than we've ever been but we carry the message they're waiting for. We must go forth from here united, determined and what a great general said a few years ago is true: "There is no substitute for victory," Mr. President.

Mr. Chairman, delegates to the Convention, my fellow citizens of this great nation. With a deep awareness of the responsibility conferred by your trust, I accept your nomination for the Presidency of the United States. I do so with deep gratitude.

I am very proud of our party tonight. This convention has shown to all America a party united, with positive programs for solving the nation's problems; a party ready to build a new consensus with all those across the land who share a community of values embodied in these words: family, work, neighborhood, peace and freedom.

I know we have had a quarrel or two in our party, but only as to the method of attaining a goal. There was no argument about the goal. As President, I will establish a liaison with the 50 Governors to encourage them to eliminate, wherever it exists, discrimination against women. I will monitor Federal laws to e nsure their implementation and to add statutes if they are needed.

More than anything else, I want my candidacy to unify our country; to renew the American spirit and sense of purpose. I want to carry our message to every American, regardless of party affiliation, who is a member of this community of shared values.

Never before in our history have Americans been called upon to face three grave threats to our very existence, any one of which could destroy us. We face a disintegrating economy, a weakened defense and an energy policy based on the sharing of scarcity.

The major issue of this campaign is the direct political, personal and moral responsibility of Democratic party leadership-in the White House and in Congress-for this unprecedented calamity which has befallen us. They tell us they have done the most that humanly could be done. They say that the United States has had its day in the sun; that our nation has passed its zenith. They expect you to tell your children that the American people no longer have the will to cope with their problems; that the future will be one of sacrifice and few opportunities.

My fellow citizens, I utterly reject that view. The American people, the most generous on earth, who created the highest standard of living, are not going to accept the notion that we can only make a better world for others by moving backwards ourselves. Those who believe we can have no business leading the nation. I will not stand by and watch this great country destroy itself under mediocre leadership that drifts from one crisis to the next, eroding our national will and purpose. We have come together here because the American people deserve better from those to whom they entrust our nation's highest offices, and we stand united in our resolve to do something about it.

We need a rebirth of the American tradition of leadership at every level of government and in private life as well. The United States of America is unique in world history because it has a genius for leaders—many leaders on many levels. But, back in 1976, Mr. Carter said, 'Trust me.' And a lot of people did. Now, many of those people are out of work. Many have seen their savings eaten away by inflation. Many others on fixed incomes, especially the elderly, have watched helplessly as the cruel tax of inflation wasted away their purchasing power. And, today a great many who trusted Mr. Carter wonder if we can survive the Carter policies of national defense.

'Trust me' government asks that we concentrate our hopes and dreams on one man; that we trust him to do what's best for us. My view of government places trust not in one person or one party, but in those values that transcend persons and parties. The trust is where it belongs, in the people. The responsibility to live up to that trust is where it belongs, in their elected leaders. That kind of relationship, between the people and their elected leaders, is a special kind of compact: an agreement among themselves to build a community and abide by its laws.

Three hundred and sixty years ago, in 1620, a group of families dared to cross a mighty ocean to build a future for themselves in a new world. When they arrived at Plymouth, Massachusetts, they formed what they called a compact: an agreement among themselves to build a community and abide by its laws. The single act the voluntary binding together of free people to live under the law set the pattern for what was to come.

A century and a half later, the descendants of those people pledged their lives, their fortunes and their sacred honor to found this nation. Some forfeited their fortunes and their lives; none sacrificed honor.

Four score and seven years later, Abraham Lincoln called upon the people of all America to renew their dedication and their commitment of, for and by the people. Isn't it once again time to renew our compact of freedom; to pledge to each other all that is best in our lives; all that gives meaning to them for the sake of this, our beloved and blessed land?

Together, let us make this a new beginning. Let us make a commitment to care for the needy; to teach our children the values and the virtues handed down to us by our families; to have the courage to defend those values and the willingness to sacrifice for them.

Let us pledge to restore, in our time, the American spirit of voluntary service, of cooperation, of private and community initiative; a spirit that flows like a deep and mighty river through the history of our nation.

As your nominee, I pledge to restore to the federal government the capacity to do the people's work without dominating their lives. I pledge to you a government that will not only work well, but wisely; its ability to act tempered by prudence, and its willingness to do good balanced by the knowledge that government is never more dangerous than when our desire to have it help us blinds us to its great power to harm us.

The first Republican President once said, While the people retain their virtue and their vigilance, no Administration by any extreme of wickedness or folly can seriously injure the government in the short space of four years.

If Mr. Lincoln could see what's happened in these last three-and-half years, he might hedge a little on that statement. But, with the virtues that are our legacy as a free people and with the vigilance that sustains liberty, we still have time to use our renewed compact to overcome the injuries that have been done to America these past three-and-a half years.

First we must overcome something the present Administration has cooked up: a new and altogether indigestible economic stew, one part inflation, one part high unemployment, one part recession, one part runaway taxes, one part deficit spending and seasoned by an energy crisis. It's an economic stew that has turned the national stomach. It is as if Mr. Carter had set out to prove, once and for all, that economics is indeed a dismal science.

Ours are not problems of abstract economic theory. These are problems of flesh and blood; problems that cause pain and destroy the moral fiber of real people who should not suffer the further indignity of being told by the White House that it is all somehow their fault. We do not have inflation because, as Mr. Carter says, we have lived too well.

The head of a government which has utterly refused to live within its means and which has, in the last few days, told us that this year's deficit will be $60 billion, dares to point the finger of blame at business and labor, both of which have been engaged in a losing struggle just trying to stay even.

High taxes, we are told, are somehow good for us, as if, when government spends our money it isn't inflationary, but when we spend it, it is. Those who preside over the worst energy shortage in our history tell us to use less, so that we will run out of oil, gasoline and natural gas a little more slowly. Conservation is desirable, of course, for we must not waste energy. But conservation is not the sole answer to our energy needs.

America must get to work producing more energy. The Republican program for solving economic problems is based on growth and productivity. Large amounts of oil and natural gas lay beneath our land and off our shores, untouched because the present Administration seems to believe the American people would rather see more regulation, taxes and controls than more energy.

Coal offers great potential. So does nuclear energy produced under rigorous safety standards. It could supply electricity for thousands of industries and millions of jobs and homes. It must not be thwarted by a tiny minority opposed to economic growth which often finds friendly ears in regulatory agencies for its obstructionist campaigns.

Make no mistake. We will not permit the safety of our people or our environmental heritage to be jeopardized, but we are going to reaffirm that the economic prosperity of our people is a fundamental part of our environment.

Our problems are both acute and chronic, yet all we hear from those in positions of leadership are the same tired proposals for more government tinkering, more meddling and more control, all of which led us to this state in the first place.

Can anyone look at the record of this Administration and say Well done? Can anyone compare the state of our economy when the Carter Administration took office with where we are today and say, Keep up the good work? Can anyone look at our reduced standing in the world today and say, Let's have four more years of this?

I believe the American people are going to answer these questions the first week of November and their answer will be, "No," we've had enough. And, when the American people have spoken, it will be up to us beginning next January 20th to offer an Administration and Congressional leadership of competence and more than a little courage.

We must have the clarity of vision to see the difference between what is essential and what is merely desirable; and then the courage to use this insight to bring our government back under control and make it acceptable to the people.

We Republicans believe it is essential that we maintain both the forward momentum of economic growth and the strength of the safety net beneath those in society who need help. We also believe it is essential that the integrity of all aspects of Social Security be preserved.

Beyond these essentials, I believe it is clear our federal government is overgrown and overweight. Indeed, it is time for our government to go no a diet. Therefore, my first act as Chief Executive will be to impose an immediate and thorough freeze on federal hiring. Then, we are going to enlist the very best minds from business, labor and whatever quarter to conduct a detailed review of every department, bureau and agency that lives by federal appropriation. We are also going to enlist the help and ideas of many dedicated and hard-working government employees at all levels who want a more efficient government as much as the rest of us do. I know that many are demoralized by the confusion and waste they confront in their work as a result of failed and failing policies.

Our instructions to the groups we enlist will be simple and direct. We will remind them that government programs exist at the sufferance of the American taxpayer and are paid for with money earned by working men and women. Any program that represents a waste of their money, a theft from their pocketbooks, ,must have that waste eliminated or the program must go by Executive Order where possible, by Congressional action where necessary. Everything that can be run more effectively by state and local governments we shall turn over to state and local government, along with the funding sources to pay for it. We are going to put an end to the money merry go round where our money becomes Washington's money, to be spent by the states and cities only if they spend it exactly the way the federal bureaucrats tell them to.

I will not accept the excuse that the federal government has grown so big and powerful that it is beyond the control of any President, any Administration or Congress. We are going to put an end to the notion that the American taxpayer exists to fund the federal government. The federal government exists to serve the American people and to be accountable to the American people. On January 20th, we are going to re-establish that truth.

Also on that date we are going to initiate action to get substantial relief for our taxpaying citizens and action to put people back to work. None of this will be based on any new form of monetary tinkering or fiscal sleight-of-hand. We will simply apply to government the common sense we all use in our daily lives.

Work and family are at the center of our lives, the foundation of our dignity as a free people. When we deprive people of what they have earned, or take away their jobs, we destroy their dignity and undermine their families. We cannot support our families unless there are jobs; and we cannot have jobs unless people have both money to invest and the faith to invest it.

These are concepts that stem from the foundation of an economic system that for more than two hundred years has helped us master a continent, create a previously undreamed of prosperity for our people and has fed millions of others around the globe. That system will continue to serve us in the future if our government will stop ignoring the basic values on which it was built and stop betraying the trust and good will of the American workers who keep it going.

The American people are carrying the heaviest peacetime tax burden in our nation's history and it will grow even heavier, under present law, next January. This burden is crushing our ability and incentive to save, invest and produce. We are taxing ourselves into economic exhaustion and stagnation. This must stop. We must halt this fiscal self-destruction and restore sanity to our economic system.

I have long advocated a 30 percent reduction in income tax rates over a period of three years. This phased tax reduction would begin with a 10 percent down payment tax cut in 1981, which the Republicans in Congress and I have already proposed.

A phased reduction of tax rates would go a long way toward easing the heavy burden on the American people. But, we should not stop here.

Within the context of economic conditions and appropriate budget priorities during each fiscal year of my Presidency, I would strive to go further. This would include improvement in business depreciation taxes so we can stimulate investment in order to get plants and equipment replaced, put more Americans back to work and put our nation back on the road to being competitive in world commerce. We will also work to reduce the cost of government as a percentage of our Gross National Product.

The first task of national leadership is to set honest and realistic priorities in our policies and our budget and I pledge that my Administration will do that.

When I talk of tax cuts, I am reminded that every major tax cut in this century has strengthened the economy, generated renewed productivity and ended up yielding new revenues for the government by creating new investment, new jobs and more commerce among our people.

The present administration has been forced by us Republicans to play follow the leader with regard to a tax cut. But, we must take with the proverbial grain of salt any tax cut proposed by those who have given us the greatest tax increase in our history.

When those in leadership give us tax increases and tell us we must also do with less, have they thought about those who have always had less especially, the minorities? This is like telling them that just as they step on the first rung of the ladder of opportunity, the ladder is being pulled up. That may be the Democratic leadership's message to the minorities, but it won't be ours. Our message will be: we have to move ahead, but we're not going to leave anyone behind.

Thanks to the economic policies of the Democratic party, millions of Americans find themselves out of work. Millions more have never even had a fair chance to learn new skills, hold a decent job, seize the opportunity to climb the ladder and secure for themselves and their families a share in the prosperity of this nation.

It is time to put Americans back to work; to make our cities and towns resound with the confident voices of men and women of all races, nationalities and faiths bringing home to their families a decent paycheck they can cash for money.

For those without skills, we'll find a way to help them get skills. For those without job opportunities, we'll stimulate new opportunities, particularly in the inner cities where they live. For those who have abandoned hope, we'll restore hope and well welcome them into a great national crusade to make America great again!

When we move from domestic affairs and cast our eyes abroad, we see an equally sorry chapter in the record of the present Administration.

A Soviet combat brigade trains in Cuba, just 90 miles from our shores.

A Soviet army of invasion occupies Afghanistan, further threatening our vital interests in the Middle East.

America's defense strength is at its lowest ebb in a generation, while the Soviet Union is vastly outspending us in both strategic and conventional arms.

Our European allies, looking nervously at the growing menace from the East, turn to us for leadership and fail to find it.

And incredibly, more than 50 of our fellow Americans have been held captive for over eight months by a dictatorial foreign power that holds us up to ridicule before the world.

Adversaries large and small test our will and seek to confound our resolve, but the Carter Administration gives us weakness when we need strength; vacillation when the times demand firmness.

Why? Because the Carter Administration lives in the world of make-believe. Every day, it dreams up a response to that day's troubles, regardless of what happened yesterday and what will happen tomorrow. The Administration lives in a world where mistakes, even very big ones, have no consequence.

The rest of us, however, live in the real world. It is here that disasters are overtaking our nation without any real response from the White House.

I condemn the Administration's make-believe; its self deceit and above all its transparent hypocrisy. For example, Mr. Carter says he supports the volunteer army, but he lets military pay and benefits slip so low that many of our enlisted personnel are actually eligible for food stamps. Re-enlistment rates drop and, just recently, after he fought all week against a proposal to increase the pay of our men and women in uniform, he helicoptered out to our carrier the USS Nimitz, which was returning from long months of duty. He told the crew that he advocated better pay for them and their comrades! Where does he really stand, now that he's back on shore?

I'll tell you where I stand. I do not favor a peacetime draft or registration, but I do favor pay and benefit levels that will attract and keep highly motivated men and women in our volunteer forces and an active reserve trained and ready for an instant call in case of an emergency.

An Annapolis graduate may be at the helm of the ship of state, but the ship has no rudder. Critical decisions are made at times almost in Marx Brothers fashion, but who can laugh? Who was not embarrassed when the Administration handed a major propaganda victory in the United Nations to the enemies of Israel, our staunch Middle East ally for three decades, and then claimed that the American vote was a mistake, the result of a failure of communication between the President, his Secretary of State and his UN Ambassador?

Who does not feel a growing sense of unease as our allies, facing repeated instances of an amateurish and confused Administration, reluctantly conclude that America is unwilling or unable to fulfill its obligations as leader of the free world?

Who does not feel rising alarm when the question in any discussion of foreign policy is no longer, "Should we do something?" but "Do we have the capacity to do anything?"

The Administration which has brought us to this state is seeking your endorsement for four more years of weakness, indecision, mediocrity and incompetence. No American should vote until he or she has asked, is the United States stronger and more respected now than it was three-and-a-half years ago? Is the world today a safer place in which we live?

It is the responsibility of the President of the United States, in working for peace, to ensure that the safety of our people cannot successfully be threatened by a hostile foreign power. As President, fulfilling that responsibility will be my Number One priority.

We are not a warlike people. Quite the opposite. We always seek to live in peace. We resort to force infrequently and with great reluctance and only after we have determined that it is absolutely necessary. We are awed and rightly so by the forces of destruction at loose in the world in this nuclear era. But neither can we be naive or foolish. Four times in my lifetime America has gone to war, bleeding the lives of its young men into the sands of beachheads, the fields of Europe and the jungles and rice paddies of Asia. We know only too well that war comes not when the forces of freedom are strong, but when they are weak. It is then that tyrants are tempted.

We simply cannot learn these lessons the hard way again without risking our destruction.

Of all the objectives we seek, first and foremost is the establishment of lasting world peace. We must always stand ready to negotiate in good faith, ready to pursue any reasonable avenue that holds forth the promise of lessening tensions and furthering the prospects of peace. But let our friends and those who may wish us ill take note: the United States has an obligation to its citizens and to the people of the world never to let those who would destroy freedom dictate the future course of human life on this planet.

I would never regard my election as proof that we have renewed our resolve to preserve world peace and freedom. This nation will once again be strong enough to do that.

This evening marks the last step save one of a campaign that has taken Nancy and me from one end of this great land to the other, over many months and thousands and thousands of miles. There are those who question the way we choose a President; who say that our process imposes difficult and exhausting burdens on those who seek the office. I have not found it so.

It is impossible to capture in words the splendor of this vast continent which God has granted as our portion of his creation. There are no words to express the extraordinary strength and character of this breed of people we call Americans.

Everywhere we have met thousands of Democrats, Independents and Republicans from all economic conditions and walks of life bound together in that community of shared values of family, work, neighborhood, peace and freedom. They are concerned, yes, but they are the kind of men and women Tom Paine had in mind when he wrote during the darkest days of the American Revolution, "We have it in our power to begin the world over again."

Nearly one-hundred-and-fifty years after Tom Paine wrote those words, an American President told the generation of the Great Depression that it had "a rendezvous with destiny." I believe this generation of Americans today also has a rendezvous with destiny.

Tonight, let us dedicate ourselves to renewing the American Compact. I ask you not simply to trust me, but to trust your values— our values and to hold me responsible for living up to them. I ask you to trust that American spirit which knows no ethnic, religious, social, political, regional or economic boundaries; the spirit that burned with zeal in the hearts of millions of immigrants from every corner of the earth who came here in search of freedom.

Some say that spirit no longer exists. But I have seen it I have felt it all across this land; in the big cities, the small towns and in rural America. The American spirit is still there, ready to blaze into life if you and I are willing to do what has to be done; the practical, down to earth things that will stimulate our economy, increase productivity and put America back to work.

The time is now to limit federal spending, to insist on a stable monetary reform, and to free ourselves from imported oil.

The time is now to resolve that the basis of a firm and principled foreign policy is one that takes the world as it is and seeks to change it by leadership and example, not by lecture and harangue.

The time is now to say that while we shall seek new friendships and expand and improve others, we shall not do so by breaking our word or casting aside old friends and allies.

And the time is now to redeem promises once made to the American people by another candidate, in another time and another place. He said, "For three long years I have been going up and down this country preaching that government—federal, state and local—costs too much. I shall not stop that preaching. As an immediate program of action, we must abolish useless offices. We must eliminate unnecessary functions of government.

"We must consolidate subdivisions of government and, like the private citizen, give up luxuries which we can no longer afford. I propose to you, my friends, and through you that government of all kinds, big and little, be made solvent and that the example be set by the President of the United States and his cabinet." So said Franklin Delano Roosevelt in his acceptance speech to the Democratic National Convention in July, 1932.

The time is now, my fellow Americans, to recapture our destiny, to take it into our own hands. But, to do this will take many of us, working together. I ask you tonight to volunteer your help in this cause so we carry our message throughout the land.

Yes, isn't now the time that we, the people, carried out these un-kept promises? Let us pledge to each other and to all America on this July day 48 years later, we intend to do just that.

*At the end, Reagan departed from his prepared text:*

I have thought of something that is not a part of my speech and I'm worried over whether I should do it. Can we doubt that only a divine providence placed this land, this island of freedom, here as a refuge for all those people in the world who yearn to breath freely: Jews and Christians enduring persecution behind the Iron Curtain, the boat people of Southeast Asia, of Cuba and of Haiti, the victims of drought and famine in Africa, the freedom fighters of Afghanistan and our own countrymen held in savage captivity?

I'll confess that I've been a little afraid to suggest what I'm going to suggest. I'm more afraid not to. Can we begin our crusade joined together in a moment of silent prayer?

God Bless America.

Father Hesburgh, I thank you very much and for so many things. The distinguished honor that you've conferred upon me here today, I must say, however, compounds a sense of guilt that I have nursed for almost 50 years. I thought the first degree I was given was honorary. [Laughter] But it's wonderful to be here today with Governor Orr, Governor Bowen, Senators Lugar and Quayle, and Representative Hiler, these distinguished honorees, the trustees, administration, faculty, students, and friends of Notre Dame and, most important, the graduating class of 1981.

Nancy and I are greatly honored to share this day with you, and our pleasure has been more than doubled because I am also sharing the platform with a longtime and very dear friend, Pat O'Brien.

Pat and I haven't been able to see much of each other lately, so I haven't had a chance to tell him that there is now another tie that binds us together. Until a few weeks ago I knew very little about my father's ancestry. He had been orphaned at age 6. But now I've learned that his grandfather, my great-grandfather, left Ireland to come to America, leaving his home in Ballyporeen, a village in County Tipperary in Ireland, and I have learned that Ballyporeen is the ancestral home of the O'Briens.

Now, if I don't watch out, this may turn out to be less of a commencement than a warm bath in nostalgic memories. Growing up in Illinois, I was influenced by a sports legend so national in scope, it was almost mystical. It is difficult to explain to anyone who didn't live in those times. The legend was based on a combination of three elements: a game, football; a university, Notre Dame; and a man, Knute Rockne. There has been nothing like it before or since.

My first time to ever see Notre Dame was to come here as a sports announcer, two years out of college, to broadcast a football game. You won or I wouldn't have mentioned it. [Laughter]

A number of years later I returned here in the company of Pat O'Brien and a galaxy of Hollywood stars for the world premiere of "Knute Rockne—All American" in which I was privileged to play George Gipp. I've always suspected that there might have been many actors in Hollywood who could have played the part better, but no one could have wanted to play it more than I did. And I was given the part largely because the star of that picture, Pat O'Brien, kindly and generously held out a helping hand to a beginning young actor.

Having come from the world of sports, I'd been trying to write a story about Knute Rockne. I must confess that I had someone in mind to play the Gipper. On one of my sports broadcasts before going to Hollywood, I had told the story of his career and tragic death. I didn't have very many words on paper when I learned that the studio that employed me was already preparing a story treatment for that film. And that brings me to the theme of my remarks.

I'm the fifth President of the United States to address a Notre Dame commencement. The temptation is great to use this forum as an address on a great international or national issue that has nothing to do with this occasion. Indeed, this is somewhat traditional. So, I wasn't surprised when I read in several reputable journals that I was going to deliver an address on foreign policy or on the economy. I'm not going to talk about either.

But, by the same token, I'll try not to belabor you with some of the standard rhetoric that is beloved of graduation speakers. For example, I'm not going to tell you that "You know more today than you've ever known before or that you will ever know again."

[Laughter] The other standby is, "When I was 14, I didn't think my father knew anything. By the time I was 21, I was amazed at how much the old gentleman had learned in 7 years." And then, of course, the traditional and the standby is that "A university like this is a storehouse of knowledge because the freshmen bring so much in and the seniors take so little away." [Laughter]

You members of the graduating class of 18—or 1981—[laughter]—I don't really go back that far—[laughter]—are what behaviorists call achievers. And while you will look back with warm pleasure on your memories of these years that brought you here to where you are today, you are also, I know, looking at the future that seems uncertain to most of you but which, let me assure you, offers great expectations.

Take pride in this day. Thank your parents, as one on your behalf has already done here. Thank those who've been of help to you over the last 4 years. And do a little celebrating; you're entitled. This is your day, and whatever I say should take cognizance of that fact. It is a milestone in life, and it marks a time of change.

Winston Churchill, during the darkest period of the "Battle of Britain" in World War II said: "When great causes are on the move in the world . . . we learn we are spirits, not animals, and that something is going on in space and time, and beyond space and time, which, whether we like it or not, spells duty."

Now, I'm going to mention again that movie that Pat and I and Notre Dame were in, because it says something about America. First, Knute Rockne as a boy came to America with his parents from Norway. And in the few years it took him to grow up to college age, he became so American that here at Notre Dame, he became an All American in a game that is still, to this day, uniquely American.

As a coach, he did more than teach young men how to play a game. He believed truly that the noblest work of man was building the character of man. And maybe that's why he was a living legend. No man connected with football has ever achieved the stature or occupied the singular niche in the Nation that he carved out for himself, not just in a sport, but in our entire social structure.

Now, today I hear very often, "Win one for the Gipper," spoken in a humorous vein. Lately I've been hearing it by Congressmen who are supportive of the programs that I've introduced. [Laughter] But let's look at the significance of that story. Rockne could have used Gipp's dying words to win a game any time. But 8 years went by following the death of George Gipp before Rock revealed those dying words, his deathbed wish.

And then he told the story at halftime to a team that was losing, and one of the only teams he had ever coached that was torn by dissension and jealousy and factionalism. The seniors on that team were about to close out their football careers without learning or experiencing any of the real values that a game has to impart. None of them had known George Gipp. They were children when he played for Notre Dame. It was to this team that Rockne told the story and so inspired them that they rose above their personal animosities. For someone they had never known, they joined together in a common cause and attained the unattainable.

We were told when we were making the picture of one line that was spoken by a player during that game. We were actually afraid to put it in the picture. The man who carried the ball over for the winning touchdown was injured on the play. We were told that as he was lifted on the stretcher and carried off the field he was heard to say, "That's the last one I can get for you, Gipper."

Now, it's only a game. And maybe to hear it now, afterward—and this is what we feared—it might sound maudlin and not the way it was intended. But is there anything wrong with young people having an experience, feeling something so deeply, thinking of someone else to the point that they can give so completely of themselves? There will come times in the lives of all of us when we'll be faced with causes bigger than ourselves, and they won't be on a playing field.

This Nation was born when a band of men, the Founding Fathers, a group so unique we've never seen their like since, rose to such selfless heights. Lawyers, tradesmen, merchants, farmers—56 men achieved security and standing in life but valued freedom more. They pledged their lives, their fortunes, and their sacred honor. Sixteen of them gave their lives. Most gave their fortunes. All preserved their sacred honor.

They gave us more than a nation. They brought to all mankind for the first time the concept that man was born free, that each of us has inalienable rights, ours by the grace of God, and that government was created by us for our convenience, having only the powers that we choose to give it. This is the heritage that you're about to claim as you come out to join the society made up of those who have preceded you by a few years, or some of us by a great many.

This experiment in man's relation to man is a few years into its third century. Saying that may make it sound quite old. But let's look at it from another viewpoint or perspective. A few years ago, someone figured out that if you could condense the entire history of life on Earth into a motion picture that would run for 24 hours a day, 365 days—maybe on leap years we could have an intermission—[laughter]—this idea that is the United States wouldn't appear on the screen until 3-1/2 seconds before midnight on December 31st. And in those 3-1/2 seconds not only would a new concept of society come into being, a golden hope for all mankind, but more than half the activity, economic activity in world history, would take place on this continent. Free to express their genius, individual Americans, men and women, in 3-1/2 seconds, would perform such miracles of invention, construction, and production as the world had never seen.

As you join us out there beyond the campus, you know there are great unsolved problems. Federalism, with its built in checks and balances, has been distorted. Central government has usurped powers that properly belong to local and State governments. And in so doing, in many ways that central government has begun to fail to do the things that are truly the responsibility of a central government.

All of this has led to the misuse of power and preemption of the prerogatives of people and their social institutions. You are graduating from a great private, or, if you will, independent university. Not too many years ago, such schools were relatively free from government interference. In recent years, government has spawned regulations covering virtually every facet of our lives. The independent and church-supported colleges and universities have found themselves enmeshed in that network of regulations and the costly blizzard of paperwork that government is demanding. Thirty-four congressional committees and almost 80 subcommittees have jurisdiction over 439 separate laws affecting education at the college level alone. Almost every aspect of campus life is now regulated—hiring, firing, promotions, physical plant, construction, recordkeeping, fundraising and, to some extent, curriculum and educational programs.

I hope when you leave this campus that you will do so with a feeling of obligation to your alma mater. She will need your help and support in the years to come. If ever the great independent colleges and universities like Notre Dame give way to and are replaced by tax-supported institutions, the struggle to preserve academic freedom will have been lost.

We're troubled today by economic stagnation, brought on by inflated currency and prohibitive taxes and burdensome regulations. The cost of stagnation in human terms, mostly among those least equipped to survive it, is cruel and inhuman.

Now, after those remarks, don't decide that you'd better turn your diploma back in so you can stay another year on the campus. I've just given you the bad news. The good news is that something is being done about all this because the people of America have said, "Enough already." You know, we who had preceded you had just gotten so busy that we let things get out of hand. We forgot that we were the keepers of the power, forgot to challenge the notion that the state is the principal vehicle of social change, forgot that millions of social interactions among free individuals and institutions can do more to foster economic and social progress than all the careful schemes of government planners.

Well, at last we're remembering, remembering that government has certain legitimate functions which it can perform very well, that it can be responsive to the people, that it can be humane and compassionate, but that when it undertakes tasks that are not its proper province, it can do none of them as well or as economically as the private sector.

For too long government has been fixing things that aren't broken and inventing miracle cures for unknown diseases.

We need you. We need your youth. We need your strength. We need your idealism to help us make right that which is wrong. Now, I know that this period of your life, you have been and are critically looking at the mores and customs of the past and questioning their value. Every generation does that. May I suggest, don't discard the time-tested values upon which civilization was built simply because they're old. More important, don't let today's doomcriers and cynics persuade you that the best is past, that from here on it's all downhill. Each generation sees farther than the generation that preceded it because it stands on the shoulders of that generation. You're going to have opportunities beyond anything that we've ever known.

The people have made it plain already. They want an end to excessive government intervention in their lives and in the economy, an end to the burdensome and unnecessary regulations and a punitive tax policy that does take "from the mouth of labor the bread it has earned." They want a government that cannot only continue to send men across the vast reaches of space and bring them safely home, but that can guarantee that you and I can walk in the park of our neighborhood after dark and get safely home. And finally, they want to know that this Nation has the ability to defend itself against those who would seek to pull it down.

And all of this, we the people can do. Indeed, a start has already been made. There's a task force under the leadership of the Vice President, George Bush, that is to look at those regulations I've spoken of. They have already identified hundreds of them that can be wiped out with no harm to the quality of life. And the cancellation of just those regulations will leave billions and billions of dollars in the hands of the people for productive enterprise and research and development and the creation of jobs.

The years ahead are great ones for this country, for the cause of freedom and the spread of civilization. The West won't contain communism, it will transcend communism. It won't bother to dismiss or denounce it, it will dismiss it as some bizarre chapter in human history whose last pages are even now being written.

William Faulkner, at a Nobel Prize ceremony some time back, said man "would not only [merely] endure: he will prevail" against the modern world because he will return to "the old verities and truths of the heart." And then Faulkner said of man, "He is immortal because he alone among creatures . . . has a soul, a spirit capable of compassion and sacrifice and endurance."

One can't say those words—compassion, sacrifice, and endurance —without thinking of the irony that one who so exemplifies them, Pope John Paul II, a man of peace and goodness, an inspiration to the world, would be struck by a bullet from a man towards whom he could only feel compassion and love. It was Pope John Paul II who warned in last year's encyclical on mercy and justice against certain economic theories that use the rhetoric of class struggle to justify injustice. He said, "In the name of an alleged justice the neighbor is sometimes destroyed, killed, deprived of liberty or stripped of fundamental human rights."

For the West, for America, the time has come to dare to show to the world that our civilized ideas, our traditions, our values, are not—like the ideology and war machine of totalitarian societies — just a facade of strength. It is time for the world to know our intellectual and spiritual values are rooted in the source of all strength, a belief in a Supreme Being, and a law higher than our own.

When it's written, history of our time won't dwell long on the hardships of the recent past. But history will ask—and our answer determine the fate of freedom for a thousand years—Did a nation borne of hope lose hope? Did a people forged by courage find courage wanting? Did a generation steeled by hard war and a harsh peace forsake honor at the moment of great climactic struggle for the human spirit?

If history asks such questions, it also answers them. And the answers are to be found in the heritage left by generations of Americans before us. They stand in silent witness to what the world will soon know and history someday record: that in the [its] third century, the American Nation came of age, affirmed its leadership of free men and women serving selflessly a vision of man with God, government for people, and humanity at peace.

A few years ago, an Australian Prime Minister, John Gorton, said, "I wonder if anybody ever thought what the situation for the comparatively small nations in the world would be if there were not in existence the United States, if there were not this giant country prepared to make so many sacrifices." This is the noble and rich heritage rooted in great civil ideas of the West, and it is yours.

My hope today is that in the years to come—and come it shall— when it's your time to explain to another generation the meaning of the past and thereby hold out to them their promise of the future, that you'll recall the truths and traditions of which we've spoken. It is these truths and traditions that define our civilization and make up our national heritage. And now, they're yours to protect and pass on.

I have one more hope for you: when you do speak to the next generation about these things, that you will always be able to speak of an America that is strong and free, to find in your hearts an unbounded pride in this much-loved country, this once and future land, this bright and hopeful nation whose generous spirit and great ideals the world still honors.

Congratulations, and God bless you.

*Note: The President spoke at 3:11 p.m. at the 136th commencement ceremony of the university, which was held in the Notre Dame Athletic and Convocation Center at the campus in South Bend, Ind. The President was introduced by Rev. Theodore M. Hesburgh, president of the university, who had presented the President with an honorary doctor of laws degree prior to the commencement address.*

*In his remarks, the President referred to Governor Robert Orr, former Governor Otis R. Bowen, Senators Richard G. Lugar and Dan Quayle, and Representative John P. Hiler, all of Indiana. The President also referred to the movie "Knute Rockne—All American," which was filmed at Notre Dame in 1940. The President played the part of All American halfback George Gipp, who died of pneumonia.*

*The occasion marked the first trip by the President outside of Washington, D.C., since the assassination attempt on March 30. Four former Presidents — Franklin D. Roosevelt, Dwight D. Eisenhower, Gerald R. Ford, and Jimmy Carter—addressed convocations or commencement exercises at the university and were awarded honorary degrees.*

# REMARKS TO MEMBERS OF THE NATIONAL PRESS CLUB
## ON ARMS REDUCTION AND NUCLEAR WEAPONS
November 18, 1981

Officers, ladies and gentlemen of the National Press Club and, as of a very short time ago, fellow members:

Back in April while in the hospital I had, as you can readily understand, a lot of time for reflection. And one day I decided to send a personal, handwritten letter to Soviet President Leonid Brezhnev reminding him that we had met about 10 years ago in San Clemente, California, as he and President Nixon were concluding a series of meetings that had brought hope to all the world. Never had peace and good will seemed closer at hand.

I'd like to read you a few paragraphs from that letter. "Mr. President: When we met, I asked if you were aware that the hopes and aspirations of millions of people throughout the world were dependent on the decisions that would be reached in those meetings. You took my hand in both of yours and assured me that you were aware of that and that you were dedicated with all your heart and soul and mind to fulfilling those hopes and dreams."

I went on in my letter to say: "The people of the world still share that hope. Indeed, the peoples of the world, despite differences in racial and ethnic origin, have very much in common. They want the dignity of having some control over their individual lives, their destiny. They want to work at the craft or trade of their own choosing and to be fairly rewarded. They want to raise their families in peace without harming anyone or suffering harm themselves. Government exists for their convenience, not the other way around.

"If they are incapable, as some would have us believe, of self-government, then where among them do we find any who are capable of governing others?

"Is it possible that we have permitted ideology, political and economic philosophies, and governmental policies to keep us from considering the very real, everyday problems of our peoples? Will the average Soviet family be better off or even aware that the Soviet Union has imposed a government of its own choice on the people of Afghanistan? Is life better for the people of Cuba because the Cuban military dictate who shall govern the people of Angola?

"It is often implied that such things have been made necessary because of territorial ambitions of the United States; that we have imperialistic designs, and thus constitute a threat to your own security and that of the newly emerging nations. Not only is there no evidence to support such a charge, there is solid evidence that the United States, when it could have dominated the world with no risk to itself, made no effort whatsoever to do so.

"When World War II ended, the United States had the only undamaged industrial power in the world. Our military might was at its peak, and we alone had the ultimate weapon, the nuclear weapon, with the unquestioned ability to deliver it anywhere in the world. If we had sought world domination then, who could have opposed us?

"But the United States followed a different course, one unique in all the history of mankind. We used our power and wealth to rebuild the war-ravished economies of the world, including those of the nations who had been our enemies. May I say, there is absolutely no substance to charges that the United States is guilty of imperialism or attempts to impose its will on other countries, by use of force."

I continued my letter by saying—or concluded my letter, I should say—by saying, "Mr. President, should we not be concerned with eliminating the obstacles which prevent our people, those you and I represent, from achieving their most cherished goals?"

Well, it's in the same spirit that I want to speak today to this audience and the people of the world about America's program for peace and the coming negotiations which begin November 30th in Geneva, Switzerland. Specifically, I want to present our program for preserving peace in Europe and our wider program for arms control.

Twice in my lifetime, I have seen the peoples of Europe plunged into the tragedy of war. Twice in my lifetime, Europe has suffered destruction and military occupation in wars that statesmen proved powerless to prevent, soldiers unable to contain, and ordinary citizens unable to escape. And twice in my lifetime, young Americans have bled their lives into the soil of those battlefields not to enrich or enlarge our domain, but to restore the peace and independence of our friends and Allies.

All of us who lived through those troubled times share a common resolve that they must never come again. And most of us share a common appreciation of the Atlantic Alliance that has made a peaceful, free, and prosperous Western Europe in the postwar era possible.

But today, a new generation is emerging on both sides of the Atlantic. Its members were not present at the creation of the North Atlantic Alliance. Many of them don't fully understand its roots in defending freedom and rebuilding a war-torn continent. Some young people question why we need weapons, particularly nuclear weapons, to deter war and to assure peaceful development. They fear that the accumulation of weapons itself may lead to conflagration. Some even propose unilateral disarmament.

I understand their concerns. Their questions deserve to be answered. But we have an obligation to answer their questions on the basis of judgment and reason and experience. Our policies have resulted in the longest European peace in this century. Wouldn't a rash departure from these policies, as some now suggest, endanger that peace?

From its founding, the Atlantic Alliance has preserved the peace through unity, deterrence, and dialog. First, we and our Allies have stood united by the firm commitment that an attack upon any one of us would be considered an attack upon us all. Second, we and our Allies have deterred aggression by maintaining forces strong enough to ensure that any aggressor would lose more from an attack than he could possibly gain. And third, we and our Allies have engaged the Soviets in a dialog about mutual restraint and arms limitations, hoping to reduce the risk of war and the burden of armaments and to lower the barriers that divide East from West.

These three elements of our policy have preserved the peace in Europe for more than a third of a century. They can preserve it for generations to come, so long as we pursue them with sufficient will and vigor.

Today, I wish to reaffirm America's commitment to the Atlantic Alliance and our resolve to sustain the peace. And from my conversations with allied leaders, I know that they also remain true to this tried and proven course.

NATO's policy of peace is based on restraint and balance. No NATO weapons, conventional or nuclear, will ever be used in Europe except in response to attack. NATO's defense plans have been responsible and restrained. The Allies remain strong, united, and resolute. But the momentum of the continuing Soviet military buildup threatens both the conventional and the nuclear balance.

Consider the facts. Over the past decade, the United States reduced the size of its Armed Forces and decreased its military spending. The Soviets steadily increased the number of men under arms. They now number more than double those of the United States. Over the same period, the Soviets expanded their real military spending by about one-third. The Soviet Union increased its inventory of tanks to some 50,000, compared to our 11,000. Historically a land power, they transformed their navy from a coastal defense force to an open ocean fleet, while the United States, a sea power with transoceanic alliances, cut its fleet in half.

During a period when NATO deployed no new intermediate-range nuclear missiles and actually withdrew 1,000 nuclear warheads, the Soviet Union deployed more than 750 nuclear warheads on the new SS - 20 missiles alone.

Our response to this relentless buildup of Soviet military power has been restrained but firm. We have made decisions to strengthen all three legs of the strategic triad: sea-, land-, and air-based. We have proposed a defense program in the United States for the next five years which will remedy the neglect of the past decade and restore the eroding balance on which our security depends.

I would like to discuss more specifically the growing threat to Western Europe which is posed by the continuing deployment of certain Soviet intermediate-range nuclear missiles. The Soviet Union has three different type such missile systems: the SS - 20, the SS - 4, and the SS - 5, all with the range capable of reaching virtually all of Western Europe. There are other Soviet weapon systems which also represent a major threat.

Now, the only answer to these systems is a comparable threat to Soviet threats, to Soviet targets; in other words, a deterrent preventing the use of these Soviet weapons by the counterthreat of a like response against their own territory. At present, however, there is no equivalent deterrent to these Soviet intermediate missiles. And the Soviets continue to add one new SS - 20 a week.

To counter this, the Allies agreed in 1979, as part of a two-track decision, to deploy as a deterrent land-based cruise missiles and Pershing II missiles capable of reaching targets in the Soviet Union. These missiles are to be deployed in several countries of Western Europe. This relatively limited force in no way serves as a substitute for the much larger strategic umbrella spread over our NATO Allies. Rather, it provides a vital link between conventional shorter-range nuclear forces in Europe and intercontinental forces in the United States.

Deployment of these systems will demonstrate to the Soviet Union that this link cannot be broken. Deterring war depends on the perceived ability of our forces to perform effectively. The more effective our forces are, the less likely it is that we'll have to use them.

So, we and our allies are proceeding to modernize NATO's nuclear forces of intermediate range to meet increased Soviet deployments of nuclear systems threatening Western Europe.

Let me turn now to our hopes for arms control negotiations. There's a tendency to make this entire subject overly complex. I want to be clear and concise. I told you of the letter I wrote to President Brezhnev last April. Well, I've just sent another message to the Soviet leadership. It's a simple, straightforward, yet, historic message. The United States proposes the mutual reduction of conventional intermediate-range nuclear and strategic forces. Specifically, I have proposed a four-point agenda to achieve this objective in my letter to President Brezhnev.

The first and most important point concerns the Geneva negotiations. As part of the 1979 two-track decision, NATO made a commitment to seek arms control negotiations with the Soviet Union on intermediate range nuclear forces. The United States has been preparing for these negotiations through close consultation with our NATO partners.

We're now ready to set forth our proposal. I have informed President Brezhnev that when our delegation travels to the negotiations on intermediate range, land-based nuclear missiles in Geneva on the 30th of this month, my representatives will present the following proposal: The United States is prepared to cancel its deployment of Pershing II and ground-launch cruise missiles if the Soviets will dismantle their SS - 20, SS - 4, and SS - 5 missiles. This would be an historic step. With Soviet agreement, we could together substantially reduce the dread threat of nuclear war which hangs over the people of Europe. This, like the first footstep on the Moon, would be a giant step for mankind.

Now, we intend to negotiate in good faith and go to Geneva willing to listen to and consider the proposals of our Soviet counterparts, but let me call to your attention the background against which our proposal is made.

During the past six years while the United States deployed no new intermediate-range missiles and withdrew 1,000 nuclear warheads from Europe, the Soviet Union deployed 750 warheads on mobile, accurate ballistic missiles. They now have 1,100 warheads on the SS - 20s, SS - 4s and 5s. And the United States has no comparable missiles. Indeed, the United States dismantled the last such missile in Europe over 15 years ago.

As we look to the future of the negotiations, it's also important to address certain Soviet claims, which left unrefuted could become critical barriers to real progress in arms control.

The Soviets assert that a balance of intermediate range nuclear forces already exists. That assertion is wrong. By any objective measure, as this chart indicates, the Soviet Union has developed an increasingly overwhelming advantage. They now enjoy a superiority on the order of six to one. The red is the Soviet buildup; the blue is our own. That is 1975, and that is 1981.

Now, Soviet spokesmen have suggested that moving their SS - 20s behind the Ural Mountains will remove the threat to Europe. Well, as this map demonstrates, the SS - 20s, even if deployed behind the Urals, will have a range that puts almost all of Western Europe—the great cities—Rome, Athens, Paris, London, Brussels, Amsterdam, Berlin, and so many more—all of Scandinavia, all of the Middle East, all of northern Africa, all within range of these missiles which, incidentally, are mobile and can be moved on shorter notice. These little images mark the present location which would give them a range clear out into the Atlantic.

The second proposal that I've made to President Brezhnev concerns strategic weapons. The United States proposes to open negotiations on strategic arms as soon as possible next year.

I have instructed Secretary Haig to discuss the timing of such meetings with Soviet representatives. Substance, however, is far more important than timing. As our proposal for the Geneva talks this month illustrates, we can make proposals for genuinely serious reductions, but only if we take the time to prepare carefully.

The United States has been preparing carefully for resumption of strategic arms negotiations because we don't want a repetition of past disappointments. We don't want an arms control process that sends hopes soaring only to end in dashed expectations.

Now, I have informed President Brezhnev that we will seek to negotiate substantial reductions in nuclear arms which would result in levels that are equal and verifiable. Our approach to verification will be to emphasize openness and creativity, rather than the secrecy and suspicion which have undermined confidence in arms control in the past.

While we can hope to benefit from work done over the past decade in strategic arms negotiations, let us agree to do more than simply begin where these previous efforts left off. We can and should attempt major qualitative and quantitative progress. Only such progress can fulfill the hopes of our own people and the rest of the world. And let us see how far we can go in achieving truly substantial reductions in our strategic arsenals.

To symbolize this fundamental change in direction, we will call these negotiations START—Strategic Arms Reduction Talks.

The third proposal I've made to the Soviet Union is that we act to achieve equality at lower levels of conventional forces in Europe. The defense needs of the Soviet Union hardly call for maintaining more combat divisions in East Germany today than were in the whole Allied invasion force that landed in Normandy on D-Day. The Soviet Union could make no more convincing contribution to peace in Europe, and in the world, than by agreeing to reduce its conventional forces significantly and constrain the potential for sudden aggression.

Finally, I have pointed out to President Brezhnev that to maintain peace we must reduce the risks of surprise attack and the chance of war arising out of uncertainty or miscalculation.

I am renewing our proposal for a conference to develop effective measures that would reduce these dangers. At the current Madrid meeting of the Conference on Security and Cooperation in Europe, we're laying the foundation for a Western-proposed conference on disarmament in Europe. This conference would discuss new measures to enhance stability and security in Europe. Agreement in this conference is within reach. I urge the Soviet Union to join us and many other nations who are ready to launch this important enterprise.

All of these proposals are based on the same fair-minded principles—substantial, militarily significant reduction in forces, equal ceilings for similar types of forces, and adequate provisions for verification.

My administration, our country, and I are committed to achieving arms reductions agreements based on these principles. Today I have outlined the kinds of bold, equitable proposals which the world expects of us. But we cannot reduce arms unilaterally. Success can only come if the Soviet Union will share our commitment, if it will demonstrate that its often-repeated professions of concern for peace will be matched by positive action.

Preservation of peace in Europe and the pursuit of arms reduction talks are of fundamental importance. But we must also help to bring peace and security to regions now torn by conflict, external intervention, and war.

The American concept of peace goes well beyond the absence of war. We foresee a flowering of economic growth and individual liberty in a world at peace.

At the economic summit conference in Cancun, I met with the leaders of 21 nations and sketched out our approach to global economic growth. We want to eliminate the barriers to trade and investment which hinder these critical incentives to growth, and we're working to develop new programs to help the poorest nations achieve self-sustaining growth.

And terms like "peace" and "security", we have to say, have little meaning for the oppressed and the destitute. They also mean little to the individual whose state has stripped him of human freedom and dignity. Wherever there is oppression, we must strive for the peace and security of individuals as well as states. We must recognize that progress and the pursuit of liberty is a necessary complement to military security. Nowhere has this fundamental truth been more boldly and clearly stated than in the Helsinki Accords of 1975. These accords have not yet been translated into living reality.

Today I've announced an agenda that can help to achieve peace, security, and freedom across the globe. In particular, I have made an important offer to forego entirely deployment of new American missiles in Europe if the Soviet Union is prepared to respond on an equal footing.

There is no reason why people in any part of the world should have to live in permanent fear of war or its spectre. I believe the time has come for all nations to act in a responsible spirit that doesn't threaten other states. I believe the time is right to move forward on arms control and the resolution of critical regional disputes at the conference table. Nothing will have a higher priority for me and for the American people over the coming months and years.

Addressing the United Nations 20 years ago, another American President described the goal that we still pursue today. He said, "If we all can persevere, if we can look beyond our shores and ambitions, then surely the age will dawn in which the strong are just and the weak secure and the peace preserved."

He didn't live to see that goal achieved. I invite all nations to join with America today in the quest for such a world.

Thank you.


*Note: The President spoke at 10 a.m. at the National Press Club Building. His address was broadcast live on radio and television.*

RADIO ADDRESS TO THE NATION ON THE
RESIGNATION OF SECRETARY OF THE INTERIOR JAMES
G. WATT
November 26, 1983

My fellow Americans:

There's a change of management over at the Department of Interior. James Watt has resigned, and Judge William Clark has taken his place.

When Jim became Secretary of Interior he told me of the things that needed doing, the things that had to be set straight. He also told me that if and when he did them, he'd probably have to resign in 18 months. Sometimes the one who straightens out a situation uses up so many brownie points he or she is no longer the best one to carry out the duties of day-to-day management. Jim understood this. But he also realized what had to be done, and he did it for more than 30 months, not 18.

Now, with the change in management, it's time to take inventory. The Federal Government owns some 730 million acres—about one-third of the total land area of the United States. The Department of Interior has jurisdiction over most of that, including our national parks, wildlife refuges, wilderness lands, wetlands, and coastal barriers. Not included in those 730 million acres are our offshore coastal waters, the Outer Continental Shelf, which is also Interior's responsibility. And I've asked Bill Clark to review policy, personnel, and process at the Department of the Interior.

Our national parks are the envy of the world, but in 1981 they were a little frayed at the edges. Since 1978 funds for upkeep and restoration had been cut in half. Jim Watt directed a billion-dollar improvement and restoration program. This 5-year effort is the largest commitment to restoration and improvement of the park system that has ever been made.

You, of course, are aware of the economic crunch we've been facing. Yet, even so, Secretary Watt set out to increase protection for fragile and important conservation lands. In 1982 he proposed that 188 areas along our gulf and Atlantic coasts be designated as undeveloped coastal areas. And that proposal became the basis for the historic Coastal Barrier Resources Act. This act covers dunes, marshes, and other coastal formations from Maine to Texas —lands that provide irreplaceable feeding and nesting grounds for hundreds of species of waterfowl and fish. And, under Secretary Watt, we've added substantial acreage to our parks and wildlife refuges and some 15,000 acres to our wilderness areas.

Interior is also in charge of preserving historic sites and structures. In the economic recovery program we launched in 1981 we gave a 25-percent tax credit for private sector restoration of historic structures. The result has been private investment in historic preservation five times as great as in the preceding 4 years. Secretary Watt has explored other ways to involve the private sector in historic preservation. And one of the efforts we're all proudest of is the campaign to restore Ellis Island and that grand lady in New York Harbor, the Statue of Liberty. This campaign is being led by Lee Iacocca, the chairman of Chrysler, and is being financed almost entirely by private contributions.

Preservation of endangered species is also a responsibility of the Department, and the approval and review of plans to bring about recovery of endangered plant and animal species has nearly tripled in the 30 months of Secretary Jim Watt. From the very first, Jim pledged to the Governors of our 50 States that the Department would be a good neighbor, that they would be included in land planning, and that small tracts of isolated Federal lands would be made available to communities needing land for hospitals, schools, parks, or housing. He also stated that isolated small tracts would be sold to farmers and ranchers.

An example of what I'm talking about is a strip of land 1 mile long and only 2 to 20 feet wide that was recently sold. I think you can imagine how these efforts must have erased some problems private landowners had with clouded title to their property.

Of course, all this was distorted and led to protests that he was selling national parks and wilderness. What he actually did was sell, in 1982, 55 tracts that totaled only 1,300 acres, and this year, 228 tracts totaling a little over 10,000 acres. The largest parcel was 640 acres; that's 1 square mile. None of it was park, wildlife refuge, wilderness, or Indian trust lands. They are not for sale. And not one acre of national parkland was leased for oil drilling or mining, contrary to what you may have read or heard.

When territories were becoming States, they were promised title to Federal lands within their borders, some lands to be used for public education. But as more and more Western States joined the Union, there began to be a delay; in fact, a permanent delay in turning over these lands. Jim Watt promised the Governors that if they'd identify lands they had a right to claim under their statehood acts, we'd make the Federal Government honest. The Governors responded, and as a result, by the end of this year more land will have been delivered to the States to support their school systems than at any time since 1969.

Changes have been made in the management of forest lands which are eligible for multiple use. Those lands will provide lumber on a sustained-yield basis. This will benefit Americans who cherish the dream of owning their own home.

We've made giant strides in implementing a national water policy which recognizes State primacy in managing water resources. People must be a part of our planning, and people need a reliable, safe drinking water supply, water for generating power, and water for irrigation.

Since I've mentioned energy, let me touch on that for a minute. It's estimated that 85 percent of the fuel we need to keep the wheels of industry turning is on Federal-owned property, including the Outer Continental Shelf. Efforts to increase the supply of energy have been carried out in full compliance with environmental stipulations. We can and will have an increased energy supply with an enhanced environment.

James G. Watt has served this nation well. And I'm sure William Clark will do the same.

Till next week, thanks for listening, and God bless you.

## REMARKS AT A CEREMONY COMMEMORATING THE 40TH ANNIVERSARY OF THE NORMANDY INVASION,

### D-DAY
June 6, 1984

We're here to mark that day in history when the Allied armies joined in battle to reclaim this continent to liberty. For 4 long years, much of Europe had been under a terrible shadow. Free nations had fallen, Jews cried out in the camps, millions cried out for liberation. Europe was enslaved, and the world prayed for its rescue. Here in Normandy the rescue began. Here the Allies stood and fought against tyranny in a giant undertaking unparalleled in human history.

We stand on a lonely, windswept point on the northern shore of France. The air is soft, but 40 years ago at this moment, the air was dense with smoke and the cries of men, and the air was filled with the crack of rifle fire and the roar of cannon. At dawn, on the morning of the 6th of June, 1944, 225 Rangers jumped off the British landing craft and ran to the bottom of these cliffs. Their mission was one of the most difficult and daring of the invasion: to climb these sheer and desolate cliffs and take out the enemy guns. The Allies had been told that some of the mightiest of these guns were here and they would be trained on the beaches to stop the Allied advance.

The Rangers looked up and saw the enemy soldiers—the edge of the cliffs shooting down at them with machineguns and throwing grenades. And the American Rangers began to climb. They shot rope ladders over the face of these cliffs and began to pull themselves up. When one Ranger fell, another would take his place. When one rope was cut, a Ranger would grab another and begin his climb again. They climbed, shot back, and held their footing. Soon, one by one, the Rangers pulled themselves over the top, and in seizing the firm land at the top of these cliffs, they began to seize back the continent of Europe. Two hundred and twenty-five came here. After 2 days of fighting, only 90 could still bear arms.

Behind me is a memorial that symbolizes the Ranger daggers that were thrust into the top of these cliffs. And before me are the men who put them there.

These are the boys of Pointe du Hoc. These are the men who took the cliffs. These are the champions who helped free a continent. These are the heroes who helped end a war.

Gentlemen, I look at you and I think of the words of Stephen Spender's poem. You are men who in your "lives fought for life . . . and left the vivid air signed with your honor."

I think I know what you may be thinking right now—thinking "we were just part of a bigger effort; everyone was brave that day." Well, everyone was. Do you remember the story of Bill Millin of the 51st Highlanders? Forty years ago today, British troops were pinned down near a bridge, waiting desperately for help. Suddenly, they heard the sound of bagpipes, and some thought they were dreaming. Well, they weren't. They looked up and saw Bill Millin with his bagpipes, leading the reinforcements and ignoring the smack of the bullets into the ground around him.

Lord Lovat was with him — Lord Lovat of Scotland, who calmly announced when he got to the bridge, "Sorry I'm a few minutes late," as if he'd been delayed by a traffic jam, when in truth he'd just come from the bloody fighting on Sword Beach, which he and his men had just taken.

There was the impossible valor of the Poles who threw themselves between the enemy and the rest of Europe as the invasion took hold, and the unsurpassed courage of the Canadians who had already seen the horrors of war on this coast. They knew what awaited them there, but they would not be deterred. And once they hit Juno Beach, they never looked back.

All of these men were part of a roll call of honor with names that spoke of a pride as bright as the colors they bore: the Royal Winnipeg Rifles, Poland's 24th Lancers, the Royal Scots Fusiliers, the Screaming Eagles, the Yeomen of England's armored divisions, the forces of Free France, the Coast Guard's "Matchbox Fleet" and you, the American Rangers.

Forty summers have passed since the battle that you fought here. You were young the day you took these cliffs; some of you were hardly more than boys, with the deepest joys of life before you. Yet, you risked everything here. Why? Why did you do it? What impelled you to put aside the instinct for self-preservation and risk your lives to take these cliffs? What inspired all the men of the armies that met here? We look at you, and somehow we know the answer. It was faith and belief; it was loyalty and love.

The men of Normandy had faith that what they were doing was right, faith that they fought for all humanity, faith that a just God would grant them mercy on this beachhead or on the next. It was the deep knowledge—and pray God we have not lost it—that there is a profound, moral difference between the use of force for liberation and the use of force for conquest. You were here to liberate, not to conquer, and so you and those others did not doubt your cause. And you were right not to doubt.

You all knew that some things are worth dying for. One's country is worth dying for, and democracy is worth dying for, because it's the most deeply honorable form of government ever devised by man. All of you loved liberty. All of you were willing to fight tyranny, and you knew the people of your countries were behind you.

The Americans who fought here that morning knew word of the invasion was spreading through the darkness back home. They fought—or felt in their hearts, though they couldn't know in fact, that in Georgia they were filling the churches at 4 a.m., in Kansas they were kneeling on their porches and praying, and in Philadelphia they were ringing the Liberty Bell.

Something else helped the men of D-day: their rock-hard belief that Providence would have a great hand in the events that would unfold here; that God was an ally in this great cause. And so, the night before the invasion, when Colonel Wolverton asked his parachute troops to kneel with him in prayer he told them: Do not bow your heads, but look up so you can see God and ask His blessing in what we're about to do. Also that night, General Matthew Ridgway on his cot, listening in the darkness for the promise God made to Joshua: "I will not fail thee nor forsake thee."

These are the things that impelled them; these are the things that shaped the unity of the Allies.

When the war was over, there were lives to be rebuilt and governments to be returned to the people. There were nations to be reborn. Above all, there was a new peace to be assured. These were huge and daunting tasks. But the Allies summoned strength from the faith, belief, loyalty, and love of those who fell here. They rebuilt a new Europe together.

There was first a great reconciliation among those who had been enemies, all of whom had suffered so greatly. The United States did its part, creating the Marshall plan to help rebuild our allies and our former enemies. The Marshall plan led to the Atlantic alliance—a great alliance that serves to this day as our shield for freedom, for prosperity, and for peace.

In spite of our great efforts and successes, not all that followed the end of the war was happy or planned. Some liberated countries were lost. The great sadness of this loss echoes down to our own time in the streets of Warsaw, Prague, and East Berlin. Soviet troops that came to the center of this continent did not leave when peace came. They're still there, uninvited, unwanted, unyielding, almost 40 years after the war. Because of this, allied forces still stand on this continent. Today, as 40 years ago, our armies are here for only one purpose—to protect and defend democracy. The only territories we hold are memorials like this one and graveyards where our heroes rest.

We in America have learned bitter lessons from two World Wars: It is better to be here ready to protect the peace, than to take blind shelter across the sea, rushing to respond only after freedom is lost. We've learned that isolationism never was and never will be an acceptable response to tyrannical governments with an expansionist intent.

But we try always to be prepared for peace; prepared to deter aggression; prepared to negotiate the reduction of arms; and, yes, prepared to reach out again in the spirit of reconciliation. In truth, there is no reconciliation we would welcome more than a reconciliation with the Soviet Union, so, together, we can lessen the risks of war, now and forever.

It's fitting to remember here the great losses also suffered by the Russian people during World War II: 20 million perished, a terrible price that testifies to all the world the necessity of ending war. I tell you from my heart that we in the United States do not want war. We want to wipe from the face of the Earth the terrible weapons that man now has in his hands. And I tell you, we are ready to seize that beachhead. We look for some sign from the Soviet Union that they are willing to move forward, that they share our desire and love for peace, and that they will give up the ways of conquest. There must be a changing there that will allow us to turn our hope into action.

We will pray forever that some day that changing will come. But for now, particularly today, it is good and fitting to renew our commitment to each other, to our freedom, and to the alliance that protects it.

We are bound today by what bound us 40 years ago, the same loyalties, traditions, and beliefs. We're bound by reality. The strength of America's allies is vital to the United States, and the American security guarantee is essential to the continued freedom of Europe's democracies. We were with you then; we are with you now. Your hopes are our hopes, and your destiny is our destiny.

Here, in this place where the West held together, let us make a vow to our dead. Let us show them by our actions that we understand what they died for. Let our actions say to them the words for which Matthew Ridgway listened: "I will not fail thee nor forsake thee."

Strengthened by their courage, heartened by their valor, and borne by their memory, let us continue to stand for the ideals for which they lived and died.

Thank you very much, and God bless you all.

*Note: The President spoke at 1:20 p.m. at the site of the U.S. Ranger Monument at Pointe du Hoc, France, where veterans of the Normandy invasion had assembled for the ceremony.*

*Following his remarks, the President unveiled memorial plaques to the 2d and 5th Ranger Battalions. Then, escorted by Phil Rivers, superintendent of the Normandy American Cemetery, the President and Mrs. Reagan proceeded to the interior of the observation bunker. On leaving the bunker, the President and Mrs. Reagan greeted each of the veterans. Other Allied countries represented at the ceremony by their heads of state and government were: Queen Elizabeth II of the United Kingdom, Queen Beatrix of The Netherlands, King Olav V of Norway, King Baudouin I of Belgium, Grand Duke Jean of Luxembourg, and Prime Minister Pierre Elliott Trudeau of Canada.*

## ADDRESS TO THE NATION ON THE EXPLOSION OF THE SPACE SHUTTLE CHALLENGER
### January 28, 1986

Ladies and gentlemen, I'd planned to speak to you tonight to report on the state of the Union, but the events of earlier today have led me to change those plans. Today is a day for mourning and remembering. Nancy and I are pained to the core by the tragedy of the shuttle Challenger. We know we share this pain with all of the people of our country. This is truly a national loss.

Nineteen years ago, almost to the day, we lost three astronauts in a terrible accident on the ground. But we've never lost an astronaut in flight; we've never had a tragedy like this. And perhaps we've forgotten the courage it took for the crew of the shuttle. But they, the Challenger Seven, were aware of the dangers, but overcame them and did their jobs brilliantly. We mourn seven heroes: Michael Smith, Dick Scobee, Judith Resnik, Ronald McNair, Ellison Onizuka, Gregory Jarvis, and Christa McAuliffe. We mourn their loss as a nation together.

For the families of the seven, we cannot bear, as you do, the full impact of this tragedy. But we feel the loss, and we're thinking about you so very much. Your loved ones were daring and brave, and they had that special grace, that special spirit that says, "Give me a challenge, and I'll meet it with joy." They had a hunger to explore the universe and discover its truths. They wished to serve, and they did. They served all of us. We've grown used to wonders in this century. It's hard to dazzle us. But for 25 years the United States space program has been doing just that. We've grown used to the idea of space, and perhaps we forget that we've only just begun. We're still pioneers. They, the members of the Challenger crew, were pioneers.

And I want to say something to the schoolchildren of America who were watching the live coverage of the shuttle's takeoff. I know it is hard to understand, but sometimes painful things like this happen. It's all part of the process of exploration and discovery. It's all part of taking a chance and expanding man's horizons. The future doesn't belong to the fainthearted; it belongs to the brave. The Challenger crew was pulling us into the future, and we'll continue to follow them.

I've always had great faith in and respect for our space program, and what happened today does nothing to diminish it. We don't hide our space program. We don't keep secrets and cover things up. We do it all up front and in public. That's the way freedom is, and we wouldn't change it for a minute. We'll continue our quest in space. There will be more shuttle flights and more shuttle crews and, yes, more volunteers, more civilians, more teachers in space. Nothing ends here; our hopes and our journeys continue. I want to add that I wish I could talk to every man and woman who works for NASA or who worked on this mission and tell them: "Your dedication and professionalism have moved and impressed us for decades. And we know of your anguish. We share it."

There's a coincidence today. On this day 390 years ago, the great explorer Sir Francis Drake died aboard ship off the coast of Panama. In his lifetime the great frontiers were the oceans, and an historian later said, "He lived by the sea, died on it, and was buried in it." Well, today we can say of the Challenger crew: Their dedication was, like Drake's, complete.

The crew of the space shuttle Challenger honored us by the manner in which they lived their lives. We will never forget them, nor the last time we saw them, this morning, as they prepared for their journey and waved goodbye and "slipped the surly bonds of earth" to "touch the face of God."

*Note: The President spoke at 5 p.m. from the Oval Office at the White House. The address was broadcast live on nationwide radio and television.*

My fellow citizens:

The matter that brings me before you today is a grave one and concerns my most solemn duty as President. It is the cause of freedom in Central America and the national security of the United States. Tomorrow the House of Representatives will debate and vote on this issue. I had hoped to speak directly and at this very hour to Members of the House of Representatives on this subject, but was unable to do so. Because I feel so strongly about what I have to say, I've asked for this time to share with you—and Members of the House—the message I would've otherwise given.

Nearly 40 years ago a Democratic President, Harry Truman, went before the Congress to warn of another danger to democracy, a civil war in a faraway country in which many Americans could perceive no national security interest. Some of you can remember the world then. Europe lay devastated. One by one, the nations of Eastern Europe had fallen into Stalin's grip. The democratic government of Czechoslovakia would soon be overthrown. Turkey was threatened, and in Greece—the home of democracy—Communist guerrillas, backed by the Soviet Union, battled democratic forces to decide the nation's fate. Most Americans did not perceive this distant danger, so the opinion polls reflected little of the concern that brought Harry Truman to the well of the House that day. But go he did, and it is worth a moment to reflect on what he said.

In a hushed Chamber, Mr. Truman said that we had come to a time in history when every nation would have to choose between two opposing ways of life. One way was based on the will of the majority—on free institutions and human rights. "The second way of life," he said, "is based upon the will of a minority forcibly imposed upon the majority. It relies upon terror and oppression, a controlled press and radio, fixed elections and the suppression of personal freedoms. I believe," President Truman said, "that it must be the policy of the United States to support free peoples who are resisting attempted subjugation by armed minorities or by outside pressures." When Harry Truman spoke, Congress was controlled by the Republican Party. But that Congress put America's interest first and supported Truman's request for military aid to Greece and Turkey—just as 4 years ago Congress put America's interest first by supporting my request for military aid to defend democracy in El Salvador.

I speak today in that same spirit of bipartisanship. My fellow Americans and Members of the House, I need your help. I ask first for your help in remembering—remembering our history in Central America, so we can learn from the mistakes of the past. Too often in the past the United States failed to identify with the aspirations of the people of Central America for freedom and a better life. Too often our government appeared indifferent when democratic values were at risk. So, we took the path of least resistance and did nothing. Today, however, with American support, the tide is turning in Central America. In El Salvador, Honduras, Costa Rica—and now in Guatemala—freely elected governments offer their people the chance for a better future, a future the United States must support.

But there's one tragic, glaring exception to that democratic tide—the Communist Sandinista government in Nicaragua. It is tragic because the United States extended a generous hand of friendship to the new revolutionary government when it came to power in 1979. Congress voted $75 million in economic aid. The United

States helped renegotiate Nicaragua's foreign debt. America offered teachers, doctors, and Peace Corps volunteers to help rebuild the country. But the Sandinistas had a different agenda.

From the very first day a small clique of Communists worked steadily to consolidate power and squeeze out their democratic allies. The democratic trade unionists who had fought Somoza's national guard in the streets were now told by the Sandinistas that the right to strike was illegal and that their revolutionary duty was to produce more for the state. The newspaper, La Prensa, whose courage and determination had inspired so much of the Nicaraguan revolution, found its pages censored and suppressed. Violeta Chamorro, widow of the assassinated editor, soon quit the revolutionary government to take up the struggle for democracy again in the pages of her newspaper. The leader of the Catholic Church in Nicaragua, Archbishop—now Cardinal—Obando y Bravo, who had negotiated the release of the Sandinista leaders from prison during the revolution, was now vilified as a traitor by the very men he helped to free.

Soviet arms and bloc personnel began arriving in Nicaragua. With Cuban, East German, and Bulgarian advisors at their side, the Sandinistas began to build the largest standing army in Central American history and to erect all the odious apparatus of the modern police state. Under the Somoza dictatorship, a single facility held all political prisoners. Today there are eleven—eleven prisons in place of one. The Sandinistas claim to defend Nicaraguan independence, but you and I know the truth. The proud people of Nicaragua did not rise up against Somoza—and struggle, fight, and die—to have Cubans, Russians, Bulgarians, East Germans, and North Koreans running their prisons, organizing their army, censoring their newspapers, and suppressing their religious faith. One Nicaraguan nationalist who fought in the revolution says, "We are an occupied country today."

I could go on, but I know that even the administration's harshest critics in Congress hold no brief for Sandinista repression. Indeed, the final verdict has already been written by Cardinal Obando himself in the Washington Post. Listen carefully to the Cardinal's words.

He says that the Sandinista regime "is a democratic government, legitimately constituted, which seeks the welfare and peace of the people and enjoys the support of the overwhelming majority" is not true. To accept this as true, the Cardinal says, "is to ignore the mass exodus of the Miskito Indians, the departure of tens of thousands of Nicaraguan men and women of every age, profession, economic status, and political persuasion. It is to ignore the most terrible violation of freedom of the press and of speech in the history of our country, the expulsion of priests, and the mass exodus of young people eligible for military service." As for the Catholic Church in Nicaragua, we have been "gagged and bound," the Cardinal says.

Many brave Nicaraguans have stayed in their country despite mounting repression—defying the security police, defying the Sandinista mobs that attack and deface their homes. Thousands— peasants, Indians, devout Christians, draftees from the Sandinista army—have concluded that they must take up arms again to fight for the freedom they thought they had won in 1979. The young men and women of the democratic resistance fight inside Nicaragua today in grueling mountain and jungle warfare. They confront a Soviet-equipped army, trained and led by Cuban officers. They face murderous helicopter gunships without any means of defense. And still they volunteer. And still their numbers grow. Who among us would tell these brave young men and women: "Your dream is dead; your democratic revolution is over; you will never live in the free Nicaragua you fought so hard to build?"

The Sandinistas call these freedom fighters contras, for counter-revolutionaries. But the real counterrevolutionaries are the Sandinista commandantes, who betrayed the hopes of the Nicaraguan revolution and sold out their country to the Soviet empire. The commandantes even betrayed the memory of the Nicaraguan rebel leader Sandino, whose legacy they falsely claim. For the real Sandino, because he was a genuine nationalist, was opposed to communism. In fact, Sandino broke with the Salvadoran Communist leader, Farbundo Marti, over this very issue. The true Nicaraguan nationalists are the leaders of the United Nicaraguan Opposition: Arturo Cruz, jailed by Somoza, a former member of the Sandinista government; Adolpho Calero, who helped organize a strike of businessmen to bring Somoza down; and Alfonso Robelo, a social democrat and once a leader of the revolutionary government. These good men refused to make any accommodation with the Somoza dictatorship. Who among us can doubt their commitment to bring democracy to Nicaragua?

So, the Nicaraguan people have chosen to fight for their freedom. Now we Americans must also choose, for you and I and every American has a stake in this struggle. Central America is vital to our own national security, and the Soviet Union knows it. The Soviets take the long view, but their strategy is clear: to dominate the strategic sealanes and vital chokepoints around the world. Half of America's imports and exports, including oil, travels through the area today. In a crisis, over half of NATO's supplies would pass through this region. And Nicaragua, just 277 miles from the Panama Canal, offers the Soviet Union ports on both the Atlantic and Pacific Oceans.

The Soviet Union already uses Cuba as an air and submarine base in the Caribbean. It hopes to turn Nicaragua into the first Soviet base on the mainland of North America. If you doubt it, ask yourself: Why have the last four Soviet leaders, with a mounting economic crisis at home, already invested over a billion dollars and dispatched thousands of Soviet-bloc advisors into a tiny country in Central America? I know that no one in Congress wants to see Nicaragua become a Soviet military base. My friends, I must tell you in all seriousness, Nicaragua is becoming a Soviet base every day that we debate and debate and debate—and do nothing. In the three months since I last asked for the House to aid the democratic resistance, four military cargo ships have arrived at Nicaraguan ports, this time directly from the Soviet Union. Recently we have learned that Russian pilots are flying a Soviet AN-30 reconnaissance plane for the Sandinistas. Now, the Sandinistas claim this is just for making civilian maps. Well, our intelligence services believe this could be the first time Soviet personnel have taken a direct role in support of military operations on the mainland of North America.

Think again how Cuba became a Soviet air and naval base. You'll see what Nicaragua will look like if we continue to do nothing. Cuba became a Soviet base gradually, over many years. There was no single, dramatic event—once the missile crisis passed—that captured the Nation's attention. And so it will be with Nicaragua. The Sandinistas will widen and deepen another port while we debate: Is it for commercial vessels or Soviet submarines? The Sandinistas will complete another airstrip while we argue: Is it for 707s or Backfire bombers? A Soviet training brigade will come to Nicaragua. Half will leave and half will stay. And we will debate: Are they soldiers or engineers?

Eventually, we Americans have to stop arguing among ourselves. We will have to confront the reality of a Soviet military beachhead inside our defense perimeters, about 500 miles from Mexico. A future President and Congress will then face nothing but bad choices, followed by worse choices. My friends in the House, for over 200 years the security of the United States has depended on the safety of unthreatened borders, north and south. Do we want to be the first elected leaders in U.S. history to put our borders at risk? Some of you may say, well, this is fearmongering. Such a danger to our security will never come to pass. Well, perhaps it won't. But in making your decisions on my request for aid tomorrow, consider this: What are the consequences for our country if you're wrong?

I know some Members of Congress who share my concern about Nicaragua have honest questions about my request for aid to the democratic resistance. Let me try to address them. Do the freedom fighters have the support of the Nicaraguan people? I urge Members of the House to ask their colleague, the chairman of the House Armed Services Committee, who recently visited a town in Nicaragua that was a Sandinista stronghold during the revolution. He heard peasants, trade unionists, farmers, workers, students, and shopkeepers all call on the United States to aid the armed resistance. Or listen to the report from Time magazine of Central American scholar Robert Leiken, who once had hopes for the Sandinista revolution. He says, "I have gone to a number of towns in Nicaragua where I have found that the youth are simply not there. I ask the parents where they've gone, and they say, they've gone off to join the contras." In Managua, Leiken reports 250 Nicaraguans stood on a breadline for 3 hours. "Who is responsible for this?" he asked. "The Sandinistas are responsible. The Sandinistas." That's what the people said. "The Sandinistas," Leiken concluded, "have not only lost support, I think they are detested by the population."

Can the democratic forces win? Consider there are 20 times as many Nicaraguans fighting the Sandinista dictatorship today as there were Sandinista fighters a year before Somoza fell. This is the largest peasant army raised in Latin America in more than 50 years. And thousands more are waiting to volunteer if American support comes through. Some Members of Congress—and I know some of you—fear that military aid to the democratic resistance will be only the first step down the slippery slope toward another Vietnam. Now, I know those fears are honest, but think where we heard them before. Just a few years ago some argued in Congress that U.S. military aid to El Salvador would lead inevitably to the involvement of U.S. combat troops. But the opposite turned out to be true.

Had the United States failed to provide aid then, we might well be facing the final Communist takeover of El Salvador and mounting pressures to intervene. Instead, with our aid, the Government of El Salvador is winning the war, and there is no prospect whatever of American military involvement. El Salvador still faces serious problems that require our attention. But democracy there is stronger, and both the Communist guerrillas and the right-wing death squads are weaker. And Congress shares credit for that accomplishment. American aid and training is helping the Salvadoran Army become a professional fighting force, more respectful of human rights. With our aid, we can help the Nicaraguan resistance accomplish the same goal.

I stress this point because I know many Members of Congress and many Americans are deeply troubled by allegations of abuses by elements of the armed resistance. I share your concerns. Even though some of those charges are Sandinista propaganda, I believe such abuses have occurred in the past, and they are intolerable. As President, I repeat to you the commitments I made to Senator Sam Nunn. As a condition of our aid, I will insist on civilian control over all military forces; that no human rights abuses are tolerated; that any financial corruption be rooted out; that American aid go only to those committed to democratic principles. The United States will not permit this democratic revolution to be betrayed nor allow a return to the hated repression of the Somoza dictatorship. The leadership of the United Nicaraguan Opposition shares these commitments, and I welcome the appointment of a bipartisan congressional commission to help us see that they are carried out.

Some ask: What are the goals of our policy toward Nicaragua? They are the goals the Nicaraguan people set for themselves in 1979: democracy, a free economy, and national self-determination. Clearly, the best way to achieve these goals is through a negotiated settlement. No humane person wants to see suffering and war. The leaders of the internal opposition and the Catholic Church have asked for dialog with the Sandinistas. The leaders of the armed resistance have called for a cease-fire and negotiations at any time, in any place. We urge the Sandinistas to heed the pleas of the Nicaraguan people for a peaceful settlement. The United States will support any negotiated settlement or Contadora treaty that will bring real democracy to Nicaragua. What we will not support is a paper agreement that sells out the Nicaraguan people's right to be free. That kind of agreement would be unworthy of us as a people; and it would be a false bargain, for internal freedom in Nicaragua and the security of Central America are indivisible. A free and democratic Nicaragua will pose no threat to its neighbors or to the United States. A Communist Nicaragua, allied with the Soviet Union, is a permanent threat to us all.

President Azcona of Honduras emphasized this point in a recent nationwide address: "As long as there is a totalitarian regime in Central America that has expansionist ambitions and is supported by an enormous military apparatus . . . the neighboring countries sharing common borders with the country that is the source of the problem will be under constant threat." If you doubt his warning, consider this: The Sandinistas have already sent two groups of Communist guerrillas into Honduras. Costa Rican revolutionaries are already fighting alongside Sandinista troops.

My friends in the Congress, with democracy still a fragile root in Central America—with Mexico undergoing an economic crisis—can we responsibly ignore the long-term danger to American interests posed by a Communist Nicaragua, backed by the Soviet Union, and dedicated—in the words of its own leaders—to a "revolution without borders"? My friends, the only way to bring true peace and security to Central America is to bring democracy to Nicaragua. And the only way to get the Sandinistas to negotiate seriously about democracy is to give them no other alternative. Seven years of broken pledges, betrayals, and lies have taught us that.

And that's why the measure the House will consider tomorrow—offered, I know, in good faith—which prohibits military aid for at least another three months, and perhaps forever, would be a tragic mistake. It would not bring the Sandinistas to the bargaining table—just the opposite. The bill, unless amended, would give the Sandinistas and the Soviet Union what they seek most: time—time to crush the democratic resistance; time to consolidate power. And it would send a demoralizing message to the democratic resistance that the United States is too divided and paralyzed to come to their aid in time.

Recently, I read the words of a leader of the internal democratic opposition. What he said made me feel ashamed. This man has been jailed, his property confiscated, and his life threatened by the security police. Still, he continues to fight. And he said: "You Americans have the strength, the opportunity, but not the will. We want to struggle, but it is dangerous to have friends like you—to be left stranded on the landing beaches of the Bay of Pigs. Either help us or leave us alone." My friends in the House of Representatives, I urge you to send a message tomorrow to this brave Nicaraguan and thousands like him. Tell them it is not dangerous to have friends like us. Tell them America stands with those who stand in defense of freedom.

When the Senate voted earlier this year for military aid, Republicans were joined by many Democratic leaders: Bill Bradley of New Jersey, Sam Nunn of Georgia, David Boren of Oklahoma, Howell Heflin of Alabama, Lloyd Bentsen of Texas, Bennett Johnston and Russell Long of Louisiana, Fritz Hollings of South Carolina, John Stennis of Mississippi, and Alan Dixon of Illinois. Today I ask the House for that kind of bipartisan support for the amendment to be offered tomorrow by Democrats Ike Skelton of Missouri and Richard Ray of Georgia and Republicans Mickey Edwards of Oklahoma and Rod Chandler of Washington. This bipartisan amendment will provide the freedom fighters with what they need — now. With that amendment, you also send another message to Central America. For democracy there faces many enemies: poverty, illiteracy, hunger, and despair. And the United States must also stand with the people of Central America against these enemies of democracy. And that's why—just as Harry Truman followed his request for military aid to Greece and Turkey with the Marshall plan—I urge Congress to support $300 million in new economic aid to the Central American democracies.

The question before the House is not only about the freedom of Nicaragua and the security of the United States but who we are as a people. President Kennedy wrote on the day of his death that history had called this generation of Americans to be "watchmen on the walls of world freedom." A Republican President, Abraham Lincoln, said much the same thing on the way to his inauguration in 1861. Stopping in Philadelphia, Lincoln spoke in Independence Hall, where our Declaration of Independence had been signed. He said far more had been achieved in that hall than just American independence from Britain. Something permanent, something unalterable, had happened. He called it "Hope to the world for all future time."

Hope to the world for all future time. In some way, every man, woman, and child in our world is tied to those events at Independence Hall, to the universal claim to dignity, to the belief that all human beings are created equal, that all people have a right to be free. We Americans have not forgotten our revolutionary heritage, but sometimes it takes others to remind us of what we ourselves believe. Recently, I read the works of a Nicaraguan bishop, Pablo Vega, who visited Washington a few weeks ago. Somoza called Pablo Vega the "communist bishop." Now the Sandinistas revile him as "the contra bishop." But Pablo Vega is really a humble man of God. "I am saddened," the good bishop said, "that so many North Americans have a vision of democracy that has only to do with materialism." The Sandinistas "speak of human rights as if they were talking of the rights of a child—the right to receive from the bountifulness of the state—but even the humblest campesino knows what it means to have the right to act. We are defending," Pablo Vega said, "the right of man to be."

Well, reverend father, we hear you. For we Americans believe with you that even the humblest campesino has the right to be free. My fellow citizens, Members of the House, let us not take the path of least resistance in Central America again. Let us keep faith with these brave people struggling for their freedom. Give them, give me, your support; and together, let us send this message to the world: that America is still a beacon of hope, still a light unto the nations. A light that casts its glow across the land and our continent and even back across the centuries—keeping faith with a dream of long ago.

Thank you, and God bless you.

*Note: The President spoke at noon from the Oval Office at the White House.*

REMARKS ON EAST-WEST RELATIONS AT THE
BRANDENBURG GATE IN WEST BERLIN
June 12, 1987

Thank you very much. Chancellor Kohl, Governing Mayor Diepgen, ladies and gentlemen: Twenty four years ago, President John F. Kennedy visited Berlin, speaking to the people of this city and the world at the city hall. Well, since then two other presidents have come, each in his turn, to Berlin. And today I, myself, make my second visit to your city.

We come to Berlin, we American Presidents, because it's our duty to speak, in this place, of freedom. But I must confess, we're drawn here by other things as well: by the feeling of history in this city, more than 500 years older than our own nation; by the beauty of the Grunewald and the Tiergarten; most of all, by your courage and determination. Perhaps the composer, Paul Lincke, understood something about American Presidents. You see, like so many Presidents before me, I come here today because wherever I go, whatever I do: *"Ich hab noch einen koffer in Berlin."* [I still have a suitcase in Berlin.]

Our gathering today is being broadcast throughout Western Europe and North America. I understand that it is being seen and heard as well in the East. To those listening throughout Eastern Europe, I extend my warmest greetings and the good will of the American people. To those listening in East Berlin, a special word: Although I cannot be with you, I address my remarks to you just as surely as to those standing here before me. For I join you, as I join your fellow countrymen in the West, in this firm, this unalterable belief: *Es gibt nur ein Berlin.* [There is only one Berlin.]

Behind me stands a wall that encircles the free sectors of this city, part of a vast system of barriers that divides the entire continent of Europe. From the Baltic, south, those barriers cut across Germany in a gash of barbed wire, concrete, dog runs, and guardtowers. Farther south, there may be no visible, no obvious wall. But there remain armed guards and checkpoints all the same—still a restriction on the right to travel, still an instrument to impose upon ordinary men and women the will of a totalitarian state. Yet it is here in Berlin where the wall emerges most clearly; here, cutting across your city, where the news photo and the television screen have imprinted this brutal division of a continent upon the mind of the world. Standing before the Brandenburg Gate, every man is a German, separated from his fellow men. Every man is a Berliner, forced to look upon a scar.

President von Weizsacker has said: "The German question is open as long as the Brandenburg Gate is closed." Today I say: As long as this gate is closed, as long as this scar of a wall is permitted to stand, it is not the German question alone that remains open, but the question of freedom for all mankind. Yet I do not come here to lament. For I find in Berlin a message of hope, even in the shadow of this wall, a message of triumph.

In this season of spring in 1945, the people of Berlin emerged from their air-raid shelters to find devastation. Thousands of miles away, the people of the United States reached out to help. And in 1947 Secretary of State—as you've been told—George Marshall announced the creation of what would become known as the Marshall plan. Speaking precisely 40 years ago this month, he said: "Our policy is directed not against any country or doctrine, but against hunger, poverty, desperation, and chaos."

In the Reichstag a few moments ago, I saw a display commemorating this 40th anniversary of the Marshall plan. I was struck by the sign on a burnt-out, gutted structure that was being rebuilt. I understand that Berliners of my own generation can remember seeing signs like it dotted throughout the Western sectors of the city. The sign read simply: "The Marshall plan is helping here to strengthen the free world." A strong, free world in the West, that dream became real. Japan rose from ruin to become an economic giant. Italy, France, Belgium—virtually every nation in Western Europe saw political and economic rebirth; the European Community was founded.

In West Germany and here in Berlin, there took place an economic miracle, the *Wirtschaftswunder*. Adenauer, Erhard, Reuter, and other leaders understood the practical importance of liberty— that just as truth can flourish only when the journalist is given freedom of speech, so prosperity can come about only when the farmer and businessman enjoy economic freedom. The German leaders reduced tariffs, expanded free trade, lowered taxes. From 1950 to 1960 alone, the standard of living in West Germany and Berlin doubled.

Where four decades ago there was rubble, today in West Berlin there is the greatest industrial output of any city in Germany-busy office blocks, fine homes and apartments, proud avenues, and the spreading lawns of park land. Where a city's culture seemed to have been destroyed, today there are two great universities, orchestras and an opera, countless theaters, and museums. Where there was want, today there's abundance—food, clothing, automobiles-the wonderful goods of the *Ku'damm*. From devastation, from utter ruin, you Berliners have, in freedom, rebuilt a city that once again ranks as one of the greatest on Earth. The Soviets may have had other plans. But, my friends, there were a few things the Soviets didn't count on Berliner *herz*, Berliner humor, *ja, und Berliner schnauze*. [Berliner heart, Berliner humor, yes, and a Berliner schnauze.] [Laughter]

In the 1950s, Khrushchev predicted: "We will bury you." But in the West today, we see a free world that has achieved a level of prosperity and well-being unprecedented in all human history. In the Communist world, we see failure, technological backwardness, declining standards of health, even want of the most basic kind—too little food. Even today, the Soviet Union still cannot feed itself. After these four decades, then, there stands before the entire world one great and inescapable conclusion: Freedom leads to prosperity. Freedom replaces the ancient hatreds among the nations with comity and peace. Freedom is the victor.

And now the Soviets themselves may, in a limited way, be coming to understand the importance of freedom. We hear much from Moscow about a new policy of reform and openness. Some political prisoners have been released. Certain foreign news broadcasts are no longer being jammed. Some economic enterprises have been permitted to operate with greater freedom from state control. Are these the beginnings of profound changes in the Soviet state? Or are they token gestures, intended to raise false hopes in the West, or to strengthen the Soviet system without changing it? We welcome change and openness; for we believe that freedom and security go together, that the advance of human liberty can only strengthen the cause of world peace.

There is one sign the Soviets can make that would be unmistakable, that would advance dramatically the cause of freedom and peace. General Secretary Gorbachev, if you seek peace, if you seek prosperity for the Soviet Union and Eastern Europe, if you seek liberalization: Come here to this gate! Mr. Gorbachev, open this gate! Mr. Gorbachev, tear down this wall!

I understand the fear of war and the pain of division that afflict this continent—and I pledge to you my country's efforts to help overcome these burdens. To be sure, we in the West must resist Soviet expansion. So we must maintain defenses of unassailable strength. Yet we seek peace; so we must strive to reduce arms on both sides. Beginning 10 years ago, the Soviets challenged the Western alliance with a grave new threat, hundreds of new and more deadly SS-20 nuclear missiles, capable of-striking every capital in Europe. The Western alliance responded by committing itself to a counter-deployment unless the Soviets agreed to negotiate a better solution;

namely, the elimination of such weapons on both sides. For many months, the Soviets refused to bargain in earnestness. As the alliance, in turn, prepared to go forward with its counter-deployment, there were difficult days—days of protests like those during my 1982 visit to this city—and the Soviets later walked away from the table.

But through it all, the alliance held firm. And I invite those who protested then—I invite those who protest today—to mark this fact: Because we remained strong, the Soviets came back to the table. And because we remained strong, today we have within reach the possibility, not merely of limiting the growth of arms, but of eliminating, for the first time, an entire class of nuclear weapons from the face of the Earth. As I speak, NATO ministers are meeting in Iceland to review the progress of our proposals for eliminating these weapons. At the talks in Geneva, we have also proposed deep cuts in strategic offensive weapons. And the Western allies have likewise made far-reaching proposals to reduce the danger of conventional war and to place a total ban on chemical weapons.

While we pursue these arms reductions, I pledge to you that we will maintain the capacity to deter Soviet aggression at any level at which it might occur. And in cooperation with many of our allies, the United States is pursuing the Strategic Defense Initiative-research to base deterrence not on the threat of offensive retaliation, but on defenses that truly defend; on systems, in short, that will not target populations, but shield them. By these means we seek to increase the safety of Europe and all the world. But we must remember a crucial fact: East and West do not mistrust each other because we are armed; we are armed because we mistrust each other. And our differences are not about weapons but about liberty. When President Kennedy spoke at the City Hall those 24 years ago, freedom was encircled, Berlin was under siege. And today, despite all the pressures upon this city, Berlin stands secure in its liberty. And freedom itself is transforming the globe.

In the Philippines, in South and Central America, democracy has been given a rebirth. Throughout the Pacific, free markets are working miracle after miracle of economic growth. In the industrialized nations, a technological revolution is taking place—a revolution marked by rapid, dramatic advances in computers and telecommunications.

In Europe, only one nation and those it controls refuse to join the community of freedom. Yet in this age of redoubled economic growth, of information and innovation, the Soviet Union faces a choice: It must make fundamental changes, or it will become obsolete. Today thus represents a moment of hope. We in the West stand ready to cooperate with the East to promote true openness, to break down barriers that separate people, to create a safer, freer world.

And surely there is no better place than Berlin, the meeting place of East and West, to make a start. Free people of Berlin: Today, as in the past, the United States stands for the strict observance and full implementation of all parts of the Four Power Agreement of 1971. Let us use this occasion, the 750th anniversary of this city, to usher in a new era, to seek a still fuller, richer life for the Berlin of the future. Together, let us maintain and develop the ties between the Federal Republic and the Western sectors of Berlin, which is permitted by the 1971 agreement.

And I invite Mr. Gorbachev: Let us work to bring the Eastern and Western parts of the city closer together, so that all the inhabitants of all Berlin can enjoy the benefits that come with life in one of the great cities of the world. To open Berlin still further to all Europe, East and West, let us expand the vital air access to this city, finding ways of making commercial air service to Berlin more convenient, more comfortable, and more economical. We look to the day when West Berlin can become one of the chief aviation hubs in all central Europe.

With our French and British partners, the United States is prepared to help bring international meetings to Berlin. It would be only fitting for Berlin to serve as the site of United Nations meetings, or world conferences on human rights and arms control or other issues that call for international cooperation. There is no better way to establish hope for the future than to enlighten young minds, and we would be honored to sponsor summer youth exchanges, cultural events, and other programs for young Berliners from the East. Our French and British friends, I'm certain, will do the same. And it's my hope that an authority can be found in East Berlin to sponsor visits from young people of the Western sectors.

One final proposal, one close to my heart: Sport represents a source of enjoyment and ennoblement, and you many have noted that the Republic of Korea—South Korea-has offered to permit certain events of the 1988 Olympics to take place in the North. International sports competitions of all kinds could take place in both parts of this city. And what better way to demonstrate to the world the openness of this city than to offer in some future year to hold the Olympic games here in Berlin, East and West?

In these four decades, as I have said, you Berliners have built a great city. You've done so in spite of threats—the Soviet attempts to impose the East-mark, the blockade. Today the city thrives in spite of the challenges implicit in the very presence of this wall. What keeps you here? Certainly there's a great deal to be said for your fortitude, for your defiant courage. But I believe there's something deeper, something that involves Berlin's whole look and feel and way of life—not mere sentiment. No one could live long in Berlin without being completely disabused of illusions. Something instead, that has seen the difficulties of life in Berlin but chose to accept them, that continues to build this good and proud city in contrast to a surrounding totalitarian presence that refuses to release human energies or aspirations. Something that speaks with a powerful voice of affirmation, that says yes to this city, yes to the future, yes to freedom. In a word, I would submit that what keeps you in Berlin is love—love both profound and abiding.

Perhaps this gets to the root of the matter, to the most fundamental distinction of all between East and West. The totalitarian world produces backwardness because it does such violence to the spirit, thwarting the human impulse to create, to enjoy, to worship.

The totalitarian world finds even symbols of love and of worship an affront. Years ago, before the East Germans began rebuilding their churches, they erected a secular structure: the television tower at Alexander Platz. Virtually ever since, the authorities have been working to correct what they view as the tower's one major flaw, treating the glass sphere at the top with paints and chemicals of every kind. Yet even today when the Sun strikes that sphere—that sphere that towers over all Berlin—the light makes the sign of the cross. There in Berlin, like the city itself, symbols of love, symbols of worship, cannot be suppressed.

As I looked out a moment ago from the Reichstag, that embodiment of German unity, I noticed words crudely spray-painted upon the wall, perhaps by a young Berliner, "This wall will fall. Beliefs become reality." Yes, across Europe, this wall will fall. For it cannot withstand faith; it cannot withstand truth. The wall cannot withstand freedom.

And I would like, before I close, to say one word. I have read, and I have been questioned since I've been here about certain demonstrations against my coming. And I would like to say just one thing, and to those who demonstrate so. I wonder if they have ever asked themselves that if they should have the kind of government they apparently seek, no one would ever be able to do what they're doing again.

Thank you and God bless you all.

The President. Thank you, Rector Logunov, and I want to thank all of you very much for a very warm welcome. It's a great pleasure to be here at Moscow State University, and I want to thank you all for turning out. I know you must be very busy this week, studying and taking your final examinations. So, let me just say *zhelayu vam uspekha* [I wish you success]. Nancy couldn't make it today because she's visiting Leningrad, which she tells me is a very beautiful city, but she, too, says hello and wishes you all good luck.

Let me say it's also a great pleasure to once again have this opportunity to speak directly to the people of the Soviet Union. Before I left Washington, I received many heartfelt letters and telegrams asking me to carry here a simple message, perhaps, but also some of the most important business of this summit: It is a message of peace and good will and hope for a growing friendship and closeness between our two peoples.

As you know, I've come to Moscow to meet with one of your most distinguished graduates. In this, our fourth summit, General Secretary Gorbachev and I have spent many hours together, and I feel that we're getting to know each other well. Our discussions, of course, have been focused primarily on many of the important issues of the day, issues I want to touch on with you in a few moments. But first I want to take a little time to talk to you much as I would to any group of university students in the United States. I want to talk not just of the realities of today but of the possibilities of tomorrow.

Standing here before a mural of your revolution, I want to talk about a very different revolution that is taking place right now, quietly sweeping the globe without bloodshed or conflict. Its effects are peaceful, but they will fundamentally alter our world, shatter old assumptions, and reshape our lives. It's easy to underestimate because it's not accompanied by banners or fanfare. It's been called the technological or information revolution, and as its emblem, one might take the tiny silicon chip, no bigger than a fingerprint. One of these chips has more computing power than a roomful of old-style computers.

As part of an exchange program, we now have an exhibition touring your country that shows how information technology is transforming our lives—replacing manual labor with robots, forecasting weather for farmers, or mapping the genetic code of DNA for medical researchers. These microcomputers today aid the design of everything from houses to cars to spacecraft; they even design better and faster computers. They can translate English into Russian or enable the blind to read or help Michael Jackson produce on one synthesizer the sounds of a whole orchestra. Linked by a network of satellites and fiber-optic cables, one individual with a desktop computer and a telephone commands resources unavailable to the largest governments just a few years ago.

Like a chrysalis, we're emerging from the economy of the Industrial Revolution—an economy confined to and limited by the Earth's physical resources—into, as one economist titled his book, "The Economy in Mind," in which there are no bounds on human imagination and the freedom to create is the most precious natural resource. Think of that little computer chip. Its value isn't in the sand from which it is made but in the microscopic architecture designed into it by ingenious human minds. Or take the example of the satellite relaying this broadcast around the world, which replaces thousands of tons of copper mined from the Earth and molded into wire. In the new economy, human invention increasingly makes physical resources obsolete. We're breaking through the material conditions of existence to a world where man creates his own destiny. Even as we explore the most advanced reaches of science, we're returning to the age-old wisdom of our culture, a wisdom contained in the book of Genesis in the Bible: In the beginning was the spirit, and it was from this spirit that the material abundance of creation issued forth.

But progress is not foreordained. The key is freedom—freedom of thought, freedom of information, freedom of communication. The renowned scientist, scholar, and founding father of this university, Mikhail Lomonosov, knew that. "It is common knowledge," he said, "that the achievements of science are considerable and rapid, particularly once the yoke of slavery is cast off and replaced by the freedom of philosophy." You know, one of the first contacts between your country and mine took place between Russian and American explorers. The Americans were members of Cook's last voyage on an expedition searching for an Arctic passage; on the island of Unalaska, they came upon the Russians, who took them in, and together with the native inhabitants, held a prayer service on the ice.

The explorers of the modern era are the entrepreneurs, men with vision, with the courage to take risks and faith enough to brave the unknown. These entrepreneurs and their small enterprises are responsible for almost all the economic growth in the United States. They are the prime movers of the technological revolution. In fact, one of the largest personal computer firms in the United States was started by two college students, no older than you, in the garage behind their home. Some people, even in my own country, look at the riot of experiment that is the free market and see only waste. What of all the entrepreneurs that fail? Well, many do, particularly the successful ones; often several times. And if you ask them the secret of their success, they'll tell you it's all that they learned in their struggles along the way; yes, it's what they learned from failing. Like an athlete in competition or a scholar in pursuit of the truth, experience is the greatest teacher.

And that's why it's so hard for government planners, no matter how sophisticated, to ever substitute for millions of individuals working night and day to make their dreams come true. The fact is, bureaucracies are a problem around the world. There's an old story about a town—it could be anywhere—with a bureaucrat who is known to be a good-for-nothing, but he somehow had always hung on to power. So one day, in a town meeting, an old woman got up and said to him: "There is a folk legend here where I come from that when a baby is born, an angel comes down from heaven and kisses it on one part of its body. If the angel kisses him on his hand, he becomes a handyman. If he kisses him on his forehead, he becomes bright and clever. And I've been trying to figure out where the angel kissed you so that you should sit there for so long and do nothing." [Laughter]

We are seeing the power of economic freedom spreading around the world.

Places such as the Republic of Korea, Singapore, Taiwan have vaulted into the technological era, barely pausing in the industrial age along the way. Low-tax agricultural policies in the subcontinent mean that in some years India is now a net exporter of food. Perhaps most exciting are the winds of change that are blowing over the People's Republic of China, where one-quarter of the world's population is now getting its first taste of economic freedom. At the same time, the growth of democracy has become one of the most powerful political movements of our age. In Latin America in the 1970s, only a third of the population lived under democratic government; today over 90 percent does. In the Philippines, in the Republic of Korea, free, contested, democratic elections are the order of the day. Throughout the world, free markets are the model for growth. Democracy is the standard by which governments are measured.

We Americans make no secret of our belief in freedom. In fact, it's something of a national pastime. Every 4 years the American people choose a new President, and 1988 is one of those years. At one point there were 13 major candidates running in the two major parties, not to mention all the others, including the Socialist and Libertarian candidates—all trying to get my job. About 1,000 local television stations, 8,500 radio stations, and 1,700 daily newspapers—each one an independent, private enterprise, fiercely independent of the Government—report on the candidates, grill them in interviews, and bring them together for debates. In the end, the people vote; they decide who will be the next President. But freedom doesn't begin or end with elections.

Go to any American town, to take just an example, and you'll see dozens of churches, representing many different beliefs—in many places, synagogues and mosques—and you'll see families of every conceivable nationality worshiping together. Go into any schoolroom, and there you will see children being taught the Declaration of Independence, that they are endowed by their Creator with certain unalienable rights—among them life, liberty, and the pursuit of happiness—that no government can justly deny; the guarantees in their Constitution for freedom of speech, freedom of assembly, and freedom of religion. Go into any courtroom, and there will preside an independent judge, beholden to no government power. There every defendant has the right to a trial by a jury of his peers, usually 12 men and women—common citizens; they are the ones, the only ones, who weigh the evidence and decide on guilt or innocence. In that court, the accused is innocent until proven guilty, and the word of a policeman or any official has no greater legal standing than the word of the accused. Go to any university campus, and there you'll find an open, sometimes heated discussion of the problems in American society and what can be done to correct them. Turn on the television, and you'll see the legislature conducting the business of government right there before the camera, debating and voting on the legislation that will become the law of the land. March in any demonstration, and there are many of them; the people's right of assembly is guaranteed in the Constitution and protected by the police. Go into any union hall, where the members know their right to strike is protected by law. As a matter of fact, one of the many jobs I had before this one was being president of a union, the Screen Actors Guild. I led my union out on strike, and I'm proud to say we won.

But freedom is more even than this. Freedom is the right to question and change the established way of doing things. It is the continuing revolution of the marketplace. It is the understanding that allows us to recognize shortcomings and seek solutions. It is the right to put forth an idea, scoffed at by the experts, and watch it catch fire among the people. It is the right to dream—to follow your dream or stick to your conscience, even if you're the only one in a sea of doubters. Freedom is the recognition that no single person, no single authority or government has a monopoly on the truth, but that every individual life is infinitely precious, that every one of us put on this world has been put there for a reason and has something to offer.

America is a nation made up of hundreds of nationalities. Our ties to you are more than ones of good feeling; they're ties of kinship. In America, you'll find Russians, Armenians, Ukrainians, peoples from Eastern Europe and Central Asia. They come from every part of this vast continent, from every continent, to live in harmony, seeking a place where each cultural heritage is respected, each is valued for its diverse strengths and beauties and the richness it brings to our lives. Recently, a few individuals and families have been allowed to visit relatives in the West. We can only hope that it won't be long before all are allowed to do so and Ukrainian-Americans, Baltic-Americans, Armenian-Americans can freely visit their homelands, just as this Irish-American visits his.

Freedom, it has been said, makes people selfish and materialistic, but Americans are one of the most religious peoples on Earth. Because they know that liberty, just as life itself, is not earned but a gift from God, they seek to share that gift with the world. "Reason and experience," said George Washington in his Farewell Address, "both forbid us to expect that national morality can prevail in exclusion of religious principle. And it is substantially true, that virtue or morality is a necessary spring of popular government." Democracy is less a system of government than it is a system to keep government limited, unintrusive; a system of constraints on power to keep politics and government secondary to the important things in life, the true sources of value found only in family and faith.

But I hope you know I go on about these things not simply to extol the virtues of my own country but to speak to the true greatness of the heart and soul of your land. Who, after all, needs to tell the land of Dostoyevski about the quest for truth, the home of Kandinski and Scriabin about imagination, the rich and noble culture of the Uzbek man of letters Alisher Navoi about beauty and heart? The great culture of your diverse land speaks with a glowing passion to all humanity. Let me cite one of the most eloquent contemporary passages on human freedom. It comes, not from the literature of America, but from this country, from one of the greatest writers of the 20th century, Boris Pasternak, in the novel "Dr. Zhivago." He writes: "I think that if the beast who sleeps in man could be held down by threats—any kind of threat, whether of jail or of retribution after death—then the highest emblem of humanity would be the lion tamer in the circus with his whip, not the prophet who sacrificed himself. But this is just the point—what has for centuries raised man above the beast is not the cudgel, but an inward music—the irresistible power of unarmed truth."

The irresistible power of unarmed truth. Today the world looks expectantly to signs of change, steps toward greater freedom in the Soviet Union. We watch and we hope as we see positive changes taking place. There are some, I know, in your society who fear that change will bring only disruption and discontinuity, who fear to embrace the hope of the future—sometimes it takes faith. It's like that scene in the cowboy movie "Butch Cassidy and the Sundance Kid," which some here in Moscow recently had a chance to see. The posse is closing in on the two outlaws, Butch and Sundance, who find themselves trapped on the edge of a cliff, with a sheer drop of hundreds of feet to the raging rapids below. Butch turns to Sundance and says their only hope is to jump into the river below, but Sundance refuses. He says he'd rather fight it out with the posse, even though they're hopelessly outnumbered. Butch says that's suicide and urges him to jump, but Sundance still refuses and finally admits, "I can't swim." Butch breaks up laughing and says, "You crazy fool, the fall will probably kill you." And, by the way, both Butch and Sundance made it, in case you didn't see the movie. I think what I've just been talking about is *perestroika* and what its goals are.

But change would not mean rejection of the past. Like a tree growing strong through the seasons, rooted in the Earth and drawing life from the Sun, so, too, positive change must be rooted in traditional values—in the land, in culture, in family and community—and it must take its life from the eternal things, from the source of all life, which is faith. Such change will lead to new understandings, new opportunities, to a broader future in which the tradition is not supplanted but finds its full flowering. That is the future beckoning to your generation.

At the same time, we should remember that reform that is not institutionalized will always be insecure. Such freedom will always be looking over its shoulder. A bird on a tether, no matter how long the rope, can always be pulled back. And that is why, in my conversation with General Secretary Gorbachev, I have spoken of how important it is to institutionalize change—to put guarantees on reform. And we've been talking together about one sad reminder of a divided world: the Berlin Wall. It's time to remove the barriers that keep people apart.

I'm proposing an increased exchange program of high school students between our countries. General Secretary Gorbachev mentioned on Sunday a wonderful phrase you have in Russian for this: "Better to see something once than to hear about it a hundred times." Mr. Gorbachev and I first began working on this in 1985. In our discussion today, we agreed on working up to several thousand exchanges a year from each country in the near future. But not everyone can travel across the continents and oceans. Words travel lighter, and that's why we'd like to make available to this country more of our 11,000 magazines and periodicals and our television and radio shows that can be beamed off a satellite in seconds. Nothing would please us more than for the Soviet people to get to know us better and to understand our way of life.

Just a few years ago, few would have imagined the progress our two nations have made together. The INF treaty, which General Secretary Gorbachev and I signed last December in Washington and whose instruments of ratification we will exchange tomorrow—the first true nuclear arms reduction treaty in history, calling for the elimination of an entire class of U.S. and Soviet nuclear missiles. And just 16 days ago, we saw the beginning of your withdrawal from Afghanistan, which gives us hope that soon the fighting may end and the healing may begin and that that suffering country may find self-determination, unity, and peace at long last.

It's my fervent hope that our constructive cooperation on these issues will be carried on to address the continuing destruction and conflicts in many regions of the globe and that the serious discussions that led to the Geneva accords on Afghanistan will help lead to solutions in southern Africa, Ethiopia, Cambodia, the Persian Gulf, and Central America. I have often said: Nations do not distrust each other because they are armed; they are armed because they distrust each other. If this globe is to live in peace and prosper, if it is to embrace all the possibilities of the technological revolution, then nations must renounce, once and for all, the right to an expansionist foreign policy. Peace between nations must be an enduring goal, not a tactical stage in a continuing conflict.

I've been told that there's a popular song in your country—perhaps you know it—whose evocative refrain asks the question, "Do the Russians want a war?" In answer it says: "Go ask that silence lingering in the air, above the birch and poplar there; beneath those trees the soldiers lie. Go ask my mother, ask my wife; then you will have to ask no more, 'Do the Russians want a war?'" But what of your one-time allies? What of those who embraced you on the Elbe? What if we were to ask the watery graves of the Pacific or the European battlefields where America's fallen were buried far from home? What if we were to ask their mothers, sisters, and sons, do Americans want war? Ask us, too, and you'll find the same answer, the same longing in every heart. People do not make wars; governments do. And no mother would ever willingly sacrifice her sons for territorial gain, for economic advantage, for ideology. A people free to choose will always choose peace.

Americans seek always to make friends of old antagonists. After a colonial revolution with Britain, we have cemented for all ages the ties of kinship between our nations. After a terrible Civil War between North and South, we healed our wounds and found true unity as a nation. We fought two world wars in my lifetime against Germany and one with Japan, but now the Federal Republic of Germany and Japan are two of our closest allies and friends.

Some people point to the trade disputes between us as a sign of strain, but they're the frictions of all families, and the family of free nations is a big and vital and sometimes boisterous one. I can tell you that nothing would please my heart more than in my lifetime to see American and Soviet diplomats grappling with the problem of trade disputes between America and a growing, exuberant, exporting Soviet Union that had opened up to economic freedom and growth.

And as important as these official people-to-people exchanges are, nothing would please me more than for them to become unnecessary, to see travel between East and West become so routine that university students in the Soviet Union could take a month off in the summer and, just like students in the West do now, put packs on their backs and travel from country to country in Europe with barely a passport check in between. Nothing would please me more than to see the day that a concert promoter in, say, England could call up a Soviet rock group, without going through any government agency, and have them playing in Liverpool the next night. Is this just a dream? Perhaps, but it is a dream that is our responsibility to have come true.

Your generation is living in one of the most exciting, hopeful times in Soviet history. It is a time when the first breath of freedom stirs the air and the heart beats to the accelerated rhythm of hope, when the accumulated spiritual energies of a long silence yearn to break free. I am reminded of the famous passage near the end of Gogol's "Dead Souls." Comparing his nation to a speeding *troika*, Gogol asks what will be its destination. But he writes, "There was no answer save the bell pouring forth marvelous sound."

We do not know what the conclusion will be of this journey, but we're hopeful that the promise of reform will be fulfilled. In this Moscow spring, this May 1988, we may be allowed that hope: that freedom, like the fresh green sapling planted over Tolstoy's grave, will blossom forth at last in the rich fertile soil of your people and culture. We may be allowed to hope that the marvelous sound of a new openness will keep rising through, ringing through, leading to a new world of reconciliation, friendship, and peace.

Thank you all very much, and *da blagoslovit vas gospod*—God bless you.

Mr. Logunov. Dear friends, Mr. President has kindly agreed to answer your questions. But since he doesn't have too much time, only 15 minutes—so, those who have questions, please ask them.

## STRATEGIC ARMS REDUCTIONS

Q. And this is a student from the history faculty, and he says that he's happy to welcome you on behalf of the students of the university. And the first question is that the improvement in the relations between the two countries has come about during your tenure as President, and in this regard he would like to ask the following question. It is very important to get a handle on the question of arms control and, specifically, the limitation of strategic arms. Do you think that it will be possible for you and the General Secretary to get a treaty on the limitation of strategic arms during the time that you are still President?

The President. Well, the arms treaty that is being negotiated now is the so-called START treaty, and it is based on taking the intercontinental ballistic missiles and reducing them by half, down to parity between our two countries. Now, this is a much more complicated treaty than the INF treaty, the intermediate-range treaty, which we have signed and which our two governments have ratified and is now in effect. So, there are many things still to be settled. You and we have had negotiators in Geneva for months working on various points of this treaty. Once we had hoped that maybe, like the INF treaty, we would have been able to sign it here at this summit meeting. It is not completed; there are still some points that are being debated. We are both hopeful that it can be finished before I leave office, which is in the coming January, but I assure you that if it isn't—I assure you that I will have impressed on my successor that we must carry on until it is signed. My dream has always been that once we've started down this road, we can look forward to a day—you can look forward to a day—when there will be no more nuclear weapons in the world at all.

YOUNG PEOPLE

Q. The question is: The universities influence public opinion, and the student wonders how the youths have changed since the days when you were a student up until now?

The President. Well, wait a minute. How you have changed since the era of my own youth?

Q. How just students have changed, the youth have changed. You were a student. [Laughter] At your time there were one type. How they have changed?

The President. Well, I know there was a period in our country when there was a very great change for the worse. When I was Governor of California, I could start a riot just by going to a campus. But that has all changed, and I could be looking out at an American student body as well as I'm looking out here and would not be able to tell the difference between you.

I think that back in our day—I did happen to go to school, get my college education in a unique time; it was the time of the Great Depression, when, in a country like our own, there was 25-percent unemployment and the bottom seemed to have fallen out of everything. But we had—I think what maybe I should be telling you from my point here, because I graduated in 1932, that I should tell you that when you get to be my age, you're going to be surprised how much you recall the feelings you had in these days here and that—how easy it is to understand the young people because of your own having been young once. You know an awful lot more about being young than you do about being old. [Laughter]

And I think there is a seriousness, I think there is a sense of responsibility that young people have, and I think that there is an awareness on the part of most of you about what you want your adulthood to be and what the country you live in—you want it to be. And I have a great deal of faith. I said the other day to 76 students—they were half American and half Russian. They had held a conference here and in Finland and then in the United States, and I faced them just the other day, and I had to say—I couldn't tell the difference looking at them, which were which, but I said one line to them. I said I believe that if all the young people of the world today could get to know each other, there would never be another war. And I think that of you. I think that of the other students that I've addressed in other places.

And of course, I know also that you're young and, therefore, there are certain things that at times take precedence. I'll illustrate one myself. Twenty-five years after I graduated, my alma mater brought me back to the school and gave me an honorary degree. And I had to tell them they compounded a sense of guilt I had nursed for 25 years because I always felt the first degree they gave me was honorary. [Laughter] You're great! Carry on.

REGIONAL CONFLICTS

Q. Mr. President, you have just mentioned that you welcome the efforts—settlement of the Afghanistan question and the difference of other regional conflicts. What conflicts do you mean? Central America conflicts, Southeast Asian, or South African?

The President. Well, for example, in South Africa, where Namibia has been promised its independence as a nation—another new African nation. But it is impossible because of a civil war going on in another country there, and that civil war is being fought on one side by some 30,000 to 40,000 Cuban troops who have gone from the Americas over there and are fighting on one side with one kind of authoritative government. When that country was freed from being a colony and given its independence, one faction seized power and made itself the government of that nation. And leaders of another— seeming the majority of the people had wanted, simply, the people to have the right to choose the government that they wanted, and that is the civil war that is going on. But what we believe is that those foreign soldiers should get out and let them settle it, let the citizens of that nation settle their problems.

And the same is true in Nicaragua. Nicaragua has been—Nicaragua made a promise. They had a dictator. There was a revolution, there was an organization that—and was aided by others in the revolution, and they appealed to the Organization of American States for help in getting the dictator to step down and stop the killing. And he did. But the Organization of American States had asked, what are the goals of the revolution? And they were given in writing, and they were the goals of pluralistic society, of the right of unions and freedom of speech and press and so forth and free elections—a pluralistic society. And then the one group that was the best organized among the revolutionaries seized power, exiled many of the other leaders, and has its own government, which violated every one of the promises that had been made. And here again, we want—we're trying to encourage the getting back those—or making those promises come true and letting the people of that particular country decide their fate.

SOVIET MIA'S IN AFGHANISTAN

Q. Esteemed Mr. President, I'm very much anxious and concerned about the destiny of 310 Soviet soldiers being missing in Afghanistan. Are you willing to help in their search and their return to the motherland?

The President. Very much so. We would like nothing better than that.

U.S. CONSTITUTION

Q. The reservation of the inalienable rights of citizens guaranteed by the Constitution faces certain problems; for example, the right of people to have arms, or for example, the problem appears, an evil appears whether spread of pornography or narcotics is compatible with these rights. Do you believe that these problems are just unavoidable problems connected with democracy, or they could be avoided?

The President. Well, if I understand you correctly, this is a question about the inalienable rights of the people—does that include the right to do criminal acts—for example, in the use of drugs and so forth? No. No, we have a set of laws. I think what is significant and different about our system is that every country has a constitution, and most constitutions or practically all of the constitutions in the world are documents in which the government tells the people what the people can do. Our Constitution is different, and the difference is in three words; it almost escapes everyone. The three words are, "We the people." Our Constitution is a document in which we the people tell the Government what its powers are. And it can have no powers other than those listed in that document. But very carefully, at the same time, the people give the government the power with regard to those things which they think would be destructive to society, to the family, to the individual and so forth—infringements on their rights. And thus, the government can enforce the laws. But that has all been dictated by the people.

PRESIDENT'S RETIREMENT PLANS

Q. Mr. President, from history I know that people who have been connected with great power, with big posts, say goodbye, leave these posts with great difficulty. Since your term of office is coming to an end, what sentiments do you experience and whether you feel like, if, hypothetically, you can just stay for another term? [Laughter]

The President. Well, I'll tell you something. I think it was a kind of revenge against Franklin Delano Roosevelt, who was elected four times—the only President. There had kind of grown a tradition in our country about two terms. That tradition was started by Washington, our first President, only because there was great talk at the formation of our country that we might become a monarchy, and we had just freed ourselves from a monarchy. So, when the second term was over, George Washington stepped down and said he would do it—stepping down—so that there would not get to be the kind of idea of an inherited aristocracy. Well, succeeding Presidents—many of them didn't get a chance at a second term; they did one term and were gone. But that tradition kind of remained, but it was just a tradition. And then Roosevelt ran the four times—died very early in his fourth term. And suddenly, in the atmosphere at that time, they added an amendment to the Constitution that Presidents could only serve two terms.

When I get out of office—I can't do this while I'm in office, because it will look as I'm selfishly doing it for myself—when I get out of office, I'm going to travel around what I call the mashed-potato circuit—that is the after-dinner speaking and the speaking to luncheon groups and so forth—I'm going to travel around and try to convince the people of our country that they should wipe out that amendment to the Constitution because it was an interference with the democratic rights of the people. The people should be allowed to vote for who they wanted to vote for, for as many times as they want to vote for him; and that it is they who are being denied a right. But you see, I will no longer be President then, so I can do that and talk for that.

There are a few other things I'm going to try to convince the people to impress upon our Congress, the things that should be done. I've always described it that if—in Hollywood, when I was there, if you didn't sing or dance, you wound up as an after-dinner speaker. And I didn't sing or dance. [Laughter] So, I have a hunch that I will be out on the speaking circuit, telling about a few things that I didn't get done in government, but urging the people to tell the Congress they wanted them done.

### AMERICAN INDIANS

Q. Mr. President, I've heard that a group of American Indians have come here because they couldn't meet you in the United States of America. If you fail to meet them here, will you be able to correct it and to meet them back in the United States?

The President. I didn't know that they had asked to see me. If they've come here or whether to see them there— laughter]—I'd be very happy to see them.

Let me tell you just a little something about the American Indian in our land. We have provided millions of acres of land for what are called preservations—or reservations, I should say. They, from the beginning, announced that they wanted to maintain their way of life, as they had always lived there in the desert and the plains and so forth. And we set up these reservations so they could, and have a Bureau of Indian Affairs to help take care of them. At the same time, we provide education for them—schools on the reservations. And they're free also to leave the reservations and be American citizens among the rest of us, and many do. Some still prefer, however, that way—that early way of life. And we've done everything we can to meet their demands as to how they want to live. Maybe we made a mistake. Maybe we should not have humored them in that wanting to stay in that kind of primitive lifestyle. Maybe we should have said, no, come join us; be citizens along with the rest of us. As I say, many have; many have been very successful.

And I'm very pleased to meet with them, talk with them at any time and see what their grievances are or what they feel they might be. And you'd be surprised: Some of them became very wealthy because some of those reservations were overlaying great pools of oil, and you can get very rich pumping oil. And so, I don't know what their complaint might be.

SOVIET DISSIDENTS

Q. Mr. President, I'm very much tantalized since yesterday evening by the question, why did you receive yesterday—did you receive and when you invite yesterday—refuseniks or dissidents? And for the second part of the question is, just what are your impressions from Soviet people? And among these dissidents, you have invited a former collaborator with a Fascist, who was a policeman serving for Fascist.

The President. Well, that's one I don't know about, or maybe the information hasn't been all given out on that. But you have to understand that Americans come from every corner of the world. I received a letter from a man that called something to my attention recently. He said, you can go to live in France, but you cannot become a Frenchman; you can go to live in Germany, you cannot become a German—or a Turk, or a Greek, or whatever. But he said anyone, from any corner of the world, can come to live in America and become an American.

You have to realize that we are a people that are made up of every strain, nationality, and race of the world. And the result is that when people in our country think someone is being mistreated or treated unjustly in another country, these are people who still feel that kinship to that country because that is their heritage. In America, whenever you meet someone new and become friends, one of the first things you tell each other is what your bloodline is. For example, when I'm asked, I have to say Irish, English, and Scotch—English and Scotch on my mother's side, Irish on my father's side. But all of them have that.

Well, when you take on to yourself a wife, you do not stop loving your mother. So, Americans all feel a kind of a kinship to that country that their parents or their grandparents or even some great-grandparents came from; you don't lose that contact. So, what I have come and what I have brought to the General Secretary—and I must say he has been very cooperative about it—I have brought lists of names that have been brought to me from people that are relatives or friends that know that—or that believe that this individual is being mistreated here in this country, and they want him to be allowed to emigrate to our country—some are separated families.

One that I met in this, the other day, was born the same time I was. He was born of Russian parents who had moved to America, oh, way back in the early 1900's, and he was born in 1911. And then sometime later, the family moved back to Russia. Now he's grown, has a son. He's an American citizen. But they wanted to go back to America and being denied on the grounds that, well, they can go back to America, but his son married a Russian young lady, and they want to keep her from going back. Well, the whole family said, no, we're not going to leave her alone here. She's a member of the family now. Well, that kind of a case is brought to me personally, so I bring it to the General Secretary. And as I say, I must say, he has been most helpful and most agreeable about correcting these things.

Now, I'm not blaming you; I'm blaming bureaucracy. We have the same type of thing happen in our own country. And every once in a while, somebody has to get the bureaucracy by the neck and shake it loose and say, Stop doing what you're doing! And this is the type of thing and the names that we have brought. And it is a list of names, all of which have been brought to me personally by either relatives or close friends and associates. [Applause]

Thank you very much. You're all very kind. I thank you very much. And I hope I answered the questions correctly. Nobody asked me what it was going to feel like to not be President anymore. I have some understanding, because after I'd been Governor for eight years and then stepped down, I want to tell you what it's like. We'd only been home a few days, and someone invited us out to dinner. Nancy and I both went out, got in the back seat of the car, and waited for somebody to get in front and drive us. [Laughter]

[At this point, Rector Logunov gave the President a gift.]

That is beautiful. Thank you very much.


*Note: The President spoke at 4:10 p.m. in the Lecture Hall at Moscow State University. Anatoliy A. Logunov was rector of the university.*

My fellow Americans:

This is the 34th time I'll speak to you from the Oval Office and the last. We've been together eight years now, and soon it'll be time for me to go. But before I do, I wanted to share some thoughts, some of which I've been saving for a long time.

It's been the honor of my life to be your President. So many of you have written the past few weeks to say thanks, but I could say as much to you. Nancy and I are grateful for the opportunity you gave us to serve.

One of the things about the Presidency is that you're always somewhat apart. You spend a lot of time going by too fast in a car someone else is driving, and seeing the people through tinted glass—the parents holding up a child, and the wave you saw too late and couldn't return. And so many times I wanted to stop and reach out from behind the glass, and connect. Well, maybe I can do a little of that tonight.

People ask how I feel about leaving. And the fact is, "parting is such sweet sorrow." The sweet part is California and the ranch and freedom. The sorrow—the goodbyes, of course, and leaving this beautiful place.

You know, down the hall and up the stairs from this office is the part of the White House where the President and his family live. There are a few favorite windows I have up there that I like to stand

and look out of early in the morning. The view is over the grounds here to the Washington Monument, and then the Mall and the Jefferson Memorial. But on mornings when the humidity is low, you can see past the Jefferson to the river, the Potomac, and the Virginia shore. Someone said that's the view Lincoln had when he saw the smoke rising from the Battle of Bull Run. I see more prosaic things: the grass on the banks, the morning traffic as people make their way to work, now and then a sailboat on the river.

I've been thinking a bit at that window. I've been reflecting on what the past eight years have meant and mean. And the image that comes to mind like a refrain is a nautical one—a small story about a big ship, and a refugee, and a sailor. It was back in the early eighties, at the height of the boat people. And the sailor was hard at work on the carrier Midway, which was patrolling the South China Sea. The sailor, like most American servicemen, was young, smart, and fiercely observant. The crew spied on the horizon a leaky little boat. And crammed inside were refugees from Indochina hoping to get to America. The Midway sent a small launch to bring them to the ship and safety. As the refugees made their way through the choppy seas, one spied the sailor on deck, and stood up, and called out to him. He yelled, "Hello, American sailor. Hello, freedom man."

A small moment with a big meaning, a moment the sailor, who wrote it in a letter, couldn't get out of his mind. And, when I saw it, neither could I. Because that's what it was to be an American in the 1980's. We stood, again, for freedom. I know we always have, but in the past few years the world again—and in a way, we ourselves—rediscovered it.

It's been quite a journey this decade, and we held together through some stormy seas. And at the end, together, we are reaching our destination.

The fact is, from Grenada to the Washington and Moscow summits, from the recession of '81 to '82, to the expansion that began in late '82 and continues to this day, we've made a difference. The way I see it, there were two great triumphs, two things that I'm proudest of. One is the economic recovery, in which the people of America created—and filled—19 million new jobs. The other is the recovery of our morale. America is respected again in the world and looked to for leadership.

Something that happened to me a few years ago reflects some of this. It was back in 1981, and I was attending my first big economic summit, which was held that year in Canada. The meeting place rotates among the member countries. The opening meeting was a formal dinner for the heads of government of the seven industrialized nations. Now, I sat there like the new kid in school and listened, and it was all Francois this and Helmut that. They dropped titles and spoke to one another on a first-name basis. Well, at one point I sort of leaned in and said, "My name's Ron." Well, in that same year, we began the actions we felt would ignite an economic comeback—cut taxes and regulation, started to cut spending. And soon the recovery began.

Two years later, another economic summit with pretty much the same cast. At the big opening meeting we all got together, and all of a sudden, just for a moment, I saw that everyone was just sitting there looking at me. And then one of them broke the silence. "Tell us about the American miracle," he said.

Well, back in 1980, when I was running for President, it was all so different. Some pundits said our programs would result in catastrophe. Our views on foreign affairs would cause war. Our plans for the economy would cause inflation to soar and bring about economic collapse. I even remember one highly respected economist saying, back in 1982, that "The engines of economic growth have shut down here, and they're likely to stay that way for years to come." Well, he and the other opinion leaders were wrong. The fact is, what they called "radical" was really "right." What they called "dangerous" was just "desperately needed."

And in all of that time I won a nickname, "The Great Communicator." But I never thought it was my style or the words I used that made a difference: it was the content. I wasn't a great communicator, but I communicated great things, and they didn't spring full bloom from my brow, they came from the heart of a great nation—from our experience, our wisdom, and our belief in the principles that have guided us for two centuries. They called it the Reagan revolution. Well, I'll accept that, but for me it always seemed more like the great rediscovery, a rediscovery of our values and our common sense.

Common sense told us that when you put a big tax on something, the people will produce less of it. So, we cut the people's tax rates, and the people produced more than ever before. The economy bloomed like a plant that had been cut back and could now grow quicker and stronger. Our economic program brought about the longest peacetime expansion in our history: real family income up, the poverty rate down, entrepreneurship booming, and an explosion in research and new technology. We're exporting more than ever because American industry became more competitive and at the same time, we summoned the national will to knock down protectionist walls abroad instead of erecting them at home.

Common sense also told us that to preserve the peace, we'd have to become strong again after years of weakness and confusion. So, we rebuilt our defenses, and this New Year we toasted the new peacefulness around the globe. Not only have the superpowers actually begun to reduce their stockpiles of nuclear weapons—and hope for even more progress is bright—but the regional conflicts that rack the globe are also beginning to cease. The Persian Gulf is no longer a war zone. The Soviets are leaving Afghanistan. The Vietnamese are preparing to pull out of Cambodia, and an American-mediated accord will soon send 50,000 Cuban troops home from Angola.

The lesson of all this was, of course, that because we're a great nation, our challenges seem complex. It will always be this way. But as long as we remember our first principles and believe in ourselves, the future will always be ours. And something else we learned: Once you begin a great movement, there's no telling where it will end. We meant to change a nation, and instead, we changed a world.

Countries across the globe are turning to free markets and free speech and turning away from the ideologies of the past. For them, the great rediscovery of the 1980's has been that, lo and behold, the moral way of government is the practical way of government: Democracy, the profoundly good, is also the profoundly productive.

When you've got to the point when you can celebrate the anniversaries of your 39th birthday you can sit back sometimes, review your life, and see it flowing before you. For me there was a fork in the river, and it was right in the middle of my life. I never meant to go into politics. It wasn't my intention when I was young. But I was raised to believe you had to pay your way for the blessings bestowed on you. I was happy with my career in the entertainment world, but I ultimately went into politics because I wanted to protect something precious.

Ours was the first revolution in the history of mankind that truly reversed the course of government, and with three little words: "We the People." "We the People" tell the government what to do; it doesn't tell us. "We the People" are the driver; the government is the car. And we decide where it should go, and by what route, and how fast. Almost all the world's constitutions are documents in which governments tell the people what their privileges are. Our Constitution is a document in which "We the People" tell the government what it is allowed to do. "We the People" are free. This belief has been the underlying basis for everything I've tried to do these past eight years.

But back in the 1960's, when I began, it seemed to me that we'd begun reversing the order of things—that through more and more rules and regulations and confiscatory taxes, the government was taking more of our money, more of our options, and more of our freedom. I went into politics in part to put up my hand and say, "Stop." I was a citizen politician, and it seemed the right thing for a citizen to do.

I think we have stopped a lot of what needed stopping. And I hope we have once again reminded people that man is not free unless government is limited. There's a clear cause and effect here that is as neat and predictable as a law of physics: As government expands, liberty contracts.

Nothing is less free than pure communism—and yet we have, the past few years, forged a satisfying new closeness with the Soviet Union. I've been asked if this isn't a gamble, and my answer is no because we're basing our actions not on words but deeds. The detente of the 1970's was based not on actions but promises. They'd promise to treat their own people and the people of the world better. But the gulag was still the gulag, and the state was still expansionist, and they still waged proxy wars in Africa, Asia, and Latin America.

Well, this time, so far, it's different. President Gorbachev has brought about some internal democratic reforms and begun the withdrawal from Afghanistan. He has also freed prisoners whose names I've given him every time we've met.

But life has a way of reminding you of big things through small incidents. Once, during the heady days of the Moscow summit, Nancy and I decided to break off from the entourage one afternoon to visit the shops on Arbat Street—that's a little street just off Moscow's main shopping area. Even though our visit was a surprise, every Russian there immediately recognized us and called out our names and reached for our hands. We were just about swept away by the warmth. You could almost feel the possibilities in all that joy. But within seconds, a KGB detail pushed their way toward us and began pushing and shoving the people in the crowd. It was an interesting moment. It reminded me that while the man on the street in the Soviet Union yearns for peace, the government is Communist. And those who run it are Communists, and that means we and they view such issues as freedom and human rights very differently.

We must keep up our guard, but we must also continue to work together to lessen and eliminate tension and mistrust. My view is that President Gorbachev is different from previous Soviet leaders. I think he knows some of the things wrong with his society and is trying to fix them. We wish him well. And we'll continue to work to make sure that the Soviet Union that eventually emerges from this process is a less threatening one. What it all boils down to is this: I want the new closeness to continue. And it will, as long as we make it clear that we will continue to act in a certain way as long as they continue to act in a helpful manner. If and when they don't, at first pull your punches. If they persist, pull the plug. It's still trust but verify. It's still play, but cut the cards. It's still watch closely. And don't be afraid to see what you see.

I've been asked if I have any regrets. Well, I do. The deficit is one. I've been talking a great deal about that lately, but tonight isn't for arguments, and I'm going to hold my tongue. But an observation: I've had my share of victories in the Congress, but what few people noticed is that I never won anything you didn't win for me. They never saw my troops, they never saw Reagan's regiments, the American people. You won every battle with every call you made and letter you wrote demanding action. Well, action is still needed. If we're to finish the job, Reagan's regiments will have to become the Bush brigades. Soon he'll be the chief, and he'll need you every bit as much as I did.

Finally, there is a great tradition of warnings in Presidential farewells, and I've got one that's been on my mind for some time. But oddly enough it starts with one of the things I'm proudest of in the past eight years: the resurgence of national pride that I called the new patriotism. This national feeling is good, but it won't count for much, and it won't last unless it's grounded in thoughtfulness and knowledge.

An informed patriotism is what we want. And are we doing a good enough job teaching our children what America is and what she represents in the long history of the world? Those of us who are over 35 or so years of age grew up in a different America. We were taught, very directly, what it means to be an American. And we absorbed, almost in the air, a love of country and an appreciation of its institutions. If you didn't get these things from your family you got them from the neighborhood, from the father down the street who fought in Korea or the family who lost someone at Anzio.

Or you could get a sense of patriotism from school. And if all else failed you could get a sense of patriotism from the popular culture. The movies celebrated democratic values and implicitly reinforced the idea that America was special. TV was like that, too, through the mid-sixties.

But now, we're about to enter the nineties, and some things have changed. Younger parents aren't sure that an unambivalent appreciation of America is the right thing to teach modern children. And as for those who create the popular culture, well-grounded patriotism is no longer the style. Our spirit is back, but we haven't re-institutionalized it. We've got to do a better job of getting across that America is freedom—freedom of speech, freedom of religion, freedom of enterprise. And freedom is special and rare. It's fragile; it needs protection.

So, we've got to teach history based not on what's in fashion but what's important—why the Pilgrims came here, who Jimmy Doolittle was, and what those 30 seconds over Tokyo meant. You know, four years ago on the 40th anniversary of D-day, I read a letter from a young woman writing to her late father, who'd fought on Omaha Beach. Her name was Lisa Zanatta Henn, and she said, "We will always remember, we will never forget what the boys of Normandy did." Well, let's help her keep her word. If we forget what we did, we won't know who we are. I'm warning of an eradication of the American memory that could result, ultimately, in an erosion of the American spirit. Let's start with some basics: more attention to American history and a greater emphasis on civic ritual.

And let me offer lesson number one about America: All great change in America begins at the dinner table. So, tomorrow night in the kitchen I hope the talking begins. And children, if your parents haven't been teaching you what it means to be an American, let 'em know and nail 'em on it. That would be a very American thing to do.

And that's about all I have to say tonight, except for one thing. The past few days when I've been at that window upstairs, I've thought a bit of the "shining city upon a hill." The phrase comes from John Winthrop, who wrote it to describe the America he imagined. What he imagined was important because he was an early Pilgrim, an early freedom man. He journeyed here on what today we'd call a little wooden boat; and like the other Pilgrims, he was looking for a home that would be free.

I've spoken of the shining city all my political life, but I don't know if I ever quite communicated what I saw when I said it. But in my mind it was a tall, proud city built on rocks stronger than oceans, wind-swept, God-blessed, and teeming with people of all kinds living in harmony and peace; a city with free ports that hummed with commerce and creativity. And if there had to be city walls, the walls had doors and the doors were open to anyone with the will and the heart to get here. That's how I saw it, and see it still.

And how stands the city on this winter night? More prosperous, more secure, and happier than it was eight years ago. But more than that: After 200 years, two centuries, she still stands strong and true on the granite ridge, and her glow has held steady no matter what storm. And she's still a beacon, still a magnet for all who must have freedom, for all the pilgrims from all the lost places who are hurtling through the darkness, toward home.

We've done our part. And as I walk off into the city streets, a final word to the men and women of the Reagan revolution, the men and women across America who for eight years did the work that brought America back. My friends: We did it. We weren't just marking time. We made a difference. We made the city stronger, we made the city freer, and we left her in good hands. All in all, not bad, not bad at all.

And so, goodbye, God bless you, and God bless the United States of America.

# INDEX